The Complete Book of Crochet Border Designs

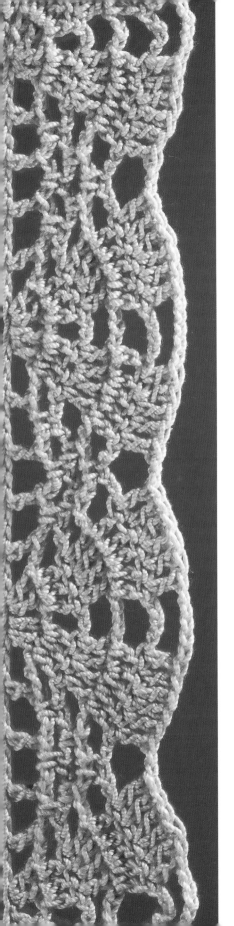

The Complete Book of Crochet Border Designs

Hundreds of Classic & Original Patterns

Revised Edition

Linda P. Schapper

LARK

Editor: Susan Mowery Kieffer

Technical Editor: Karen Manthey

Art Director: Shannon Yokeley

Cover Designer: Cindy LaBreacht

Assistant Designer: Travis Medford

Art Production Assistants: Bradley Norris, Jeff Hamilton, and Avery Johnson

Editorial Assistance: Dawn Dillingham, Rosemary Kast, and Kathleen McCafferty

Art Intern: Michael Foreman

Illustrator: Orrin Lundgren

Diagrams: Karen Manthey

Photographer: Steve Mann

An Imprint of Sterling Publishing
387 Park Avenue South
New York, NY 10016

First Paperback Edition 2013
Text © 2007, Linda P. Schapper
Photography © 2007, Lark Books, an Imprint of Sterling Publishing Co., Inc.
Illustrations © 2007, Lark Books, an Imprint of Sterling Publishing Co., Inc.;
unless otherwise specified
First published in 1987 by Sterling Publishing Co., Inc.

ISBN 978-1-57990-914-7 (hardcover) 978-1-4547-0810-0 (paperback)

The Library of Congress has cataloged the hardcover edition as follows:

Schäpper, Linda.
  The complete book of crochet border designs hundreds of original & classic patterns / Linda P. Schapper. -- Rev. ed.
     p. cm.
  Includes index.
  ISBN-13: 978-1-57990-914-7 (hc-plc with jacket : alk. paper)
  ISBN-10: 1-57990-914-0 (hc-plc with jacket : alk. paper)
  1. Crocheting--Patterns. 2. Borders, Ornamental (Decorative arts) I.
Title.
  TT820.S278 2007
  746.43'4041--dc22

                                   2007015682

Distributed in Canada by Sterling Publishing
c/o Canadian Manda Group, 165 Dufferin Street
Toronto, Ontario, Canada M6K 3H6
Distributed in the United Kingdom by GMC Distribution Services
Castle Place, 166 High Street, Lewes, East Sussex, England BN7 1XU
Distributed in Australia by Capricorn Link (Australia) Pty. Ltd.
P.O. Box 704, Windsor, NSW 2756, Australia

For information about custom editions, special sales, and premium and corporate purchases, please contact Sterling Special Sales at 800-805-5489 or specialsales@sterlingpublishing.com.

Email academic@larkbooks.com for information about desk and examination copies. The complete policy can be found at larkcrafts.com.

Every effort has been made to ensure that all the information in this book is accurate. However, due to differing conditions, tools, and individual skills, the publisher cannot be responsible for any injuries, losses, and other damages that may result from the use of the information in this book.

Printed in Canada

2 4 6 8 10 9 7 5 3 1

larkcrafts.com

■ Contents ■

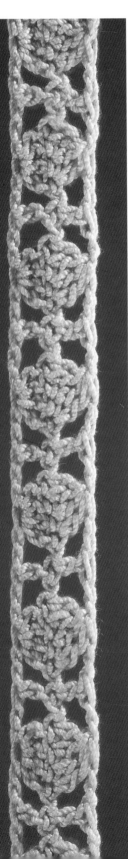

■ Introduction ■

There is not much of a written record about the history of crochet. As with many handcrafts, it grew and flourished, but no one thought it important enough to write about.

We believe crochet originated as early as the Stone Age era, perhaps when a rough hook was used to join sections of clothing. And, most likely, we adopted the French word for hook—*crochet*—as the name of the craft itself because the French did more than people in any other country to record crochet patterns.

Without written instructions available, patterns survived by being handed down through families over generations. Patterns were copied and new ones created by examining designs with a magnifying glass. Then, in the 19th century, written instructions became popular as more women began to read. Instructions, however, can be long and tedious, and although perfectly clear to the writer, can be unintelligible to the crocheter.

This book includes diagrams of individual stitches based on what is known as the International Crochet Symbol system. The system is easy to understand after you have worked out a few of the basic stitches. By using this system, it's easier to see the whole pattern in proportion, and it is a rewarding experience to be able to pick up a crochet book in Russian, French, or Japanese and understand the crochet symbols. The symbols look a great deal like the crochet stitches themselves, and are not difficult to follow.

Crochet is based on a few simple stitches used in endless variation. It begins with a chain, and the way the stitches are formed determines the pattern. You need only a crochet hook, your hand, and the thread. It's easy to carry with you and do anywhere. Unlike knitting and weaving, it's difficult to make a mistake that can't be corrected immediately.

Crochet is versatile. You can make generous lace patterns, mimic knitting, patchwork, or weaving, and you can create any number of textile patterns. I found the challenge of making over 300 different patterns with the same off-white thread to be exhilarating.

This book focuses on bands and borders. Patterns range from small in size to large, flamboyant, lace designs. You can use crocheted borders to finish projects in weaving, knitting, sewing, and in many other handcrafts. You can utilize bands to decorate clothing, household textiles, or any type of sewing. In Switzerland, crocheted filet bands were used to piece together sheets and tablecloths before looms were large enough to make one wide piece.

Use borders to embellish blankets, place mats, towels, or sheets. Decorate handkerchiefs, altar cloths, curtains, or children's clothing with them. Enlarge the pattern, and you could use a border design as a curtain. Smaller versions could be perfect as doll clothes or collars. There is no limit to the number of ideas and uses for crocheted borders. All you have to do is vary the size of your needle, the material you use, and the way you use it.

My hope is that this book will inspire you and that you will enjoy many happy hours of crocheting bands and borders for your projects.

Notes for those using the written instructions
- Stitch is always counted from the last stitch used, unless otherwise specified.
- The abbreviations used throughout are ones used in the United States.
- Learn to read the diagrams. Any new behavior is uncomfortable in the beginning, but the diagrams are much easier than the written explanations. When in doubt about the written explanations, check them against the drawings.
- Work a foundation chain for the desired length of the finished border, making your foundation chain a multiple of the number of stitches indicated at the beginning of the instruction, plus any additional stitches noted to complete the pattern.
- Although the instructions for the vertical bands begin with row 1, instructions for repetition usually begin with row 2. The first row is not standard because it is all worked on a base row of chains.
- The division of stitches into chapters is somewhat arbitrary because many of the patterns could fit into several chapters. I tried to place them where they were most typical.

Basic Stitches

SLIP KNOT

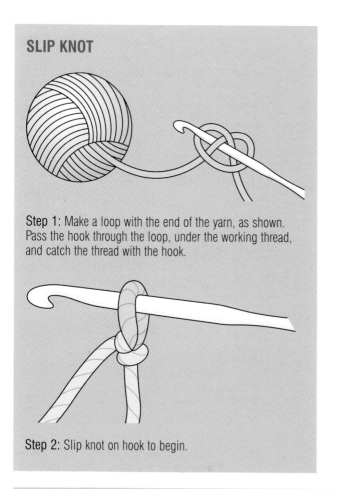

Step 1: Make a loop with the end of the yarn, as shown. Pass the hook through the loop, under the working thread, and catch the thread with the hook.

Step 2: Slip knot on hook to begin.

CHAIN (ch)

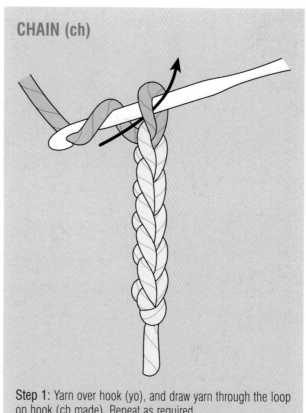

Step 1: Yarn over hook (yo), and draw yarn through the loop on hook (ch made). Repeat as required.

SLIP STITCH (sl st)

Step 1: Insert hook in designated stitch.

Step 2: Yo, draw yarn through stitch and the loop on hook (sl st made).

SINGLE CROCHET (sc)

This is a short, tight stitch.

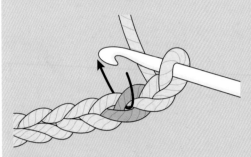

Make a chain of desired length.
Step 1: Insert hook in designated st (2nd ch from hook for first sc).

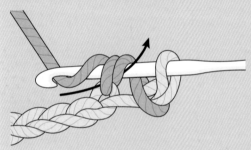

Step 2: Draw yarn through stitch.

Step 3: Yo, draw yarn through 2 loops on hook (sc made).

Step 4: Insert hook in next chain, and repeat steps to create another single crochet.

HALF DOUBLE CROCHET (hdc)

This stitch gives a lot of body and structure and resembles knitting.

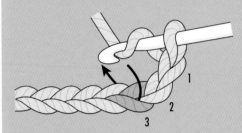

Make a chain of desired length.
Step 1: Yo, insert hook in designated st (3rd ch from hook for first hdc).

Step 2: Yo, draw through stitch (3 loops on hook).

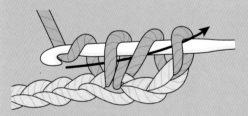

Step 3: Yo, draw yarn through 3 loops on hook (hdc made).

Step 4: You will have one loop left on the hook. Yo, insert hook in next ch, and repeat sequence across row.

DOUBLE CROCHET (dc)

This is perhaps the most popular and frequently used crochet stitch.

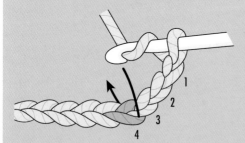

Make a chain of desired length.
Step 1: Yo, insert hook in designated st (4th ch from hook for first dc).

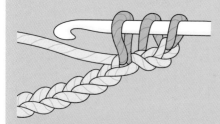

Step 2: Yo, draw through stitch (3 loops on hook).

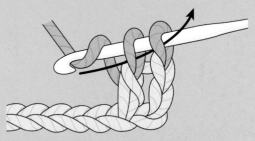

Step 3: Yo, draw yarn through first 2 loops on hook.

Step 4: Yo, draw yarn through last 2 loops on hook (dc made).

Step 5: Yo, insert hook in next st, and repeat steps to continue across row. Repeat steps 2-4 to work next dc.

TREBLE CROCHET (tr)

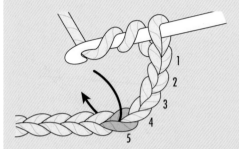

Make a chain of desired length.
Step 1: Yo twice, insert hook in designated st (5th ch from hook for first tr).

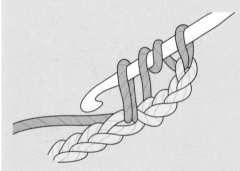

Step 2: Yo, draw through stitch (4 loops on hook).

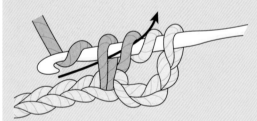

Step 3: Yo, draw yarn through 2 loops on hook (3 loops on hook).

Step 4: Yo, draw yarn through 2 loops on hook (2 loops on hook).

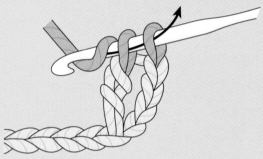

Step 5: Yo, draw yarn through 2 loops on hook (tr made).

Step 6: Yo twice, and repeat steps in next ch st.

DOUBLE TREBLE CROCHET (dtr)

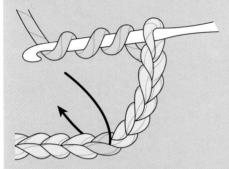

Make a chain of desired length.

Step 1: Double Treble Crochet (dtr) is worked the same as Treble Crochet, with an additional yarn over (yo 3 times) at the beginning.

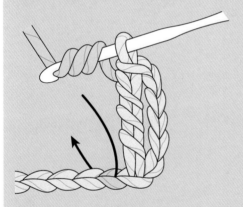

Step 2

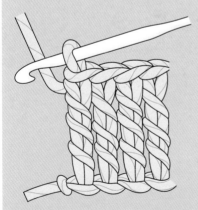

Step 3: To complete the stitch, work Step 4 of Treble Crochet one additional time.

TRIPLE TREBLE CROCHET (trtr)

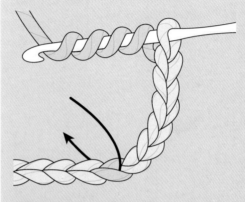

Step 1: Triple Treble Crochet (trtr) is worked the same as Treble Crochet, with two additional yarn overs (yo 4 times) at the beginning.

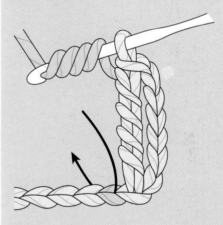

Step 2

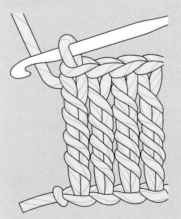

Step 3: To complete the stitch, work Step 4 of Treble Crochet two additional times.

BOBBLE

Can be made with 2 to 6 loops. Shown for 4 loops.

Step 1: Yo, insert hook in designated st.

Step 2: Yo, draw yarn through st and up to level of work (first loop).

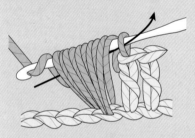

Step 3: (Yo, insert hook in same st, yo, draw yarn through st) as many times as required (3 more times for 4-looped bobble st–11 loops on hook).

Step 4: Yo, draw yarn through all loops on hook (bobble made).

PUFF STITCH

Can be made with 2 to 6 sts. Shown for 3 dc.

Step 1: Yo, insert hook in designated st (4th ch from hook for first puff st), yo, draw yarn through st, yo, draw yarn through 2 loops on hook (half-closed dc made–2 loops remain on hook).

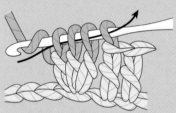

Step 2: Yo, insert hook in same st, yo, draw yarn through st, yo, draw yarn through 2 loops on hook for each additional dc required (2 more times for 3-dc puff stitch—4 loops on hook).

Step 3: Yo, draw yarn through all loops on hook (puff stitch made).

POPCORN (pop)

Can be made with 2 to 6 sts. Shown with 5 dc.

Pop on RS rows:
Step 1: Work 5 dc in designated st (4th ch from hook for first pop).

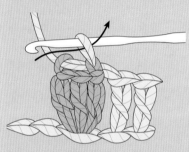

Step 2: Drop loop from hook, insert hook from front to back in top of first dc of group, pick up dropped loop, and draw through st, ch 1 tightly to secure (pop made).

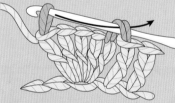

Pop on WS rows:
Step 1: Work 5 dc in designated st (4th ch from hook for first pop).

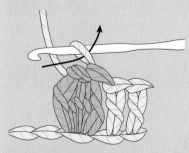

Step 2: Drop loop from hook, insert hook from back to front in top of first dc of group, pick up dropped loop, and draw through st, ch 1 tightly to secure (pop made).

CLUSTER

Shown for 4-dc cluster.

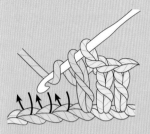

Step 1: Yo, insert hook in designated st, yo, draw yarn through st, yo, draw yarn through 2 loops on hook (half-closed dc made—2 loops remain on hook).

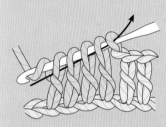

Step 2: (Yo, insert hook in next designated st, yo, draw yarn through st, yo, draw yarn through 2 loops on hook) as many times as required (3 more times for 4-dc cluster—4 half-closed dc made—5 loops on hook).

Step 3: Yo, draw yarn through all loops on hook (cluster made).

PICOT
Shown for ch-3 picot.

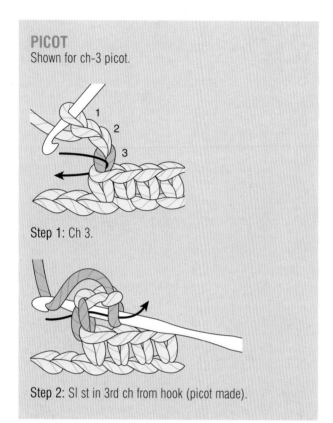

Step 1: Ch 3.

Step 2: Sl st in 3rd ch from hook (picot made).

CROSSED STITCH (CROSSED tr SHOWN)

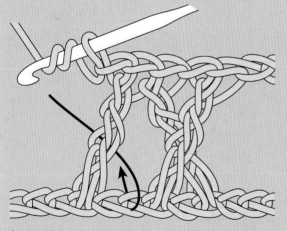

Step 1: Skip required number of sts (skip 2 sts shown), tr in next st, ch required number of sts (ch 1 shown), working behind tr just made, tr in first skipped st.

V-STITCH (V-st), OR SHELL
A designated number of stitches (frequently worked with double crochet stitches) worked in same stitch (shown for 4-dc shell). V-sts are comprised of 2 dc (with or without a ch space). Shells can be made with 3 or more dc (with or without ch spaces).

Work 4 dc in designated st (shell made).

Y-STITCH (OPEN VERSION SHOWN)

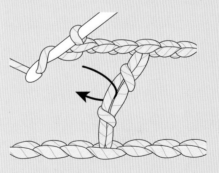

Step 1: Work tr in designated st.

Step 2: Ch required number of sts (ch 3 shown), yo, work dc in 2 strands at center of tr just made (Y-st made).

JOINING BORDERS TO FABRIC
Illustrations © Karen Manthey

All these borders patterns give directions for a stand-alone border, worked across a foundation chain. As written, they are designed to be sewn onto fabric after completion. Borders can also be worked directly onto the fabric. To do so, eliminate the foundation chain and work a row of single crochet with the necessary multiple of stitches, then work pattern row 1 across sc row. Alternately, work row 1 of the pattern directly onto the fabric, evenly spacing stitches and loops, as per photograph of finished border.

CROCHETING BORDERS ONTO FABRIC

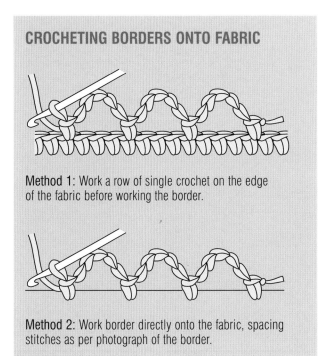

Method 1: Work a row of single crochet on the edge of the fabric before working the border.

Method 2: Work border directly onto the fabric, spacing stitches as per photograph of the border.

BORDER WORKED ON EDGE OF FABRIC DIAGRAM

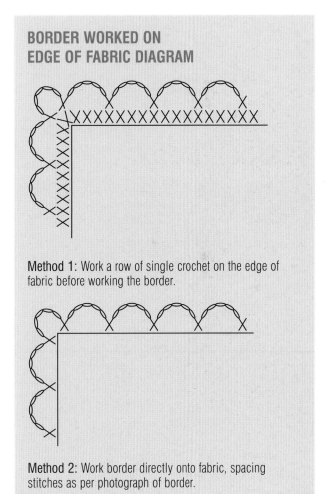

Method 1: Work a row of single crochet on the edge of fabric before working the border.

Method 2: Work border directly onto fabric, spacing stitches as per photograph of border.

▪ International Crochet Symbols ▪

chain stitch (ch)	⬯	⬯⬯⬯⬯
slip stitch (sl st)	•	• • • • •
single crochet (sc)	X	X X X X X
half double crochet (hdc)	T	T T T T T
double crochet (dc)	⟊	⟊ ⟊ ⟊ ⟊ ⟊
treble crochet (tr)	⟤	⟤ ⟤ ⟤ ⟤ ⟤
double treble crochet (dtr)	⟤	⟤ ⟤ ⟤ ⟤ ⟤
triple treble crochet (trtr)	⟤	⟤ ⟤ ⟤ ⟤ ⟤
ch-3 picot	⌓	⌓ ⌓ ⌓ ⌓ ⌓
ch-4 picot	⬠	⬠ ⬠ ⬠ ⬠ ⬠
3-dc popcorn (pop)	⬭	⬭ ⬭ ⬭ ⬭ ⬭
4-dc popcorn (pop)	⬭	⬭ ⬭ ⬭ ⬭ ⬭
5-dc popcorn (pop)	⬭	⬭ ⬭ ⬭ ⬭ ⬭
2-looped bobble	⬭	⬭ ⬭ ⬭ ⬭ ⬭
3-looped bobble	⬭	⬭ ⬭ ⬭ ⬭ ⬭
4-looped bobble	⬭	⬭ ⬭ ⬭ ⬭ ⬭
5-looped bobble	⬭	⬭ ⬭ ⬭ ⬭ ⬭

2-dc puff st	
3-dc puff st	
4-dc puff st	
5-dc puff st	
crossed dc	
wraparound dc	
2-dc cluster	
3-dc cluster	
4-dc cluster	
5-dc cluster	
V-st	or
3-dc shell	
4-dc shell	
5-dc shell	
4-dc shell with ch-2 space	
6-dc shell with ch-2 space	
working over previous rows	or
Y-stitch	

.1.
Single Crochet & Chains

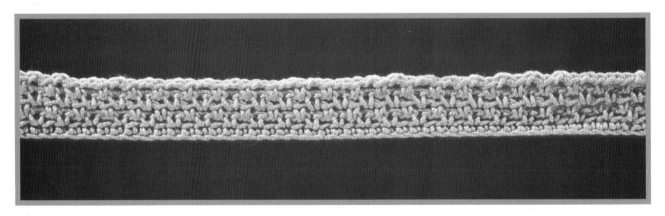

1 Chain multiples of 2.

Row 1 (RS): Sc in 2nd ch from hook, sc in each ch across, turn.

Row 2: Ch 1, sc in first sc, *ch 1, skip next sc, sc in next sc; rep from * across, turn.

Row 3: Ch 1, sc in first sc, sc in next ch-1 space, (ch 1, sc) in each ch-1 space across, sc in last sc, turn.

Row 4: Rep Row 2.

Row 5: Ch 1, sc in first sc, sc in next ch-1 space, (ch 2, sc) in each ch-1 space across, sc in last sc. Fasten off.

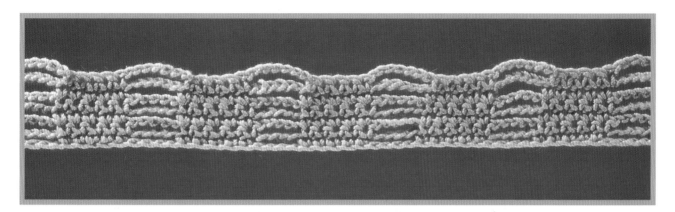

2

Chain multiples of 9 plus 6.

Row 1 (RS): Sc in 2nd ch from hook, sc in each of next 4 ch, *ch 4, skip next 4 ch, sc in each of next 5 ch; rep from * across, turn.

Row 2: Ch 1, sc in each of first 5 sc, *ch 5, skip next ch-4 loop, sc in each of next 5 sc; rep from * across, turn.

Rows 3-4: Ch 1, sc in each of first 5 sc, *ch 5, skip next ch-5 loop, sc in each of next 5 sc; rep from * across, turn.

Row 5: Ch 1, sc in each of first 5 sc, *ch 6, skip next ch-5 loop, sc in each of next 5 sc; rep from * across, turn.

Row 6: Ch 1, sc in each of first 5 sc, *ch 7, skip next ch-6 loop, sc in each of next 5 sc; rep from * across. Fasten off.

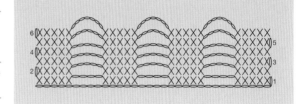

3

Chain multiples of 4 plus 2.

Row 1 (RS): Sc in 2nd ch from hook, sc in each ch across, turn.

Row 2: Ch 1, sc in first sc, *ch 5, skip next 3 sc, sc in next sc; rep from * across, turn.

Row 3: Ch 1, sl st in first sc, *ch 6, skip next ch-5 loop, sl st in next sc; rep from * across. Fasten off.

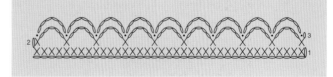

4 Chain multiples of 4 plus 2.

Row 1 (RS): Sc in 2nd ch from hook, sc in each ch across, turn.

Row 2: Ch 1, sc in first sc, *ch 5, skip next 3 sc, sc in next sc; rep from * across, turn.

Row 3: Ch 1, sc in first sc, *ch 7, skip next ch-5 loop, sc in next sc; rep from * across, turn.

Row 4: Ch 1, sl st in first sc, *ch 9, skip next ch-7 loop, sl st in next sc; rep from * across. Fasten off.

5 Chain multiples of 7 plus 6..

Row 1 (WS): Sc in 2nd ch from hook, sc in each of next 4 ch, *ch 6, skip next 2 ch, sc in each of next 5 ch; rep from * across, turn.

Row 2: Ch 1, sc in each of first 3 sc, *ch 8, skip next ch-6 loop, sl st in next sc, sc in each of next 2 sc; rep from * across to last 2 sts, sc in each of last 2 sc. Fasten off.

6 Chain multiples of 5 plus 1.

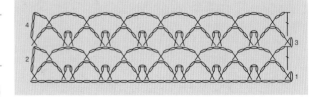

Row 1 (RS): Sc in 2nd ch from hook, *ch 5, skip next 3 ch, sc in next ch**, ch 3, sc in next ch; rep from * across, ending last rep at **, turn.

Row 2: Ch 5 (counts as dc, ch 2), (sc, ch 5) in each ch-5 loop across to within last ch-5 loop, sc in last ch-5 loop, ch 2, dc in last sc, turn.

Row 3: Ch 1, sc in first dc, (ch 5, sc, ch 3, sc) in each ch-5 loop across, ending with ch-5, sc in 3rd ch of turning ch, turn.

Row 4: Rep Row 2. Fasten off.

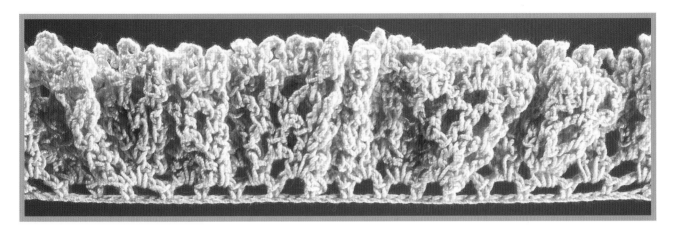

7 **Chain** multiples of 3.

Row 1 (RS): Sc in 7th ch from hook, *ch 4, skip next 2 ch, sc in next ch; rep from * across to within last 2 ch, ch 2, dc in last ch, turn.

Row 2: Ch 5 (counts as dc, ch 2), sc in next ch-2 space, *ch 4, (sc, ch 4, sc) in next ch-4 loop; rep from * across to last ch-4 loop, ch 4, sc in ch-2 space of turning ch, ch 2, dc in 4th ch of turning ch, turn.

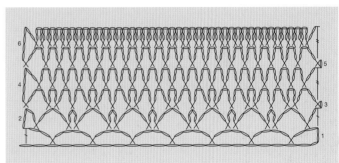

Row 3: Ch 1, sc in first dc, *ch 5, (sc, ch 5, sc) in next ch-4 loop, ch 5, sc in next ch-4 loop; rep from * across, ending with last sc in 3rd ch of turning ch, turn.

Row 4: Ch 6 (counts as tr, ch 2), sc in next ch-5 loop, (ch 5, sc) in each ch-5 loop across to last ch-5 loop, ch 2, tr in last sc, turn.

Row 5: Ch 1, sc in first tr, skip next ch-2 space, (ch 5, sc) in each ch-5 loop across, ending with last sc in 4th ch of turning ch, turn.

Row 6: Ch 6 (counts as tr, ch 2), (sc, ch 5, sc) in next ch-5 loop, (ch 5, sc, ch 5, sc) in each ch-5 loop across to last ch-5 loop, ch 2, tr in last sc. Fasten off.

8 **Chain** multiples of 12.

Row 1 (RS): Sc in 2nd ch from hook, *(ch 5, skip next 4 ch, sc in next ch) twice**, (ch 5, sc) in each of next 2 ch; rep from * across, ending last rep at **, turn.

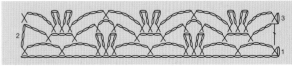

Row 2: Ch 6 (counts as dc, ch 3), (sc, ch 3) in each ch-5 loop across to last ch-5 loop, dc in last sc, turn.

Row 3: Ch 1, sc in first dc, *ch 5, skip next ch-3 loop, (sc, ch 5, sc, ch 5, sc) in next ch-3 loop, ch 5, skip next ch-3 loop, sc in next ch-3 loop; rep from * across, ending with last sc in 3rd ch of turning ch. Fasten off.

9 **Chain** multiples of 6.

Row 1 (WS): Sc in 9th ch from hook, *ch 7, skip next 5 ch, sc in next ch; rep from * across to within last 3 ch, ch 3, skip next 2 ch, dc in last ch, turn.

Row 2: Ch 1, sc in first dc, (ch 3, sc, ch 3, sc) in next ch-2 space, (sc, ch 3, sc, ch 3, sc, ch 3, sc) in each ch-7 loop across to turning ch, (sc, ch 3, sc, ch 3, sc) in ch-3 loop of turning ch, turn.

Row 3: Ch 1, sc in first sc, ch 7, skip next 3 ch-3 loops, sc in next ch-3 loop, *ch 7, skip next 2 ch-3 loops, sc in next ch-3 loop; rep from * across to within last 3 ch-3 loops, ch 7, skip next 3 ch-3 loops, sc in last sc, turn.

Row 4: Ch 7 (counts as tr, ch 3), sc in next ch-7 loop, (ch 7, sc) in each ch-7 loop across to last ch-7 loop, ch 3, tr in last sc. Fasten off.

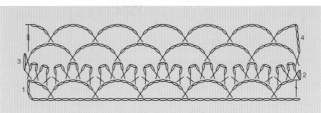

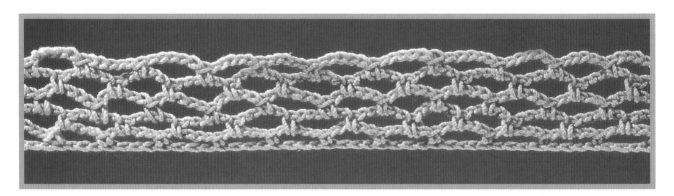

10 **Chain** multiples of 4 plus 2.

Row 1 (RS): Sc in 2nd ch from hook, *ch 5, skip next 3 ch, sc in next ch; rep from * across, turn.

Row 2: Ch 5 (counts as dc, ch 2), sc in next ch-5 loop, (ch 5, sc) in each ch-5 loop across to last ch-5 loop, ch 2, dc in last sc, turn.

Row 3: Ch 1, sc in first dc, (ch 5, sc) in each ch-5 loop across, ending with last sc in 3rd ch of turning ch, turn.

Rows 4-5: Rep Rows 2-3. Fasten off.

11

Chain multiples of 4 plus 2.

Row 1 (RS): (Sc, ch 3, sc) in 2nd ch from hook, *ch 3, skip next 3 ch, (sc, ch 3, sc) in next ch; rep from * across, turn.

Row 2: Ch 2, (sc, ch 3, sc) in next ch-3 loop, *ch 3, skip next ch-3 loop, (sc, ch 3, sc) in next ch-3 loop; rep from * across, turn.

Rows 3-5: Rep Row 2. Fasten off.

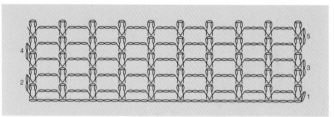

12

Chain multiples of 6 plus 4.

Row 1 (RS): Dc in 4th ch from hook, *ch 5, skip next 5 ch, (sc, ch 5, sc) in next ch; rep from * across to within last 6 ch, ch 5, skip next 5 ch, dc in last ch, turn.

Row 2: Ch 3, dc in first dc, *ch 5, skip next ch-5 loop, (sc, ch 5, sc) in next ch-5 loop; rep from * across to within last ch-5 loop, ch 5, skip next ch-5 loop, skip next dc, dc in 3rd ch of turning ch, turn.

Rows 3-5: Rep Row 2. Fasten off.

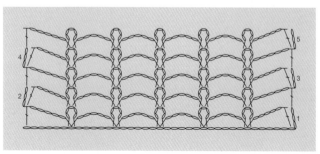

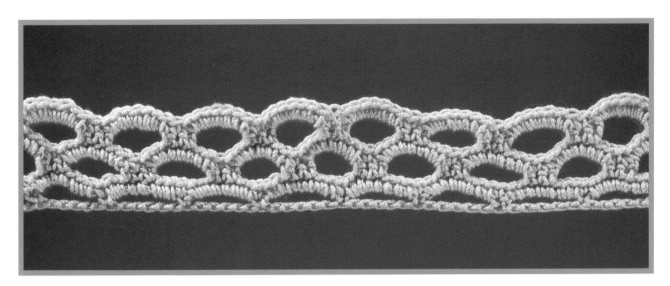

13

Chain multiples of 6 plus 2.

Row 1 (WS): Sc in 2nd ch from hook, *ch 6, skip next 5 ch, sc in next ch; rep from * across, turn.

Row 2: Ch 1, sc in first sc, *7 sc in next ch-6 loop, sc in next sc; rep from * across, turn.

Row 3: Ch 7 (counts as tr, ch 3), skip first 3 sc, *sc in each of next 3 sc**, ch 6, skip next 5 sc; rep from * across, ending last rep at **, ch 3, skip next 2 sc, tr in last sc, turn.

Row 4: Ch 1, sc in first tr, 3 sc in next ch-3 loop, *skip next sc, sc in next sc**, 7 sc in next ch-6 loop; rep from * across, ending last rep at **, 3 sc in ch-3 loop of turning ch, sc in 4th ch of turning ch, turn.

Row 5: Ch 1, sc in each of first 2 sc, *ch 6, skip next 5 sc, sc in each of next 3 sc; rep from * across, ending with sc in each of last 2 sc, turn.

Row 6: Ch 1, sc in first sc, *7 sc in next ch-6 loop, skip next sc, sc in next sc; rep from * across. Fasten off.

14

Chain multiples of 6 plus 4.

Row 1 (RS): Sc in 2nd ch from hook, sc in each ch across, turn.

Row 2: Ch 1, sc in each of first 3 sc, *ch 7, skip next 3 sc, sc in each of next 5 sc; rep from * across, ending with sc in each of last 3 sc, turn.

Row 3: Ch 1, sc in each of first 2 sc, *ch 3, 3 sc in next ch-7 loop, ch 3, skip next sc, sc in each of next 3 sc; rep from * across, ending with sc in each of last 2 sc, turn.

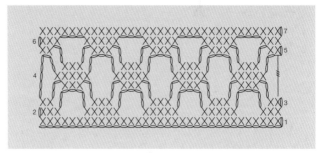

Row 4: Ch 8 (counts as dtr, ch 3), skip first 2 sc, *sc in next ch-3 loop, sc in each of next 3 sc, sc in next ch-3 loop**, ch 7; rep from * across, ending last rep at **, ch 3, skip next sc, dtr in last sc, turn.

Row 5: Ch 1, sc in first dtr, sc in next ch-3 loop, *ch 3, skip next sc, sc in each of next 3 sc, ch 3**, 3 sc in next ch-7 loop; rep from * across, ending last rep at **, sc in ch-3 loop of turning ch, sc in 5th ch of turning ch, turn.

Row 6: Ch 1, sc in each of first 2 sc, *sc in next ch-3 loop, ch 3, sc in next ch-3 loop, sc in each of next 3 sc; rep from * across, ending with sc in each of last 2 sc, turn.

Row 7: Ch 1, sc in each of first 3 sc, *3 sc in next ch-3 loop, sc in each of next 5 sc; rep from * across, ending with sc in each of last 3 sc. Fasten off.

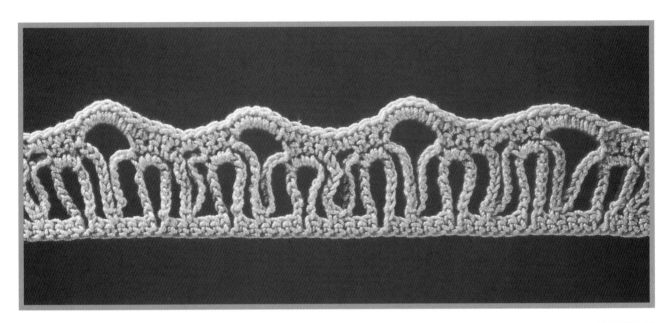

15

Chain multiples of 12 plus 9.

Row 1 (WS): Sc in 2nd ch from hook, *ch 15, sc in each of next 6 ch; rep from * across to within last ch, ch 15, sc in last ch, turn. Fasten off.

Row 2: With RS facing, rejoin thread in first ch-5 loop, ch 1, 3 sc in first ch-15 loop, ch 8, skip next 3 sc, sc between next 2 sc, ch 8, 3 sc in next ch-15 loop**, ch 3, 3 sc in next ch-15 loop; rep from * across, ending last rep at **, turn.

Row 3: Ch 1, sc in each of first 3 sc, *sc in next ch-8 loop, ch 2, sc in next ch-8 loop, sc in each of next 3 sc**, ch 5, skip next ch-3 loop, sc in each of next 3 sc; rep from * across, ending last rep at **, turn.

Row 4: Ch 1, sc in each of first 4 sc, *sc in next ch-2 space, sc in each of next 4 sc**, 7 sc in next ch-5 loop, sc in each of next 4 sc; rep from * across, ending last rep at **. Fasten off.

.2.
Single Crochet, Chains & Picots

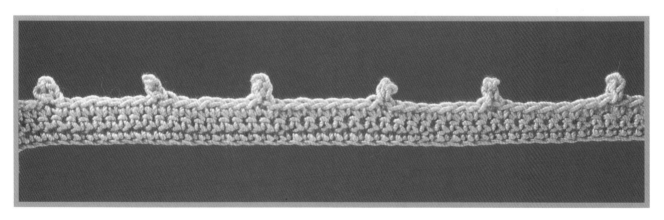

16

Picot: Ch 4, sl st in 4th ch form hook.

Chain multiples of 8 plus 1.

Row 1 (RS): Sc in 2nd ch from hook, sc in each ch across, turn.

Row 2: Ch 1, sc in each sc across, turn.

Row 3: Ch 1, sc in each of first 8 sc, *picot, sc in each of next 8 sc; rep from * across. Fasten off.

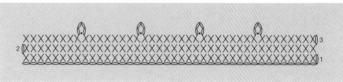

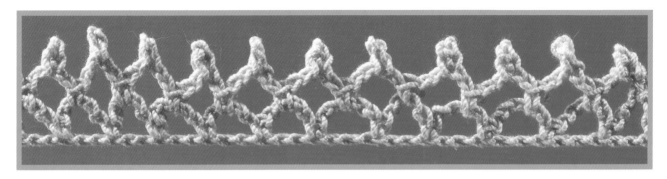

17   *Picot: Ch 3, sl st in 3rd ch from hook.*

Chain multiples of 3.

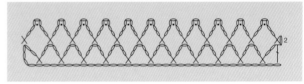

Row 1 (WS): Sc in 7th ch from hook, *ch 5, skip next 2 ch, sc in next ch; rep from * across to within last 2 ch, ch 2, skip next ch, dc in last ch, turn.

Row 2: Ch 1, sc in first dc, *ch 2, picot, ch 2**, sc in next ch-5 loop; rep from * across, ending with sc in 4th ch of turning ch. Fasten off.

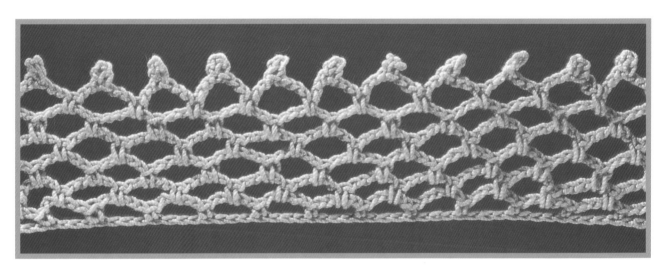

18   *Picot: Ch 3, sl st in 3rd ch from hook.*

Chain multiples of 4 plus 2.

Row 1 (WS): Sc in 2nd ch from hook, *ch 5, skip next 3 ch, sc in next ch; rep from * across, turn.

Row 2: Ch 5 (counts as dc, ch 2), sc in next ch-5 loop, (ch 5, sc) in each ch-5 loop across to last ch-5 loop, ch 2, dc in last sc, turn.

Row 3: Ch 1, sc in first dc, (ch 5, sc) in each ch-5 loop across, ending with last sc in 3rd ch of turning ch, turn.

Rows 4-5: Rep Rows 2-3.

Row 6: Ch 4 (counts as dc), picot, ch 3, sc in next ch-5 loop, *ch 3, picot, ch 3, sc in next ch-5 loop; rep from * across to last ch-5 loop, ch 3, dc in last sc. Fasten off.

19

Picot: Ch 4, sl st in 4th ch from hook.

Chain multiples of 8 plus 4.

Row 1 (WS): Sc in 2nd ch from hook, sc in each of next 2 ch, *ch 7, skip next 5 ch, sc in each of next 3 ch; rep from * across, turn.

Row 2: Ch 1, sc in each of first 2 sc, *ch 4, sc in next ch-7 loop, picot, ch 4, skip next sc, sc in next sc; rep from * across to within last sc, sc in last sc. Fasten off.

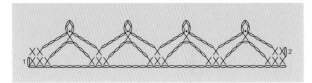

20

Picot: Ch 3, sl st in 3rd ch from hook.

Chain multiples of 5 plus 2.

Row 1 (RS): Sc in 2nd ch from hook, sc in each ch across, turn.

Row 2: Ch 1, sc in first sc, *ch 2, picot, ch 2, skip next 4 sc, sc in next sc; rep from * across, turn.

Row 3: Ch 1, sc in first sc, *ch 3, picot, ch 3, sc in next sc; rep from * across. Fasten off.

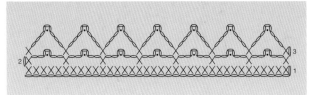

21

Picot: Ch 6, sl st in 6th ch from hook.

No foundation ch required.

Row 1 (WS): *Work picot, work 2nd picot, sl st in sl st of last picot, work 3rd picot, sl st in sl st of first picot, ch 8; rep from * for desired length, work picot, work 2nd picot, sl st in sl st of last picot, turn.

Row 2: Ch 4, sc in next picot, *ch 8, work picot, work 2nd picot, sl st in sl st

of last picot, work 3rd picot, sl st in sl st of first picot, ch 8, skip next 2 picots, sc in center picot of next 3-picot group; rep from * across. Fasten off.

22

Picot: Ch 3, sl st in 3rd ch from hook.

Chain multiples of 8 plus 4.

Row 1 (RS): Sc in 2nd ch from hook, sc in each ch across, turn.

Row 2: Ch 1, sc in each of first 3 sc, *ch 8, skip next 5 sc, sc in each of next 3 sc; rep from * across, turn.

Row 3: Ch 1, sc in each of first 2 sc, *(3 sc, picot, 3 sc, picot, 3 sc, picot, 3 sc) in next ch-8 loop, skip next sc, sc in next sc; rep from * across, sc in last sc. Fasten off.

23

Picot: Ch 3, sl st in 3rd ch from hook.

Chain multiples of 6 plus 2.

Row 1 (RS): Sc in 2nd ch from hook, *ch 5, skip next 5 ch, sc in next ch; rep from * across, turn.

Row 2: Ch 1, sc in first sc, (ch 5, sc) in each sc across, turn.

Row 3: Ch 1, sc in first sc, (ch 7, sc) in each sc across, turn.

Row 4: Ch 1, sc in first sc, (ch 8, sc) in each sc across, turn.

Row 5: Ch 1, sc in first sc, (ch 9, sc) in each sc across, turn.

Row 6: Ch 1, sc in first sc, *(5 sc, picot, 4 sc) in next ch-9 loop, sc in next sc; rep from * across. Fasten off.

24

Picot: Ch 3, sl st in 3rd ch from hook.

Chain multiples of 8 plus 2.

Row 1 (WS): Sc in 2nd ch from hook, sc in each ch across, turn.

Row 2: Ch 1, sc in each sc across, turn.

Row 3: Ch 1, sc in each of first 3 sc, *ch 9, skip next 3 sc, sc in each of next 5 sc; rep from * across, ending with sc in each of last 3 sc, turn.

Row 4: Ch 1, sc in each of first 2 sc, *ch 5, sc in next ch-9 loop, ch 5, skip next sc**, sc in each of next 3 sc; rep from * across, ending with sc in each of last 2 sc, turn.

Row 5: Ch 1, sc in first sc, *ch 6, skip next ch-5 loop, sc in next sc, ch 6, skip next sc, sc in next sc; rep from * across, turn.

Row 6: Ch 1, sc in first sc, *ch 6, skip next ch-6 loop, sc in next sc, picot, turn, work 10 sc in picot just made, ch 6, skip next ch-6 loop, sc in next sc; rep from * across. Fasten off.

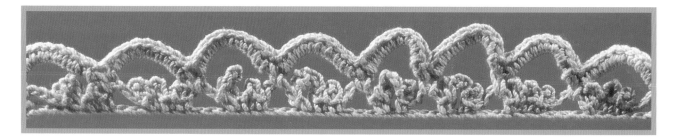

25

Picot: Ch 3, sl st in 3rd ch from hook.

Chain multiples of 6 plus 5.

Row 1 (WS): Sc in 7th ch from hook, picot, ch 5, sc in next ch, picot, sc in next ch, *ch 5, skip next 3 ch, sc in next ch, picot, ch 5, sc in next ch, picot, sc in next ch; rep from * across to within last 2 ch, ch 2, skip next ch, dc in last ch, turn.

Row 2: Ch 1, sc in first dc, *ch 9, skip next (picot, ch-5, picot), sc in next ch-5 loop; rep from * across, ending with last sc in 4th ch of turning ch, turn.

Row 3: Ch 1, sc in first sc, *11 sc in next ch-9 loop, sc in next sc; rep from * across. Fasten off.

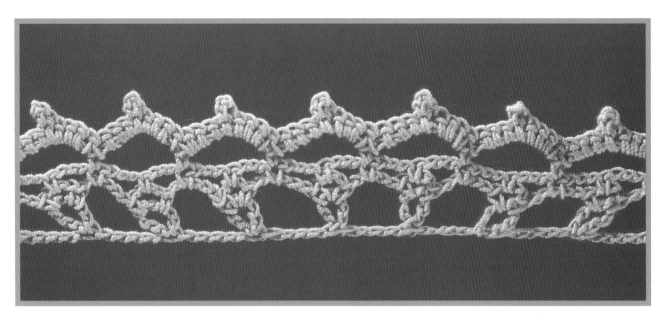

26

Picot: Ch 3, sl st in 3rd ch from hook.

No foundation ch required.

Row 1 (WS): Ch 16, sl st in 8th ch from hook, *ch 12, sl st in 8th ch from hook; rep from * for desired length, working an even number of ch-8 loops, turn.

Row 2: Ch 5, (sc, ch 3, sc) in next ch-8 loop *ch 5, (sc, ch 3, sc) in next ch-8 loop; rep from * across, ending with (sc, ch 3, sc) in first ch of previous row, turn.

Row 3: Ch 3, sc in next ch-3 loop, *ch 3, sc in next ch-5 loop, ch 3, sc in next ch-3 loop; rep from * across, turn.

Row 4: Ch 8 (counts as dtr, ch 3), skip next ch-3 loop, sc in next sc, *ch 7, skip next 2 ch-3 loops, sc in next sc; rep from * across to within last ch-3 loop, ch 3, skip next ch-3 loop, dtr in 3rd ch of turning ch, turn.

Row 5: Ch 1, sc in first dtr, picot, 4 sc in next ch-3 loop, (4 sc, picot, 4 sc) in each ch-7 loop across to turning ch, 4 sc in ch-3 loop of turning ch, picot. Fasten off.

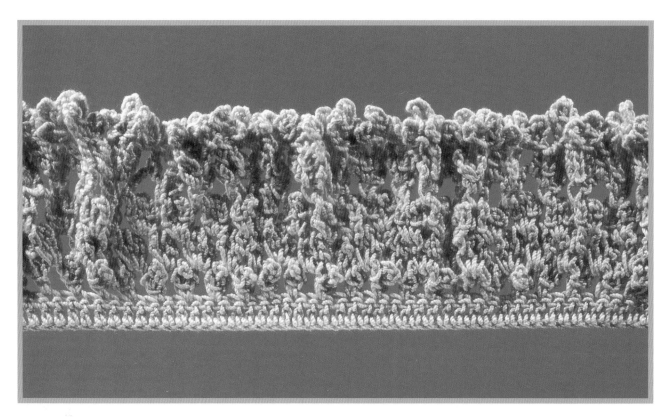

27

Picot: Ch 5, sl st in 5th ch from hook.

Chain multiples of 2.

Row 1 (WS): Dc in 4th ch from hook, dc in each ch across, turn.

Row 2: Ch 1, sc in first dc, picot, ch 5, skip next dc, sc in next dc, *ch 1, picot, ch 4, skip next dc, sc in next dc; rep from * across to turning ch, ch 2, dc in 3rd ch of turning ch, turn.

Row 3: Ch 5, sc in first dc, *(sc, ch 5, sc) in next ch-4 loop, ch 5, skip next picot; rep from * across to within last ch-5 loop, (sc, ch 5, sc) in next ch-5 loop, ch 5, sc in last picot, turn.

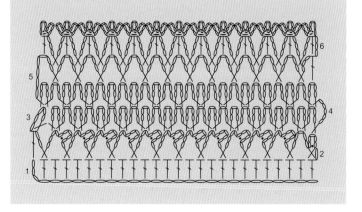

Row 4: Ch 5, *(sc, ch 5, sc) in next ch-5 loop**, ch 5, skip next ch-5 loop; rep from * across, ending last rep at **, turn.

Row 5: Ch 7, skip next ch-5 loop, sc in next ch-5 loop, *ch 5, skip next ch-5 loop, sc in next ch-5 loop; rep from * across to within last ch-5 loop, ch 3, dc in last ch-5 loop, turn.

Row 6: Ch 3, dc in first dc, work picot, work 2nd picot, sl st in sl st of first picot, ch 3, skip next ch-3 loop, sc in next sc, *ch 3, dc in next ch-5 loop, work picot, work 2nd picot, sl st in sl st of first picot, work 3rd picot, sl st in sl st of first picot, ch 3, sc in next sc; rep from * across to turning ch, ch 3, dc in turning ch, work picot, work 2nd picot, sl st in sl st of first picot. Fasten off.

.3.

Double Crochet, Single Crochet, Chains & Picots

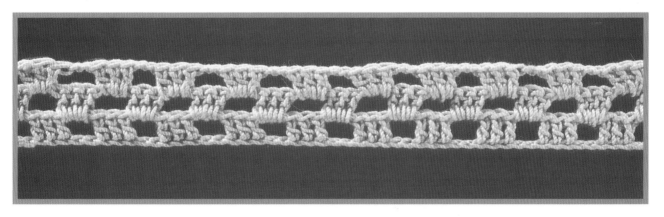

28

Chain multiples of 6.

Row 1 (RS): Dc in 4th ch from hook, dc in each of next 2 ch, *ch 2, skip next 2 ch, dc in each of next 4 ch; rep from * across, turn.

Row 2: Ch 5 (counts as dc, ch 2), skip first 3 dc, *dc in next dc, 2 dc in next ch-2 space, dc in next dc, ch 2, skip next 2 dc; rep from * across to turning ch, dc in 3rd ch of turning ch, turn.

Row 3: Ch 3 (counts as dc), *2 dc in next ch-2 space, dc in next dc, ch 2, skip next 2 dc, dc in next dc; rep from * across to turning ch, 2 dc in ch-2 space of turning ch, dc in 3rd ch of turning ch. Fasten off.

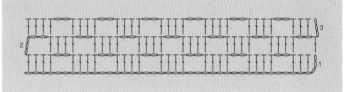

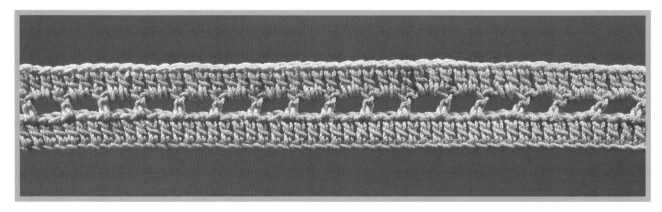

29

Chain multiples of 3.

Row 1 (RS): Dc in 4th ch from hook, dc in each ch across, turn.

Row 2: Ch 5 (counts as dc, ch 2), skip first 3 dc, dc in next dc, *ch 2, skip next 2 dc, dc in next dc; rep from * across, ending with last dc in 3rd ch of turning ch, turn.

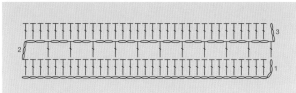

Row 3: Ch 3 (counts as dc), *2 dc in next ch-2 space, dc in next dc; rep from * across, ending with last dc in 3rd ch of turning ch. Fasten off.

30

Chain multiples of 9 plus 3.

Row 1 (RS): Dc in 4th ch from hook, dc in next ch, *ch 2, skip next 2 ch, dc in each of next 7 ch; rep from * across, ending with dc in each of last 5 ch, turn.

Row 2: Ch 3 (counts as dc), skip first dc, dc in each of next 4 dc, *2 dc in next ch-2 space, ch 2, skip next 2 dc**, dc in each of next 5 dc; rep from * across, ending ending last rep at **, dc in 3rd ch of turning ch, turn.

Row 3: Ch 3 (counts as dc), *2 dc in next ch-2 space, dc in each of next 5 dc**, ch 2, skip next 2 dc; rep from * across, ending last rep at **, ch 1, skip next dc, dc in 3rd ch of turning ch, turn.

Row 4: Ch 3 (counts as dc), dc in next ch-1 space, *ch 2, skip next 2 dc, dc in each of next 5 dc**, 2 dc in next ch-2 space; rep from * across, ending last rep at **, dc in 3rd ch of turning ch. Fasten off.

31

Chain multiples of 5 plus 3.

Row 1 (WS): Sc in 2nd ch from hook, sc in next ch, *ch 3, skip next 3 ch, sc in each of next 2 ch; rep from * across, turn.

Row 2: Ch 3 (counts as dc), skip first sc, dc in next sc, *ch 3, skip next ch-3 loop, dc in each of next 2 sc; rep from * across, turn.

Row 3: Ch 1, sc in each of first 2 dc, *ch 3, skip next ch-3 loop, sc in each of next 2 dc; rep from * across, ending with last sc in 3rd ch of turning ch, turn.

Rows 4-7: Rep Rows 2-3 (twice). Fasten off.

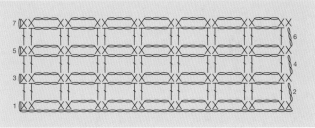

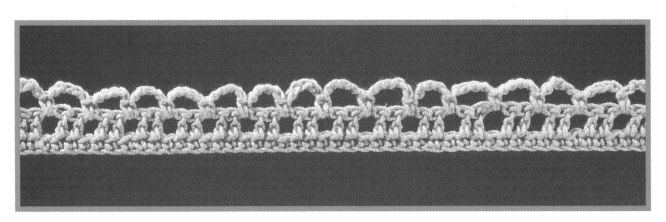

32

Chain multiples of 3 plus 1.

Row 1 (RS): Sc in 2nd ch from hook, sc in each ch across, turn.

Row 2: Ch 4 (counts as dc, ch 1), skip first 2 sc, *dc in each of next 2 sc, ch 1, skip next sc; rep from * across to within last sc, dc in last sc, turn.

Row 3: Ch 1, sc in first dc, sc in next ch-1 space, (ch 5, sc) in each ch-1 space across, sc in 3rd ch of turning. Fasten off.

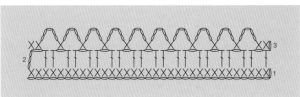

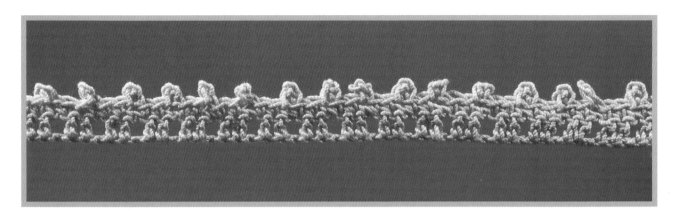

33

Picot: Ch 3, sl st in 3rd ch from hook.

Chain multiples of 3 plus 1.

Row 1 (WS): Dc in 4th ch from hook, *ch 1, skip next ch, dc in each of next 2 ch; rep from * across, turn.

Row 2: Ch 1, sc in each of first 2 dc, *picot, skip next ch-1 space, sc in each of next 2 dc; rep from * across, ending with last sc in 3rd ch of turning ch. Fasten off.

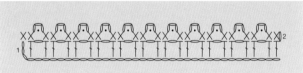

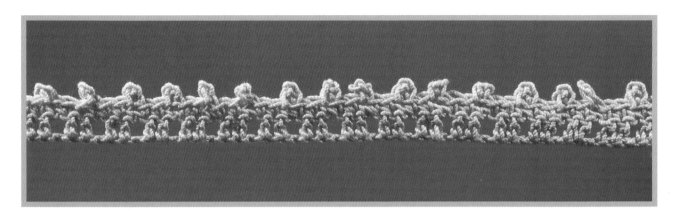

34

Chain multiples of 6 plus 4.

Row 1 (RS): Dc in 6th ch from hook, dc in each of next 2 ch, *ch 5, turn, skip next 2 dc, sl st in next dc, ch 3, turn, sc in next ch-5 loop, ch 3, sl st in last ch of ch-5 loop**, ch 3, skip next 3 ch, dc in each of next 3 ch; rep from * across, ending last rep at **, ch 1, skip next ch, dc in last ch. Fasten off.

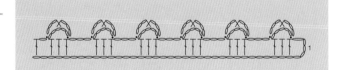

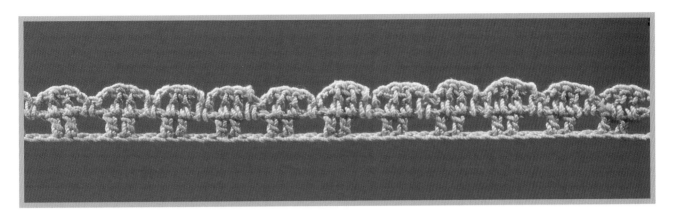

35

Chain multiples of 4.

Row 1 (WS): Dc in 4th ch from hook, *ch 2, skip next 2 ch, dc in each of next 2 ch; rep from * across, turn.

Row 2: Ch 3 (counts as dc), skip first dc, dc in next dc, *ch 2, sc in next ch-2 space, ch 2, dc in each of next 2 dc; rep from * across, ending with last dc in 3rd ch of turning ch. Fasten off.

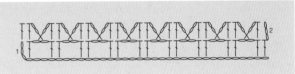

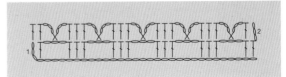

36

Chain multiples of 6 plus 3.

Row 1 (WS): Dc in 4th ch from hook, *ch 3, skip next 3 ch, dc in each of next 3 ch; rep from * across, ending with dc in each of last 2 ch, turn.

Row 2: Ch 3 (counts as dc), skip first dc, dc in next dc, *ch 3, sc in next ch-3 loop, ch 3**, dc in each of next 3 dc; rep from * across, ending last rep at **, dc in next dc, dc in 3rd ch of turning ch. Fasten off.

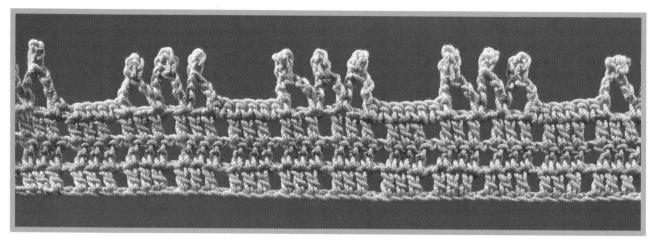

37

Chain multiples of 4 plus 1.

Row 1 (WS): Dc in 4th ch from hook, dc in next ch, *ch 1, skip next ch, dc in each of next 3 ch; rep from * across, turn.

Rows 2-3: Ch 3 (counts as dc), skip first dc, dc in each of next 2 dc, *ch 1, skip next ch-1 space, dc in each of next 3 dc; rep from * across, ending with last dc in 3rd ch of turning ch.

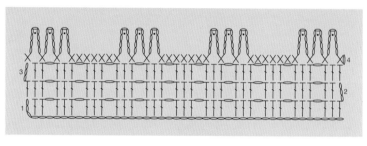

Row 4: Ch 1, sc in first dc, *(ch 3, picot, ch 3, skip next st, sc in next dc) 3 times**, sc in each of next 6 sts; rep from * across, ending last rep at **, with last sc in 3rd ch of turning ch. Fasten off.

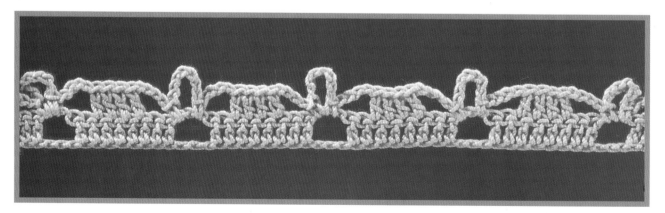

38

Chain multiples of 11 plus 2.

Row 1 (WS): Dc in 4th ch from hook, dc in each of next 2 ch, *ch 3, skip next 3 ch, dc in each of next 8 ch; rep from * across, ending with dc in each of last 4 ch turn.

Row 2: Ch 3 (counts as dc), skip first dc, dc in next dc, *ch 4, skip next 2 dc, (sc, ch 7, sc) in next ch-3 loop, ch 4, skip next 2 dc**, dc in each of next 4 dc; rep from * across, ending last rep at **, dc in next dc, dc in 3rd ch of turning ch. Fasten off.

39

Picot: Ch 3, sl st in 3rd ch from hook.

Chain multiples of 12 plus 8.

Row 1 (RS): Sc in 2nd ch from hook, *ch 5, skip next 5 ch, sc in next ch; rep from * across, turn.

Row 2: Ch 3 (counts as dc), *5 dc in next ch-5 loop**, ch 3, sc in next ch-5 loop, ch 3; rep from * across, ending last rep at **, dc in last sc, turn.

Row 3: Ch 3 (counts as dc), skip first dc, *dc in each of next 5 dc**, ch 3, skip next ch-3 loop, sc in next sc, ch 3, skip next ch-3 loop; rep from * across, ending last rep at **, dc in 3rd ch of turning, turn.

Row 4: Ch 3 (counts as dc), skip first dc, *dc in each of next 5 dc**, ch 3, skip next ch-3 loop, sc in next sc, picot, ch 3, skip next ch-3 loop; rep from * across, ending last rep at **, dc in 3rd ch of turning, turn. Fasten off.

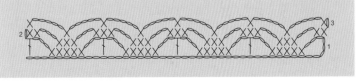

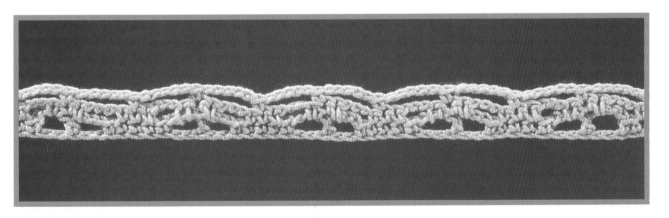

40

Chain multiples of 10 plus 6.

Row 1 (RS): Sc in 9th ch from hook, sc in each of next 4 ch, *ch 3, skip next 2 ch, dc in next ch**, ch 3, skip next 2 ch, sc in each of next 5 ch; rep from * across, ending last rep at **, turn.

Row 2: Ch 1, sc in first dc, sc in first ch of next ch-3 loop, *ch 3, skip next sc, sc in each of next 3 sc, ch 3, sc in last ch of next ch-3 loop**, sc in next dc, sc in first ch of next ch-3 loop; rep from * across, ending last rep at ** in ch-3 loop of turning ch, sc in next ch of turning ch, turn.

Row 3: Ch 1, sc in first sc, *ch 5, skip next (sc, ch 3, sc), sc in next sc; rep from * across. Fasten off.

41

Chain multiples of 9 plus 2.

Row 1 (RS): Dc in 8th ch from hook, *ch 2, skip next 2 ch, dc in next ch; rep from * across, turn.

Row 2: Ch 1, sc in first dc, *2 sc in next ch-2 space, sc in next dc; rep from * across, ending with last sc in 3rd ch of turning ch, turn.

Row 3: Ch 1, sc in first 7 sc, *ch 5, skip next 2 sc, sc in each of next 7 sc; rep from * across, turn.

Row 4: Ch 1, sc in each of first 5 sc, ch 5, skip next 2 sc, sc in next ch-5 loop, ch 5, skip next 2 sc, sc in each of next 3 sc; rep from * across to within last 2 sc, sc in each of last 2 sc, turn.

Row 5: Ch 1, sc in each of first 4 sc, *skip next sc, 3 sc in next ch-5 loop, ch 7, 3 sc in next ch-5 loop, skip next sc, sc in next sc; rep from * across to within last 3 sc, sc in last 3 sc. Fasten off.

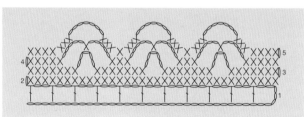

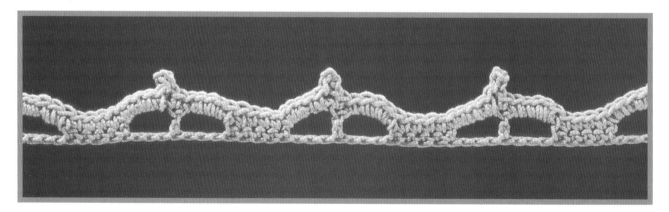

42

Picot: Ch 4, sl st in 4th ch from hook.

Chain multiples of 12 plus 6.

Row 1 (WS): Sc in 2nd ch from hook, sc in each of next 4 ch, *ch 5, skip next 3 ch, dc in next ch, ch 5, skip next 3 ch, sc in each of next 5 ch; rep from * across, turn.

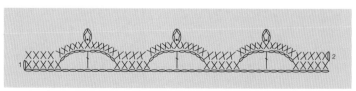

Row 2: Ch 1, sc in each of first 5 sc, *5 sc in next ch-5 loop, sc in next dc, picot, 5 sc in next ch-5 loop, skip next sc, sc in each of next 4 sc; rep from * across, turn. Fasten off.

43

Chain multiples of 6 plus 3.

Row 1 (RS): Dc in 4th ch from hook, dc in each ch across, turn.

Row 2: Ch 8 (counts as dc, ch 5), skip first 6 dc, dc in next dc, *ch 5, skip next 5 dc, dc in next dc; rep from * across, ending with last dc in 3rd ch of turning ch, turn.

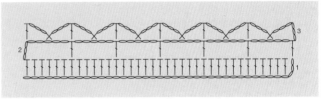

Row 3: Ch 6 (counts as dc, ch 3), *sc in next ch-5 loop, ch 3, dc in next dc**, ch 3; rep from * across, ending last rep at **, with last dc in 3rd ch of turning ch. Fasten off.

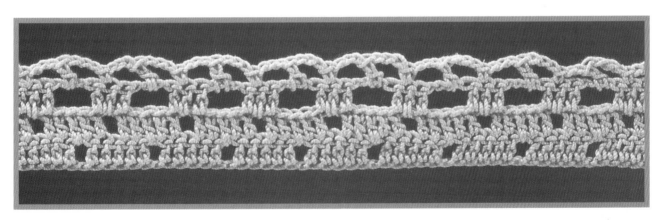

44

Chain multiples of 6 plus 3.

Row 1 (WS): Dc in 4th ch from hook, dc in next ch, *ch 1, skip next ch, dc in each of next 5 ch; rep from * across, ending with dc in each of last 3 ch, turn.

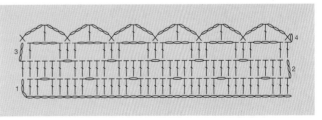

Row 2: Ch 3 (counts as dc), skip first dc, *dc in each of next 5 sts or spaces**, ch 1, skip next dc; rep from * across, ending last rep at **, dc in 3rd ch of turning ch, turn.

Row 3: Ch 3 (counts as dc), skip first dc, dc in next dc, *ch 3, skip next 3 dc, dc in next dc**, dc in next ch-1 space, dc in next dc; rep from * across, ending last rep at **, dc in 3rd ch of turning ch, turn.

Row 4: Ch 1, sc in first dc, *ch 3, skip next dc, dc in next ch-3 loop, ch 3, skip next dc, sc in next dc; rep from * across, ending with last sc in 3rd ch of turning ch. Fasten off.

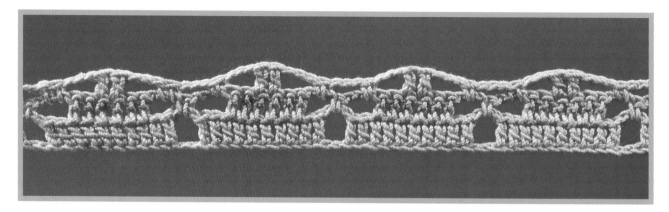

45

Chain multiples of 12 plus 2.

Row 1 (WS): Dc in 4th ch from hook, dc in each of next 3 ch, *ch 3, skip next 2 ch, dc in each of next 10 ch; rep from * across, ending with dc in each of last 5 ch, turn.

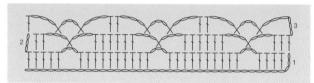

Row 2: Ch 3 (counts as dc), skip first dc, dc in each of next 2 dc, *ch 3, skip next 2 dc, sc in next ch-3 loop, ch 3, skip next 2 dc**, dc in each of next 6 dc; rep from * across, ending last rep at **, dc in each of next 2 dc, dc in 3rd ch of turning ch, turn.

Row 3: Ch 6 (counts as dc, ch 3), skip first 3 dc, *(sc, ch 3) in each of next 2 ch-3 loops, skip next 2 dc**, dc in each of next 2 dc; rep from * across, ending last rep at **, dc in 3rd ch of turning ch. Fasten off.

46

Chain multiples of 10 plus 2.

Row 1 (RS): Sc in 2nd ch from hook, *ch 3, skip next 2 ch, dc in each of next 5 ch, ch 3, skip next 2 ch, sc in next ch; rep from * across, turn.

Row 2: Ch 5 (counts as dc, ch 2), skip next ch-3 loop, *sc in each of next 5 dc, ch 2, skip next ch-3 loop, dc in next sc**, ch 2, skip next ch-3 loop; rep from * across, ending last rep at **, turn.

Row 3: Ch 1, sc in first sc, *ch 3, skip next ch-2 space, dc in each of next 5 sc, ch 3, skip next ch-2 space, sc in next dc; rep from * across, ending with last sc in 3rd ch of turning ch. Fasten off.

47

Chain multiples of 7 plus 3.

Row 1 (RS): Sc in 2nd ch from hook, sc in each ch across, turn.

Row 2: Ch 3 (counts as dc), skip first sc, dc in next sc, *ch 5, skip next 5 sc, dc in each of next 2 sc; rep from * across, turn.

Row 3: Ch 3 (counts as dc), skip first dc, dc in next dc, *ch 2, sc in next ch-5 loop, ch 2, dc in each of next 2 dc; rep from * across, ending with last dc in 3rd ch of turning ch, turn.

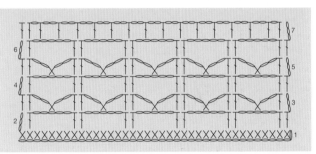

Row 4: Ch 3 (counts as dc), skip first dc, dc in next dc, *ch 5, skip next 2 ch-2 spaces, dc in each of next 2 dc; rep from * across, ending with last dc in 3rd ch of turning ch, turn.

Rows 5-6: Rep Rows 3-4.

Row 7: Ch 3 (counts as dc), skip first dc, dc in next dc, *ch 1, (dc, ch 2) twice in next ch-5 loop, dc between next 2 dc, ch 2; rep from * across to within last ch-5 loop, (dc, ch 3, dc) in last ch-5 loop, ch 1, dc in next dc, dc in 3rd ch of turning ch. Fasten off.

48

Chain multiples of 3.

Row 1 (RS): Dc in 4th ch from hook, dc in each ch across, turn.

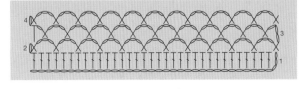

Row 2: Ch 1, sc in first dc, *ch 3, skip next 2 dc, sc in next dc; rep from * across, ending with last sc in 3rd ch of turning ch, turn.

Row 3: Ch 3 (counts as hdc, ch 1), sc in next ch-3 loop, (ch 3, sc) in each ch-3 loop across to last ch-3 loop, ch 1, hdc in last sc, turn.

Row 4: Ch 1, sc in first hdc, (ch 3, sc) in each ch-3 loop across, ending with last sc in 2nd ch of turning ch. Fasten off.

49

Chain multiples of 6 plus 4.

Row 1 (RS): Dc in 6th ch from hook, *ch 1, skip next ch, dc in next ch; rep from * across, turn.

Row 2: Ch 1, sc in first dc, *ch 9, skip next 3 ch-1 spaces, sc in next dc; rep from * across, ending with last sc in 4th ch of turning ch, turn.

Row 3: Ch 7 (counts as dtr, ch 2), (5 dc, ch 5) in each ch-9 loop across to within last ch-9 loop, 5 dc in last ch-9 loop, ch 2, dtr in last sc, turn.

Row 4: Ch 1, sc in first dtr, (ch 5, sc) in each ch-5 loop across, ending with last sc in 5th ch of turning ch, turn.

Row 5: Ch 4 (counts as dc, ch 1), *(dc, ch 1, dc, ch 1) in next ch-5 loop, dc in next sc**, ch 1; rep from * across, ending last rep at **. Fasten off.

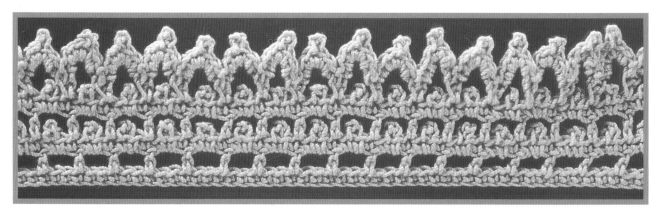

50

Picot: Ch 3, sl st in 3rd ch from hook.

Chain multiples of 3 plus 2.

Row 1 (RS): Sc in 2nd ch from hook, sc in each ch across, turn.

Row 2: Ch 5 (counts as dc, ch 2), skip first 3 sc, dc in next sc, *ch 2, skip next 2 sc, dc in next sc; rep from * across, turn.

Row 3: Ch 1, sc in first sc, *(sc, picot, sc) in next ch-2 space, sc in next dc; rep from * across, ending with last sc in 3rd ch of turning ch, turn.

Rows 4-5: Rep Rows 2-3.

Row 6: Ch 1, sc in first sc, *ch 6, skip next 2 sc, sc in next sc; rep from * across, turn.

Row 7: Ch 1, sl st in first sc, *(3 sc, picot, 3 sc) in next ch-6 loop, sl st in next sc; rep from * across. Fasten off

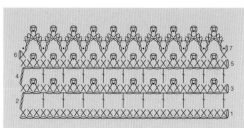

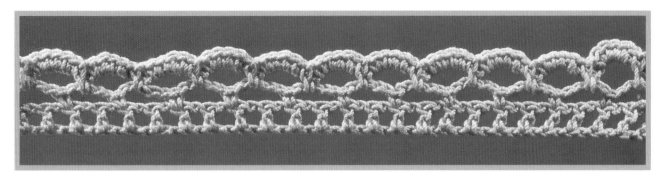

51

Chain multiples of 4.

Row 1 (WS): Dc in 6th ch from hook, *ch 1, skip next ch, dc in next ch; rep from * across, turn.

Row 2: Ch 1, sc in first dc, *ch 5, skip next 2 ch-1 spaces, sc in next dc; rep from * across, ending with last sc in 4th ch of turning ch, turn.

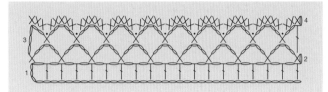

Row 3: Ch 5 (counts as dc, ch 2), sc in next ch-5 loop, (ch 5, sc) in each ch-5 loop across to last ch-5 loop, ch 2, dc in last sc, turn.

Row 4: Ch 1, sc in first dc, 2 sc in next ch-2 space, sl st in next sc, *5 sc in next ch-5 loop, sl st in next sc; rep from * across to turning ch, 2 sc in ch-2 space of turning ch, sc in 3rd ch of turning ch. Fasten off.

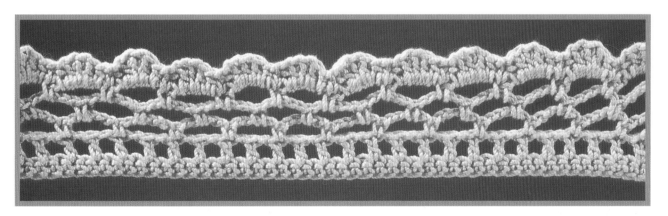

52

Chain multiples of 4 plus 2.

Row 1 (WS): Sc in 2nd ch from hook, sc in each ch across, turn.

Row 2: Ch 4 (counts as dc, ch 1), skip first 2 sc, dc in next sc, *ch 1, skip next sc, dc in next sc; rep from * across, turn.

Row 3: Ch 1, sc in first sc, *ch 5, skip next 2 ch-1 spaces, sc in next dc; rep from * across, ending with last sc in 3rd ch of turning ch, turn.

Row 4: Ch 5 (counts as dc, ch 2), sc in next ch-5 loop, (ch 5, sc) in each ch-5 loop across to last ch-5 loop, ch 2, dc in last sc, turn.

Row 5: Ch 1, sc in first dc, (ch 5, sc) in each ch-5 loop across, ending with last sc in 3rd ch of turning ch, turn.

Row 6: Ch 1, sc in first sc, *(hdc, 3 dc, hdc) in next ch-5 loop, sc in next sc; rep from * across. Fasten off.

53

Chain multiples of 8 plus 2.

Row 1 (RS): Sc in 2nd ch from hook, *ch 5, skip next 3 ch, sc in next ch; rep from * across, turn.

Row 2: Ch 5 (counts as dc, ch 2), sc in next ch-5 loop, (ch 5, sc) in each ch-5 loop across to last ch-5 loop, ch 2, dc in last sc, turn.

Row 3: Ch 5 (counts as dc, ch 2), skip next ch-2 space, *4 dc in next ch-5 loop, ch 2**, dc in next ch-5 loop, ch 2; rep from * across, ending last rep at **, dc in 3rd ch of turning ch. Fasten off.

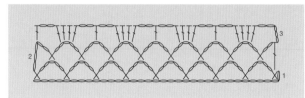

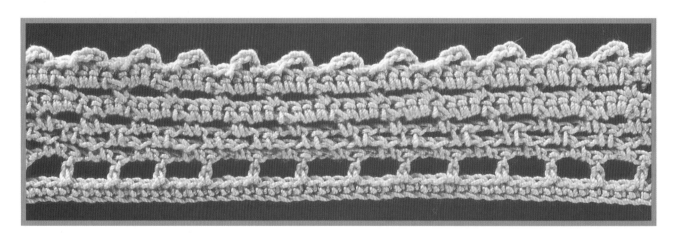

54

Chain multiples of 4 plus 2.

Row 1 (RS): Sc in 2nd ch from hook, sc in each ch across, turn.

Row 2: Ch 6 (counts as dc, ch 3), skip first 4 sc, dc in next sc, *ch 3, skip next 3 sc, dc in next sc; rep from * across, turn.

Row 3: Ch 3 (counts as hdc, ch 1), sc in next ch-3 loop, (ch 3, sc) in each ch-3 loop across to last ch-3 loop, ch 1, hdc in 3rd ch of turning ch, turn.

Row 4: Ch 1, sc in first hdc, (ch 3, sc) in each ch-3 loop across, ending with last sc in 2nd ch of turning ch, turn.

Row 5: Rep Row 3.

Row 6: Ch 1, sc in first hdc, sc in next ch-1 space, sc in next sc, *3 sc in next ch-3 loop, sc in next sc; rep from * across to turning ch, sc in ch-1 space of turning ch, sc in 2nd ch of turning ch, turn.

Row 7: Ch 1, sc in first sc, *ch 3, skip next 3 sc, sc in next sc; rep from * across, turn.

Row 8: Ch 1, sc in first sc, *3 sc in next ch-3 loop, sc in next sc; rep from * across, turn.

Row 9: Ch 1, sl st in each of first 2 sc, *ch 4, skip next sc, sl st in each of next 3 sc; rep from * across, ending with sl st in each of last 2 sc. Fasten off.

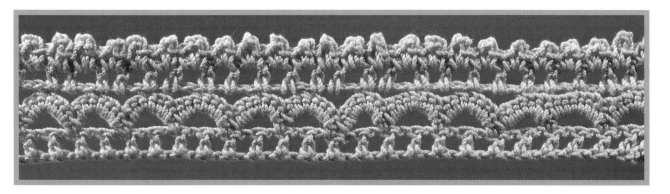

55

Chain multiples of 4.

Row 1 (WS): Dc in 6th ch from hook, *ch 1, skip next ch, dc in next ch; rep from * across, turn.

Row 2: Ch 1, sc in first dc, *ch 5, skip next 2 ch-1 spaces, sc in next dc; rep from * across, ending with last sc in 4th ch of turning ch, turn.

Row 3: Ch 1, sc in first sc, 7 sc in each ch-5 loop across to last ch-5 loop, sc in last sc, turn.

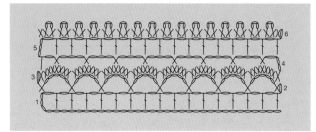

Row 4: Ch 3 (counts as hdc, ch 1), skip first 4 sc, sc in next sc, *ch 3, skip next 6 sc, sc in next sc; rep from * across to within last 4 sc, ch 1, skip next 3 sc, hdc in last sc, turn.

Row 5: Ch 4 (counts as dc, ch 1), skip next ch-1 space, dc in next sc, *ch 1, dc in next ch-3 loop, ch 1, dc in next sc; rep from * across to turning ch, ch 1, dc in 2nd ch of turning ch, turn.

Row 6: Ch 1, sc in first dc, (sc, ch 3, sc) in each ch-1 space across to turning ch, (sc, ch 3, sc) in ch-1 space of turning ch, sc in 3rd ch of turning ch. Fasten off.

56

Picot: Ch 4, sl st in 4th ch from hook.

Chain multiples of 6 plus 5.

Row 1 (WS): Dc in 8th ch from hook, *ch 2, skip next 2 ch, dc in next ch; rep from * across, turn.

Row 2: Ch 1, sc in first dc, *ch 13, skip next 2 ch-2 spaces, sc in next dc; rep from * across, ending with last sc in 5th ch of turning ch, turn.

Row 3: Ch 1, (6 sc, picot, 6 sc) in each ch-13 loop across. Fasten off.

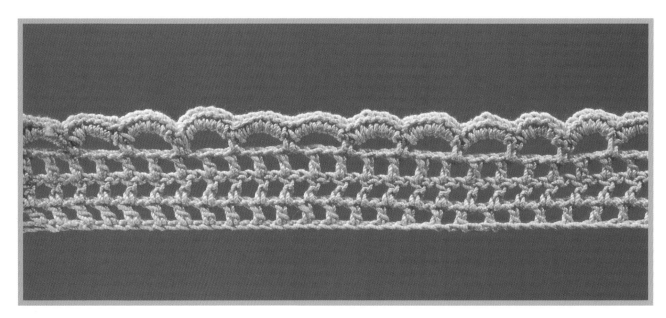

57

Chain multiples of 4.

Row 1 (RS): Dc in 6th ch from hook, *ch 1, skip next ch, dc in next ch; rep from * across, turn.

Row 2: Ch 4 (counts as dc, ch 1), skip next ch-1 space, dc in next dc, (ch 1, dc) in each dc across, ending with last dc in 4th ch of turning ch, turn.

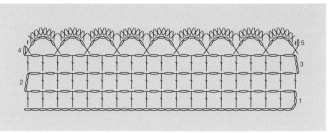

Row 3: Ch 4 (counts as dc, ch 1), skip next ch-1 space, dc in next dc, (ch 1, dc) in each dc across, ending with last dc in 3rd ch of turning ch, turn.

Row 4: Ch 1, sc in first dc, *ch 5, skip next 2 ch-1 spaces, sc in next dc; rep from * across, ending with last sc in 3rd ch of turning ch, turn.

Row 5: Ch 1, sl st in first sc, 7 sc in each ch-5 loop across, sl st in last sc. Fasten off.

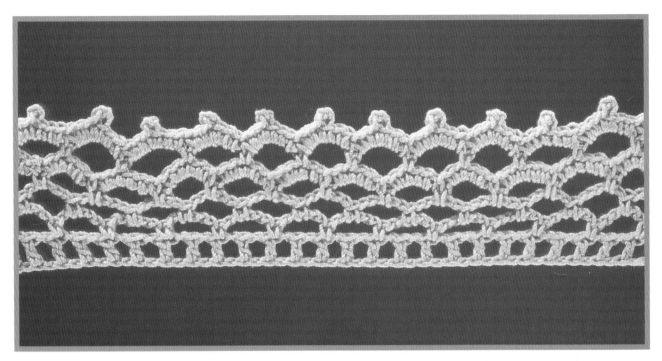

58

Picot: Ch 3, sl st in 3rd ch from hook.

Chain multiples of 4.

Row 1 (RS): Dc in 6th ch from hook, *ch 1, skip next ch, dc in next ch; rep from * across, turn.

Row 2: Ch 1, sc in first dc, *ch 5, skip next 2 ch-1 spaces, sc in next dc; rep from * across, ending with last sc in 4th ch of turning ch, turn.

Row 3: Ch 5 (counts as dc, ch 2), sc in next ch-5 loop, (ch 5, sc) in each-5 loop across to last ch-5 loop, ch 2, dc in last sc, turn.

Row 4: Ch 1, sc in first dc, (ch 5, sc) in each ch-5 loop across, ending with last sc in 3rd ch of turning ch, turn.

Row 5: Ch 1, sc in first sc, *5 sc in next ch-5 loop, sl st in next sc; rep from * across, ending with sc in last sc, turn.

Row 6: Ch 6 (counts as tr, ch 2), skip first 3 sc, sc in next sc, *ch 5, skip next 4 sc, sc in next sc; rep from * across to within last 3 sc, ch 2, skip next 2 sc, dc in last sc, turn.

Row 7: Ch 1, sc in first dc, picot, 3 sc in next ch-2 space, (3 sc, picot, 3 sc) in each ch-5 loop across to turning ch, 3 sc in ch-2 space of turning ch, sc in 4th ch of turning ch, picot. Fasten off.

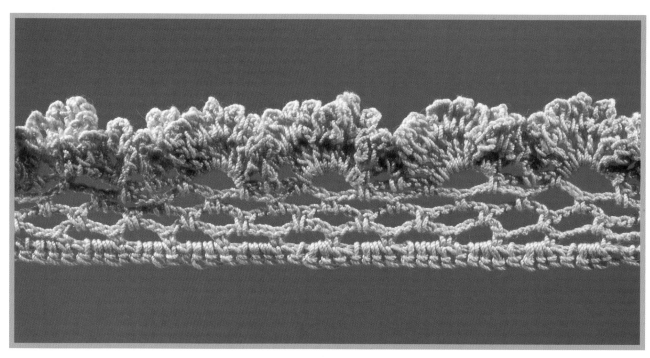

59

Chain multiples of 4 plus 2.

Row 1 (RS): Sc in 2nd ch from hook, *ch 5, skip next 3 ch, sc in next ch; rep from * across, turn.

Row 2: Ch 5 (counts as dc, ch 2), sc in next ch-5 loop, (ch 5, sc) in each ch-5 loop across to last ch-5 loop, ch 2, dc in last sc, turn.

Row 3: Ch 1, sc in first dc, (ch 5, sc) in each ch-5 loop across, ending with last sc in 3rd ch of turning ch, turn.

Row 4: Rep Row 2.

Row 5: Ch 1, sc in first sc, *ch 2, (dc, ch 2) 10 times in next ch-5 loop, sc in next ch-5 loop; rep from * across, ending with last sc in 3rd ch of turning ch, turn.

Row 6: Ch 1, sc in first sc, (ch 4, sc) in each ch-2 space across to last ch-2 space, ch 2, sc in last sc. Fasten off.

Bottom Edging: With WS facing, working across opposite side of foundation ch, join yarn in first ch, ch 1, sc in first ch, *3 sc in next ch-3 loop, sc in next ch; rep from * across. Fasten off.

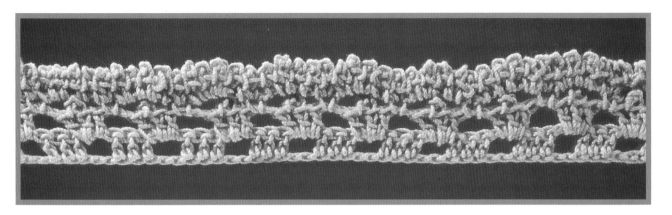

60

Picot: Ch 3, sl st in 3rd ch form hook.

Chain multiples of 5.

Row 1 (WS): Dc in 4th ch from hook, dc in next ch, *ch 2, skip next 2 ch, dc in each of next 3 ch; rep from * across, turn.

Row 2: Ch 5 (counts as dc, ch 2), skip first 3 dc, *(2 dc, picot, dc) in next ch-2 space**, ch 2; rep from * across, ending last rep at **, ch 1, skip next 2 dc, dc in 3rd ch of turning ch.

Row 3: Ch 1, sc in first dc, sc in next ch-1 space, (ch 5, sc) in each ch-2 space across to turning ch, ch 5, sc in ch-2 space of turning ch, sc in 3rd ch of turning ch.

Row 4: Ch 1, sc in each of first 2 sc, picot, *(sc, picot) 4 times in next ch-5 loop, sc in next sc, picot; rep from * across to within last sc, sc in last sc. Fasten off.

61

Picot: Ch 3, sl st in 3rd ch form hook.

Chain multiples of 8 plus 3.

Row 1 (RS): Dc in 4th ch from hook, *ch 2, skip next 2 ch, dc in next ch, ch 2, skip next 2 ch, dc in each of next 3 ch; rep from * across, ending with dc in each of last 2 ch, turn.

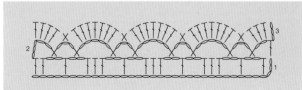

Row 2: Ch 5 (counts as dc, ch 2), skip first 2 dc, *sc in next ch-2 space, ch 3, sc in next ch-2 space**, ch 5; rep from * across, ending last rep at **, ch 2, skip next dc, dc in 3rd ch of turning ch.

Row 3: Ch 3 (counts as dc), 3 dc in next ch-3 loop, sc in next ch-3 loop, *7 dc in next ch-5 loop, sc in next ch-3 loop; rep from * across to last ch-3 loop, 3 dc in ch-2 space of turning ch, dc in 3rd ch of turning ch. Fasten off.

62

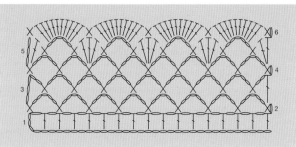

Chain multiples of 8 plus 4.

Row 1 (WS): Dc in 6th ch from hook, *ch 1, skip next ch, dc in next ch; rep from * across, turn.

Row 2: Ch 1, sc in first dc, *ch 5, skip next 2 ch-1 spaces, sc in next dc; rep from * across, ending with last sc in 4th ch of turning ch, turn.

Row 3: Ch 5 (counts as dc, ch 2), sc in next ch-5 loop, (ch 5, sc) in each ch-5 loop across to last ch-5 loop, ch 2, dc in last sc, turn.

Row 4: Ch 1, sc in first dc, (ch 5, sc) in each ch-5 loop across, ending with last sc in 3rd ch of turning ch, turn.

Row 5: Ch 3 (counts as dc), dc in first sc, *sc in next ch-5 loop, ch 5, sc in next ch-5 loop, 3 dc in next sc; rep from * across, ending with 2 dc in last sc, turn.

Row 6: Ch 1, sc in first dc, *10 dc in next ch-5 loop, skip next (sc, dc), sc in next dc; rep from * across, ending with last sc in 3rd ch of turning ch. Fasten off.

63

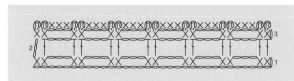

Picot: Ch 3, sl st in next sc.

Chain multiples of 5 plus 3.

Row 1 (RS): Sc in 2nd ch from hook, sc in next ch, *ch 3, skip next 3 ch, sc in each of next 2 ch; rep from * across, turn.

Row 2: Ch 3 (counts as dc), skip first sc, dc in next sc, *ch 3, skip next ch-3 loop, dc in each of next 2 sc; rep from * across, turn.

Row 3: Ch 1, sc in each of first 2 dc, *ch 3, skip next ch-3 loop, sc in each of next 2 dc; rep from * across, turn.

Row 4: Work picot in each of first 2 sc, *3 sc in next ch-3 loop, work picot in each of next 2 sc; rep from * across. Fasten off.

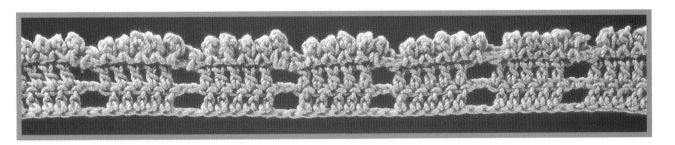

64

Picot: Ch 3, sl st in 3rd ch form hook.

Chain multiples of 7 plus 3.

Row 1 (WS): Dc in 4th ch from hook, dc in next ch, *ch 2, skip next 2 ch, dc in each of next 5 ch; rep from * across, ending with dc in each of last 3 ch, turn.

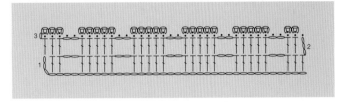

Row 2: Ch 3 (counts as dc), skip first dc, dc in each of next 2 dc, *ch 2, skip next ch-2 space**, dc in each of next 5 dc; rep from * across, ending last rep at **, dc in next 2 dc, dc in 3rd ch of turning ch.

Row 3: Ch 1, (sl st, picot) in each of first 3 dc, *sl st in each of next 2 ch**, (sl st, picot) in each of next 5 dc; rep from * across, ending last rep at **, (sl st, picot) in each of next 2 dc, sl st in 3rd ch of turning ch. Fasten off.

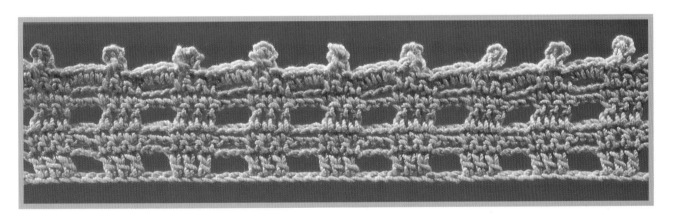

65

Picot: Ch 4, sl st in 4th ch form hook.

Chain multiples of 6 plus 5.

Row 1 (RS): Dc in 4th ch from hook, dc in next ch, *ch 3, skip next 3 ch, dc in each of next 3 ch; rep from * across, turn.

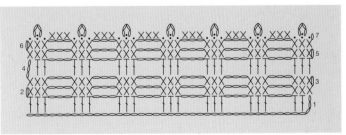

Row 2: Ch 1, sc in each of first 3 dc, *ch 3, skip next ch-3 loop, sc in each of next 3 dc; rep from * across, ending with last sc in 3rd ch of turning ch.

Row 3: Ch 1, sc in each of first 3 sc, *ch 3, skip next ch-3 loop, sc in each of next 3 sc; rep from * across, turn.

Row 4: Ch 3 (counts as dc), skip first sc, dc in each of next 2 sc, *ch 3, skip next ch-3 loop, dc in each of next 3 sc; rep from * across, turn.

Rows 5-6: Rep Rows 2-3.

Row 7: Ch 1, sl st in each of first 2 sc, picot, sl st in next sc, *3 sc in next ch-3 loop, sl st in each of next 2 sc, picot, sl st in next sc; rep from * across. Fasten off.

66

Picot: Ch 4, sl st in 4th ch from hook.

Chain multiples of 26 plus 18.

Row 1 (WS): Sc in 2nd ch from hook, sc in each ch across, turn.

Row 2: Ch 6 (counts as dc, ch 3), skip first 4 sc, *dc in each of next 9 sc, ch 3, skip next 3 sc, dc in next sc**, ch 3, skip next 3 sc, dc in each of next 3 sc, ch 3, skip next 3 sc, dc in next dc, ch 3, skip next 3 sc; rep from * across, ending last rep at **, turn.

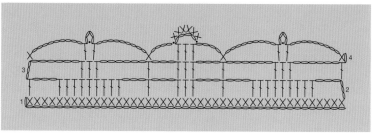

Row 3: Ch 9 (counts as dc, ch 6), *skip next ch-3 loop, skip next 3 dc, dc in each of next 3 dc, ch 6**, skip next ch-3 loop, dc in next dc, ch 3, skip next ch-3 loop, dc in each of next 3 dc, ch 3, skip next ch-3 loop, dc in next dc, ch 6; rep from * across, ending last rep at **, skip next 3 ch of turning ch, dc in 3rd ch of turning ch, turn.

Row 4: Ch 1, sc in first sc, *ch 9, skip next ch-6 loop, dc between next 2 dc, picot, dc between next 2 dc, ch 9**, skip next ch-6 loop, sc in next dc, ch 4, skip next ch-3 loop, dc in each of next 3 dc, ch 4, turn, skip next 3 dc, sl st in next ch, turn, work 5 sc in next ch-4 loop, sl st in 3rd dc of 3-dc group, ch 4, skip next ch-3 loop, sc in next dc; rep from * across, ending last rep at **, skip next 6 ch of turning ch, sc in next ch of turning ch. Fasten off.

67

Ch-3 picot: Ch 3, sl st in 3rd ch from hook.

Ch-4 picot: Ch 4, sl st in 4th ch from hook.

Chain multiples of 13 plus 6.

Row 1 (WS): Sc in 2nd ch from hook, sc in each ch across, turn.

Row 2: Ch 3 (counts as dc), skip first sc, dc in next sc, *ch 1, ch-3 picot, ch 1, skip next sc, dc in each of next 2 sc**, ch 8, skip next 8 sc, dc in each of next 2 sc; rep from * across, ending last rep at **, turn.

Row 3: Ch 3 (counts as dc), skip first dc, dc in next dc, *ch 1, ch-3 picot, ch 1, skip next picot, dc in each of next 2 dc**, 8 dc in next ch-8 loop, dc in each of next 2 dc; rep from * across, ending last rep at **, with last dc in 3rd ch of turning ch, turn.

Row 4: Ch 3 (counts as dc), skip first dc, dc in next dc, *ch 1, ch-3 picot, ch 1, skip next picot, dc in each of next 2 dc**, ch 4, skip next 3 dc, dc in next dc, ch-4 picot, dc in next dc, ch 4, skip next 3 dc, dc in each of next 2 dc; rep from * across, ending last rep at ** with last dc in 3rd on of turning ch. Fasten off.

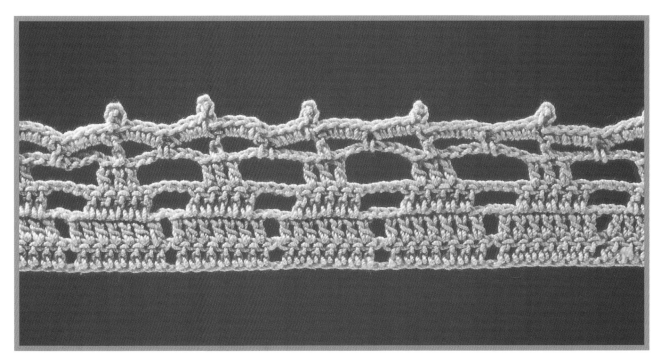

68

Picot: Ch 4, sl st in 4th ch from hook.

Chain multiples of 8 plus 1.

Row 1 (WS): Dc in 4th ch from hook, dc in each of next 5 ch, *ch 1, skip next ch, dc in each of next 7 ch; rep from * across, turn.

Row 2: Ch 3 (counts as dc), skip first dc, dc in each of next 6 dc, *ch 2, skip next ch-1 space, dc in each of next 7 dc; rep from * across, ending with last dc in 3rd ch of turning ch, turn.

Row 3: Ch 3 (counts as dc), skip first dc, dc in each of next 5 dc, *ch 4, skip next (dc, ch-2 space, dc), dc in each of next 5 dc; rep from * across to turning ch, dc in 3rd ch of turning ch, turn.

Row 4: Ch 5 (counts as dc, ch 2), skip first 2 dc, dc in each of next 3 dc, *ch 7, skip next (dc, ch-4 loop, dc), dc in each of next 3 dc; rep from * across to within last 2 sts, ch 2, skip next dc, dc in 3rd ch of turning ch, turn.

Row 5: Ch 5 (counts as dc, ch 2), skip next (ch-2 space, dc), dc in next dc, ch 4, sl st in next ch-7 loop, ch 4, skip next dc, dc in next dc; rep from * across to within last 4 sts, ch 2, skip next 2 ch of turning ch, dc in 3rd ch of turning ch, turn.

Row 6: Ch 1, sc in first dc, 2 sc in next ch-2 space, picot, *4 sc in each of next 2 ch-4 loops, picot; rep from * across to turning ch, 2 sc in ch-2 space of turning ch, sc in 3rd ch of turning ch. Fasten off.

69

Picot: Ch 3, sl st in 3rd ch from hook.

Chain multiples of 12 plus 2.

Row 1 (RS): Dc in 8th ch from hook, *ch 2, skip next 2 ch, dc in next ch; rep from * across, turn.

Row 2: Ch 3 (counts as dc), *2 dc in next ch-2 space, dc in next dc, ch 2, skip next ch-2 space, dc in next dc; rep from * across to turning ch, 2 dc in ch-2 space of turning ch, dc in next ch of turning ch, turn.

Rows 3-4: Ch 3 (counts as dc), skip first dc, dc in each of next 3 dc, *ch 2, skip next ch-2 space, dc in each of next 4 dc; rep from * across, ending with last dc in 3rd ch of turning ch, turn.

Row 5: Ch 1, *sl st in each of next 4 dc, 2 sc in next ch-2 space, sl st in next dc, ch 5, turn, skip next 2 sc, sl st in next dc in Row 4, ch 3, skip next 2 dc, sl st in next dc in Row 4, turn, (3 dc, picot, 2 dc, picot, 2 dc, picot, 4 dc) in next ch-5 loop, skip next 3 dc in Row 4, sl st in next dc**, 2 sc in next ch-2 space; rep from * across, ending last rep at ** with last sl st in 3rd ch of turning ch, turn. Fasten off.

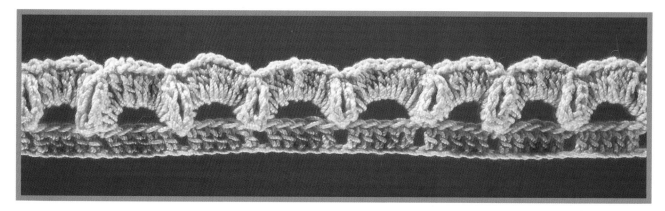

70

Chain multiples of 6 plus 3.

Row 1 (RS): Dc in 4th ch from hook, dc in each of next 4 ch, *ch 1, skip next ch, dc in each of next 5 ch; rep from * across to within last ch, dc in last ch, turn.

Row 2: Ch 1, sc in first dc, *ch 6, skip next 5 dc, sc in next ch-1 space; rep from * across, ending with last sc in 3rd ch of turning ch, turn.

Row 3: Ch 3 (counts as dc), work 20 dc in each ch-6 loop across. Fasten off.

Row 4: *With RS facing, join 16th dc of first shell to 5th dc of next shell with sl st, fasten off; rep from * across to last shell. Fasten off.

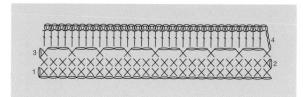

71

Picot: Ch 3, sl st in 3rd ch from hook.

Chain multiples of 3 plus 2.

Row 1 (WS): Sc in 2nd ch from hook, sc in each ch across, turn.

Row 2: Ch 1, sc in each sc across, turn.

Row 3: Ch 1, sc in first sc, *ch 2, skip next 2 sc, sc in next sc; rep from * across, turn.

Row 4: Ch 3 (counts as dc), picot, *(dc, picot) 3 times in next ch-2 space, dc in next sc**, picot; rep from * across, ending last rep at **. Fasten off.

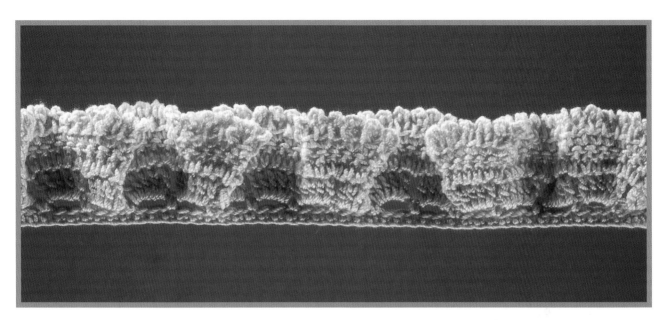

72

Picot: Ch 4, sl st in 4th ch from hook.

Chain multiples of 3 plus 2.

Row 1 (RS): Sc in 2nd ch from hook, sc in each ch across, turn.

Row 2: Ch 1, sc in first sc, *ch 3, skip next 2 sc, sc in next sc; rep from * across, turn.

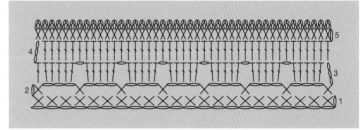

Row 3: Ch 3 (counts as dc), *5 dc in next ch-3 loop**, ch 1; rep from * across, ending last rep at **, dc in last sc, turn.

Row 4: Ch 3 (counts as dc), skip first dc, *dc in each of next 5 dc**, dc in next ch-1 space; rep from * across, ending last rep at **, dc in 3rd ch of turning ch, turn.

Row 5: Ch 1, (sc, picot) in each dc across. Fasten off.

.4.

Half-Double Crochet

73

Picot: Ch 3, sl st in 3rd ch from hook.

Chain multiples of 2.

Row 1 (WS): Sc in 2nd ch from hook, sc in each ch across, turn.

Row 2: Ch 2, skip first sc, *picot, skip next sc, hdc in next sc; rep from * across. Fasten off.

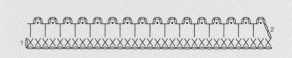

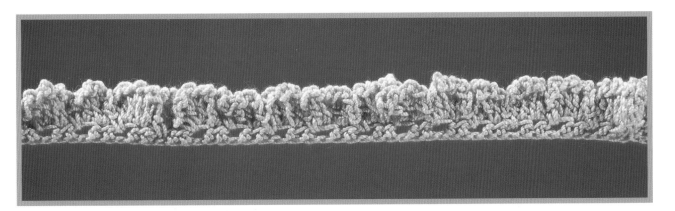

74

Chain multiples of 3.

Row 1 (WS): Hdc in 3rd ch from hook, *ch 1, skip next ch, hdc in each of next 2 ch; rep from * across, turn.

Row 2: Ch 5 (counts as dc, ch 2), dc in first hdc, *(dc, ch 2, dc) in next hdc, ch 2, sc in next ch-1 space, ch 2, (dc, ch 2, dc) in next hdc, ch 2; rep from * across to turning ch, (dc, ch 2, dc) in 2nd ch of turning ch. Fasten off.

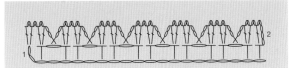

75

Chain multiples of 9 plus 2.

Row 1 (WS): Sc in 2nd ch from hook, sc in each of next 3 ch, * (sc, ch 2, 2 dc) in next ch, ch 2**, sc in each of next 8 ch; rep from * across, ending last rep at **, sc in each of last 5 ch, turn.

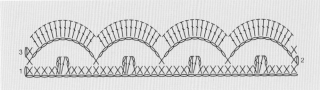

Row 2: Ch 1, sc in first sc, *ch 11, skip next 8 sc, sc in next sc; rep from * across, turn.

Row 3: Ch 1, sc in first sc, 16 dc in each ch-11 loop across, sc in last sc. Fasten off.

76

Picot: Ch 6, sl st in 6th ch from hook.

No foundation ch required.

Row 1 (RS): Ch 10, sl st in in 6th ch from hook for picot, *ch 11, picot; rep from * for desired length, ch 4, turn.

Row 2: Ch 6 (counts as dc, ch 3), *(sc, hdc, 5 dc, hdc, sc) in next picot**, ch 7; rep from * across, ending last rep at **, ch 3, skip next 3 ch, dc in last ch, turn.

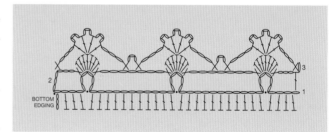

Row 3: Ch 1, sc in first dc, ch 3, *skip next (ch-3 loop and 4 sts of next shell), (dc, ch 3) 4 times in center dc of next shell, ch 3**, (sc, ch 3, sc) in next ch-7 loop; rep from * across, ending last rep at **, sc in 3rd ch of turning ch. Fasten off.

Bottom Edging: With RS facing, working across bottom edge, join yarn in first ch-4 loop, ch 3 (counts as dc), 3 dc in first ch-4 loop, 11 dc in each ch-11 loop across, ending with 4 dc in last ch-3 loop. Fasten off.

.5.
Treble Crochet Variations

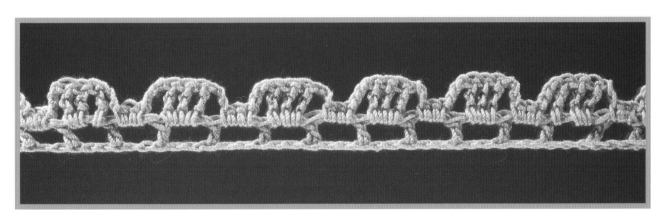

77

Chain multiples of 6 plus 2.

Row 1 (RS): Dc in 8th ch from hook, *ch 2, skip next 2 ch, dc in next ch; rep from * across, turn.

Row 2: Ch 1, 3 sc in next ch-2 space, *ch 3, 3 tr in next ch-2 space, ch 3, 3 sc in next ch-2 space; rep from * across. Fasten off.

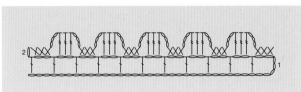

78

Picot: Ch 3, sl st in 3rd ch from hook.

Chain multiples of 6 plus 2.

Row 1 (WS): Sc in 2nd ch from hook, *ch 7, skip next 5 ch, sc in next ch; rep from * across, turn.

Row 2: Ch 5 (counts as tr, ch 1), (4 tr, ch 1) in each ch-7 loop across to last ch-7 loop, tr in last sc, turn.

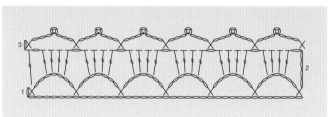

Row 3: Ch 1, sc in first tr, *ch 3, picot, ch 3, skip next 4 tr, sc in next ch-1 space; rep from * across, ending with last sc in 4th ch of turning ch. Fasten off.

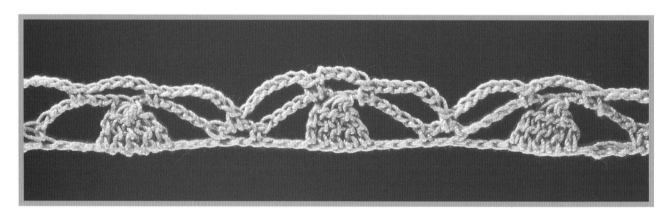

79

Chain multiples of 14 plus 4.

Row 1 (RS): Sc in 2nd ch from hook, ch 3, skip next ch, sc in next ch, *ch 7, skip next 3 ch, 5-tr cluster worked across next 5 ch, ch 7, skip next 3 ch, sc in next ch, ch 3, skip next ch, sc in next ch; rep from * across, turn.

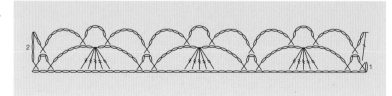

Row 2: Ch 5 (counts as dc, ch 2), sc in next ch-3 loop, *ch 7, sc in next ch-7 loop, ch 5, sc in next ch-7 loop, ch 7, sc in next ch-3 loop; rep from * across, ch 2, dc in last sc. Fasten off.

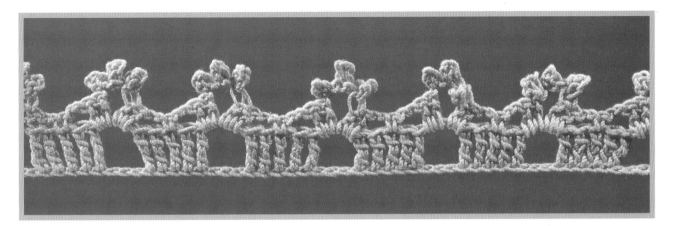

80

Picot: Ch 4, sl st in 4th ch from hook.

Chain multiples of 8.

Row 1 (RS): Tr in 5th ch from hook, tr in each of next 3 ch, *ch 3, skip next 3 ch, tr in each of next 5 ch; rep from * across, turn.

Row 2: Ch 1, sl st in each of first 2 tr, sc in next tr, *ch 2, 2 dc in next ch-3 loop, work picot, work 2nd picot, sl st in sl st of first picot, work 3rd picot, sl st in sl st of first picot, 2 dc in same ch-3 loop, ch 2, skip next 2 tr, sc in next tr; rep from * across to within last 2 sts, sl st in next tr, sl st in 4th ch of turning ch. Fasten off.

81

Picot: Ch 3, sl st in 3rd ch from hook.

Chain multiples of 8 plus 6.

Row 1 (WS): Dc in 6th ch from hook, *ch 1, skip next ch, dc in next ch; rep from * across, turn.

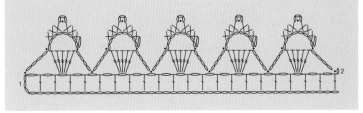

Row 2: Ch 1, sl st in first dc, ch 4, skip next 2 ch-1 spaces, *5 tr in next ch-1 space, ch 8, turn, sl st in next ch-4 loop, ch 1, turn, (3 sc, picot, 3 sc) in next ch-8 loop, sl st in last tr of 5-tr group, ch 4, skip next ch-1 space**, sl st in next ch-1 space, ch 4, skip next ch-1 space; rep from * across, ending last rep at **, sl st in 4th ch of turning ch. Fasten off.

82

Picot: Ch 4, sl st in 4th ch from hook.

Chain multiples of 9 plus 5.

Row 1 (RS): Tr in 5th ch from hook, picot, *ch 2, skip next 2 ch, tr in each of next 4 ch, ch 7, turn, skip next 4 tr, sl st in next ch-2 space, turn, (6 sc, ch 5, 6 sc) in next ch-7 loop, sl st in last tr of 4-tr group, ch 2, skip next 2 ch, tr in next ch, picot; rep from * across. Fasten off.

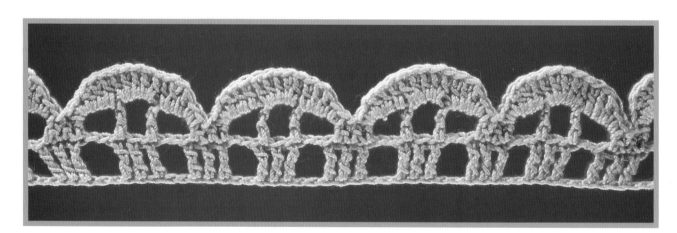

83

Chain multiples of 10 plus 6.

Row 1 (RS): Tr in 5th ch from hook, tr in next ch, *ch 2, skip next 2 ch, tr in each of next 3 ch; rep from * across, turn.

Row 2: Ch 1, sc in each of first 3 tr, *ch 4, skip next ch-2 space, tr in next tr, ch 2, skip next tr, tr in next tr, ch 4, skip next ch-2 space, sc in each of next 3 tr; rep from * across, ending with last sc in 4th ch of turning ch, turn.

Row 3: Ch 1, skip first sc, sl st in 2nd sc, (2 sc, 3 dc) in next ch-4 loop, dc in next tr, 3 dc in next ch-2 space, dc in next tr, (3 dc, 2 sc) in next ch-4 loop, skip next sc, sl st in next sc; rep from * across. Fasten off.

84

No foundation ch required.

Row 1 (RS): Ch 8, dc in 6th from hook, *ch 10, dc in 6th ch from hook; rep from * for desired length, ch 3, turn.

Row 2: Ch 7 (counts as tr, ch 3), tr in 8th ch from hook, *ch 2, in next ch-5 loop, (sc, ch 2, 2 dc, ch 2, sc) ch 2, skip next 2 ch**, (tr, ch 5, tr) in next ch; rep from * across, ending last rep at **, (tr, ch 3, tr) in last ch, turn.

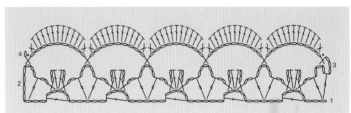

Row 3: Ch 3, sc in next ch-3 loop, *ch 9, skip next 2 ch-2 spaces, sc in next ch-5 loop; rep from * across, ending with last sc in ch-3 loop of turning ch, turn.

Row 4: Ch 1, sl st in first sc, (sc, hdc, 9 dc, hdc, sc) in each ch-9 loop across to last ch-9 loop, sl st in last sc. Fasten off.

85

Picot: Ch 4, sl st in 4th ch from hook.

Chain multiples of 12 plus 2.

Row 1 (WS): Sc in 2nd ch from hook, *ch 5, skip next 5 ch, sc in next ch; rep from * across, turn.

Row 2: Ch 1, sc in first sc, *ch 5, skip next ch-5 loop, sc in next sc; rep from * across, turn.

Row 3: Ch 1, sc in first sc, *ch 7, skip next ch-5 loop, 2 dtr in next sc, ch 7, skip next ch-5 loop, sc in next sc; rep from * across, turn.

Row 4: Ch 4 (counts as tr), 4 dc in next ch-7 loop, 3 dc in next dtr, picot, 3 dc in next dtr, 4 dc in next ch-4 loop; rep from * across to last ch-7 loop, dc in last sc. Fasten off.

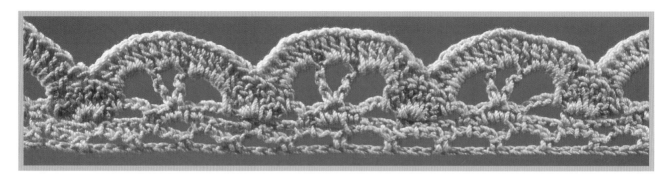

86

Chain multiples of 12 plus 5.

Row 1 (RS): Sc in 7th ch from hook, *ch 5, skip next 3 ch, sc in next ch; rep from * across to within last 2 ch, ch 2, skip next ch, dc in last ch, turn.

Row 2: Ch 1, sc in first dc, (ch 3, sc) in each ch-5 loop across, ending with last sc in 4th ch of turning ch, turn.

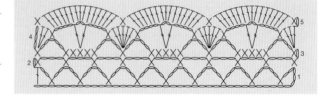

Row 3: Ch 1, sc in first sc, *ch 5, skip next ch-3 loop, sc in next sc, 3 sc in next ch-3 loop, sc in next sc, ch 5, skip next ch-3 loop, sc in next sc; rep from * across, turn.

Row 4: Ch 3 (counts as dc), 2 dc in first sc, *sc in next ch-5 loop, ch 4, skip next 2 sc, (tr, ch 2, tr) in next sc, ch 4, sc in next ch-5 loop, 5 dc in next sc; rep from * across, ending with 3 dc in last sc, turn.

Row 5: Ch 1, sc in first dc, *5 dc in next ch-4 loop, dc in next dc, 3 dc in next ch-2 space, dc in next dc, 5 dc in next ch-5 loop, skip next 3 sts, sc in next dc; rep from * across, ending with last sc in 3rd ch of turning ch. Fasten off.

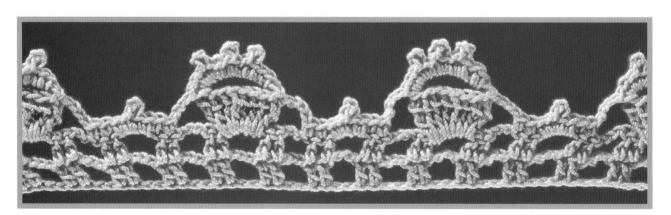

87

Picot: Ch 3, sl st in 3rd ch from hook.

Chain multiples of 16 plus 8.

Row 1 (RS): Dc in 4th ch from hook, *ch 3, skip next 2 ch, dc in each of next 2 ch; rep from * across, turn.

Row 2: Ch 3 (counts as dc), skip first dc, dc in next dc, *ch 3, skip next ch-3 loop, dc in each of next 2 dc; rep from * across, ending with last dc in 3rd ch of turning ch, turn.

Row 3: Ch 1, sc in each of first 2 dc, *(2 sc, ch 3, 2 sc) in next ch-3 loop, sc in each of next 2 dc**, ch 4, skip next ch-3 loop, 8 tr in next ch-3 loop, ch 7, turn, sl st in next ch-4 loop, turn, (3 sc, picot, 2 sc, picot, 3 sc) in next ch-7 loop, sl st in last tr of 8-tr group, ch 4, skip next ch-3 loop, sc in each of next 2 dc; rep from * across, ending last rep at **, with last sc in 3rd ch of turning ch. Fasten off.

88

Picot: Ch 5, sl st in 5th ch from hook.

Chain multiples of 9 plus 3.

Row 1 (WS): Tr in 9th ch from hook, *ch 2, skip next 2 ch, tr in next ch; rep from * across, turn.

Row 2: Ch 5 (counts as dc, ch 1), picot, skip next ch-2 space, tr in next tr, ch 2, skip next ch-2 space, tr in next tr, *2 tr in next ch-2 space, tr in next tr, ch 7, turn, sl st in next ch-2 space, ch 3, turn, (3 dc, picot) 3 times in next ch-7 loop, 3 dc in same ch-7 loop, ch 2, sl st in last tr of 4-tr group, ch 1, picot, skip next ch-2 space, tr in next tr, ch 2, skip next ch-2 space, tr in next tr; rep from * across, ending with last tr in next ch of turning ch. Fasten off.

89

Chain multiples of 5.

Row 1 (WS): Dc in 5th ch from hook, *skip next ch, dc in next ch, skip next ch, dc in next ch**, ch 3, dc in next ch; rep from * across, ending last rep at **, ch 1, dc in last ch, turn.

Row 2: Ch 1, sc in first dc, sc in next ch-1 space, *ch 5, skip next 3 dc**, (sc, ch 3, sc) in next ch-3 loop; rep from * across, ending last rep at **, sc in ch-1 space of turning ch, sc in 3rd ch of turning ch, turn.

Row 3: Ch 1, sc in first sc, *ch 4, tr in next ch-5 loop, ch 4, sc in next ch-3 loop; rep from * across, ending with last sc in last sc, turn.

Row 4: Ch 1, *5 sc in next ch-4 loop, ch 5, 5 sc in next ch-4 loop; rep from * across. Fasten off.

90

Chain multiples of 8 plus 6.

Row 1 (RS): Sc in 10th ch from hook, *ch 3, skip next 3 ch, dc in next ch**, ch 3, skip next 3 ch, sc in next ch; rep from * across, ending last rep at **, turn.

Row 2: Ch 1, sc in first dc, *ch 2, skip next ch-3 loop, (3 tr, ch 3, 3 tr) in next sc, ch 2, skip next ch-3 loop, sc in next dc; rep from * across, ending with last sc in next ch of turning ch, turn.

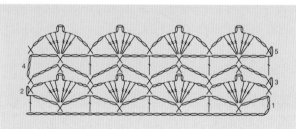

Row 3: Ch 1, sc in first sc, *ch 4, skip next ch-2 space, sc in next ch-3 loop, ch 4, skip next ch-2 space, sc in next sc; rep from * across, turn.

Row 4: Ch 6 (counts as dc, ch 3), skip next ch-4 loop, sc in next sc, *ch 3, skip next ch-4 loop, dc in next sc**, ch 3, skip next ch-4 loop, sc in next sc; rep from * across, ending last rep at **, turn.

Row 5: Rep Row 2. Fasten off.

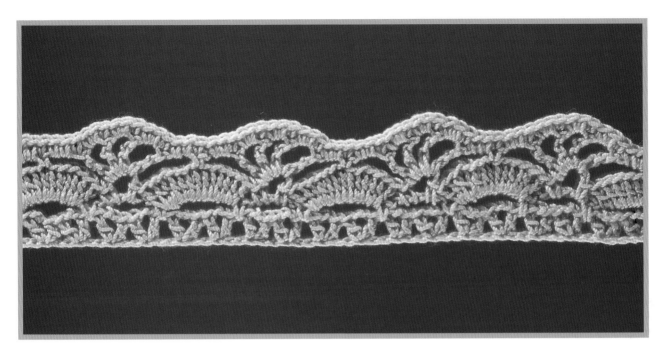

91

Chain multiples of 12 plus 4.

Row 1 (RS): (Dc, ch 1, dc) in 5th ch from hook, *skip next 2 ch, (dc, ch 1, dc) in next ch; rep from * across to within last 2 ch, skip next ch, dc in last ch, turn.

Row 2: Ch 5 (counts as dc, ch 2), skip next ch-1 space, sc between next 2 dc, *ch 5, skip next 2 ch-1 spaces, sc between next 2 dc; rep from * across to within last ch-1 space, ch 2, skip next ch-1 space, skip next dc, dc in 3rd ch of turning ch, turn.

Row 3: Ch 3 (counts as dc), 6 dc in next ch-2 space, *(sc, ch 5, sc) in next ch-5 loop**, 13 dc in next ch-5 loop; rep from * across, ending last rep at **, 6 dc in ch-2 space of turning ch, dc in 3rd ch of turning ch, turn.

Row 4: Ch 1, sc in first dc, *ch 2, (tr, ch 2) 4 times in next ch-5 loop, skip next 7 sts, sc in next dc; rep from * across, ending with last sc in 3rd ch of turning ch, turn.

Row 5: Ch 1, sc in first sc, *2 sc in next ch-2 space, (sc in next tr, 2 sc in next ch-2 space) 4 times, sc in next sc; rep from * across. Fasten off.

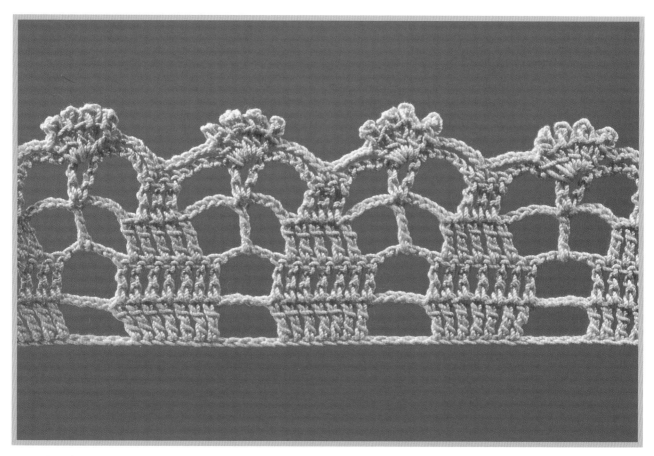

92

Chain multiples of 12 plus 10.

Row 1 (RS): Tr in 5th ch from hook, tr in each of next 5 ch, *ch 5, skip next 5 ch, tr in each of next 7 ch; rep from * across, turn.

Row 2: Ch 4 (counts as tr), skip first tr, tr in each of next 6 tr, *ch 5, skip next ch-5 loop, tr in each of next 7 tr; rep from * across, ending with last tr in 4th ch of turning ch, turn.

Row 3: Ch 4 (counts as tr), skip first tr, tr in each of next 5 tr, *ch 5, tr in next ch-5 loop, ch 5, skip next tr, tr in each of next 5 tr; rep from * across, tr in 4th ch of turning ch, turn.

Row 4: Ch 5 (counts as tr, ch 1), skip first 2 tr, tr in each of next 3 tr, *ch 6, skip next ch-5 loop, 2 tr in next tr, ch 6, skip next tr, tr in each of next 3 tr; rep from * across to within last 2 sts, ch 1, skip next tr, tr in 4th ch of turning ch, turn.

Row 5: Ch 6 (counts as dc, ch 3), skip next ch-1 space and next tr, sc in next tr, *ch 5, skip next ch-6 loop, (tr, picot) 4 times between next 2 tr, tr in between same 2 tr, ch 5, skip next ch-6 loop and next tr, sc in next tr; rep from * across to within last 3 sts, ch 3, dc in 4th ch of turning ch. Fasten off.

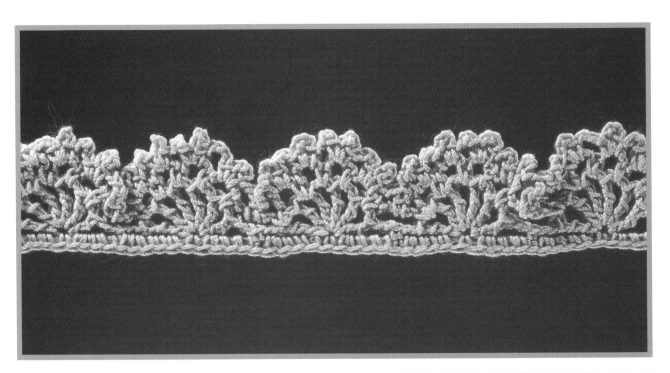

93

Chain multiples of 10 plus 2.

Row 1 (RS): Sc in 2nd ch from hook, *ch 2, skip next 4 ch, (tr, ch 2) 7 times in next ch, skip next 4 ch, sc in next ch; rep from * across, turn.

Row 2: Ch 4 (counts as dc, ch 1), skip next ch-2 space, *(sc, ch 4) in each of next 6 ch-2 space, skip next 2 ch-2 spaces; rep from * across, omitting last ch-4 loop, ch 1, skip next ch-2 space, dc in last sc, turn.

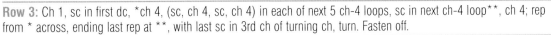

Row 3: Ch 1, sc in first dc, *ch 4, (sc, ch 4, sc, ch 4) in each of next 5 ch-4 loops, sc in next ch-4 loop**, ch 4; rep from * across, ending last rep at **, with last sc in 3rd ch of turning ch, turn. Fasten off.

Bottom Edging: With RS facing, working across opposite side of foundation ch, join yarn in first ch, ch 1, sc in first ch, *4 sc in next ch-4 loop, sc in next ch; rep from * across. Fasten off.

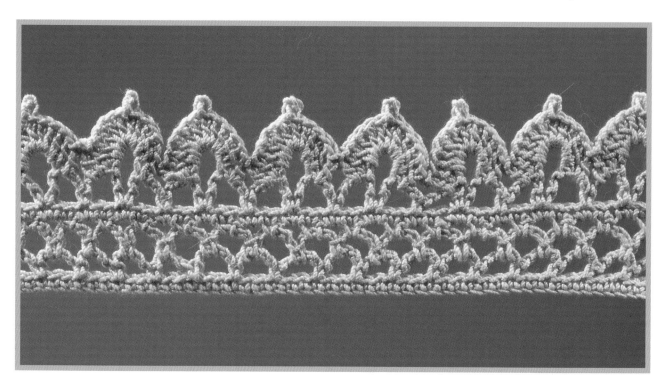

94

Picot: Ch 3, sl st in 3rd ch from hook.

Chain multiples of 3 plus 2.

Row 1 (RS): Sc in 2nd ch from hook, sc in each ch across, turn.

Row 2: Ch 1, sc in first sc, *ch 5, skip next 2 sc, sc in next sc; rep from * across, turn.

Row 3: Ch 5 (counts as dc, ch 2), sc in next ch-5 loop, (ch 5, sc) in each ch-5 loop across to last ch-5 loop, ch 2, dc in last sc, turn.

Row 4: Ch 1, sc in first dc, (ch 2, sc) in each ch-5 loop across, ending with last sc in 3rd ch of turning ch, turn.

Row 5: Ch 1, sc in first sc, *2 sc in next ch-2 space, sc in next sc; rep from * across, turn.

Row 6: Ch 1, sc in first sc, *ch 3, skip next 2 sc, (tr, ch 5, tr) in next sc, ch 3, skip next 2 sc, sc in next sc; rep from * across, turn.

Row 7: Ch 1, sc in first sc, *dc in next ch-3 loop, dc in next dc, (4 dc, picot, 4 dc) in next ch-5 loop, dc in next dc, dc in next ch-3 loop, sc in next sc; rep from * across. Fasten off.

95

Chain multiples of 8 plus 2.

Row 1 (WS): Sc in 2nd ch from hook, sc in each ch across, turn.

Row 2: Ch 3 (counts as dc), skip first 4 sc, *(tr, ch 1, tr, ch 1, tr, ch 1, tr, ch 1, tr) in next sc**, skip next 7 sc; rep from * across, ending last rep at **, skip next 3 sc, dc in last sc, turn.

Row 3: Ch 5 (counts as dc, ch 2), sc in next ch-1 space, (ch 4, sc) in each ch-1 space across to last ch-1 space, ch 2, dc in 3rd ch of turning ch, turn.

Row 4: Ch 1, sc in first dc, (ch 4, sc) in each ch-4 loop across, ending with last sc in 3rd ch of turning ch. Fasten off.

.6.
Mixed Stitches

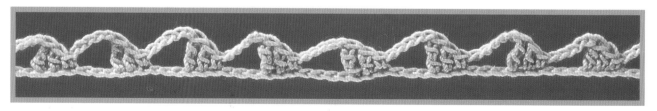

96 **Chain** multiples of 12 plus 2.

Row 1 (RS): Sc in 2nd ch from hook, *ch 2, skip next ch, dc in next ch, ch 2, skip next ch, tr in next ch, ch 2, skip next ch, dtr in next ch, ch 2, skip next ch, tr in next ch, ch 2, skip next ch, dc in next ch, ch 2, skip next ch, sc in next ch; rep from * across. Fasten off.

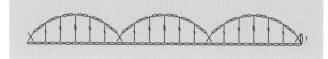

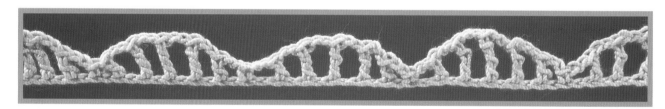

97 **Chain** multiples of 6 plus 4.

Row 1 (RS): Sc in 2nd ch from hook, *dc in next ch, tr in next ch**, ch 5, skip next 3 ch, sc in next ch; rep from * across, ending last rep at **. Fasten off.

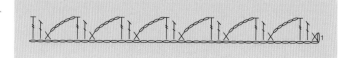

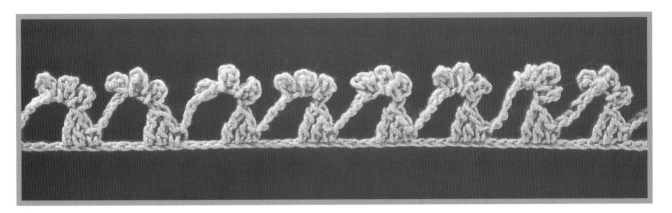

98

Picot: Ch 5, sl st in 5th ch from hook.

Chain multiples of 6 plus 4.

Row 1 (RS): Sc in 2nd ch from hook, *dc in next ch, tr in next ch, work picot, work 2nd picot, sl st in sl st of first picot, work 3rd picot, sl st in sl st of first picot**, ch 5, skip next 3 ch, sc in next ch; rep from * across, ending last rep at **. Fasten off.

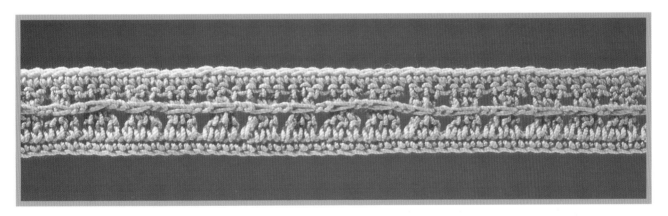

99

Chain multiples of 3.

Row 1 (RS): Sc in 2nd ch from hook, sc in each ch across, turn.

Row 2: Ch 5 (counts as dtr), skip first sc, dtr in each sc across, turn.

Row 3: Ch 1, sc in each dtr across, ending with last sc in 5th ch of turning ch. Fasten off.

Trim Row: Make a slip knot with yarn, with RS facing, insert hook between last 2 dtr in Row 2, place slip knot on hook, *insert hook over posts of next 3 dtr, yo, draw yarn through st and loop on hook**, keeping working yarn in back, ch 2; rep from * across, ending last rep at ** in space before turning ch. Fasten off.

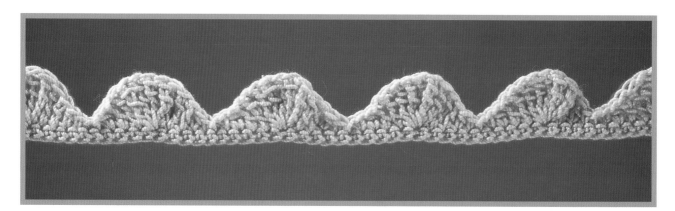

100

Chain multiples of 10 plus 2.

Row 1 (WS): Sc in 2nd ch from hook, sc in each ch across, turn.

Row 2: Ch 1, sl st in first sc, *sc in next sc, hdc in next sc, dc in next sc, tr in next sc, 5 dtr in next sc, tr in next sc, dc in next sc, hdc in next sc, sc in next sc, sl st in next sc; rep from * across. Fasten off.

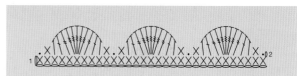

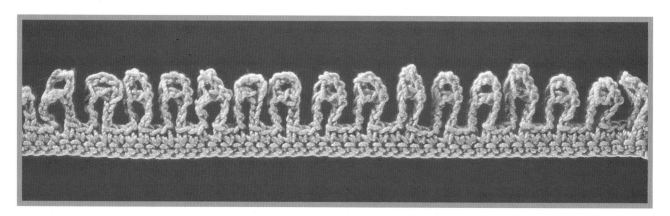

101

Chain multiples of 3 plus 2.

Row 1 (WS): Sc in 2nd ch from hook, sc in each ch across, turn.

Row 2: Ch 1, sc in each of first 2 sc, *ch 8, dc in 5th ch from hook, ch 3, sc in each of next 3 sc; rep from * across, ending with sc in each of last 2 sc. Fasten off.

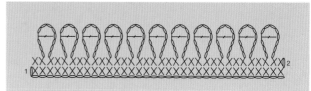

102

Chain multiples of 10 plus 8.

Row 1 (WS): Sc in 2nd ch from hook, sc in each ch across, turn.

Row 2: Ch 4 (counts as dc, ch 1), skip first 2 sc, dc in next sc, (ch 1, skip next sc, dc in next sc) twice, *ch 4, skip next next 3 sc, dc in next sc, (ch 1, skip next sc, dc in next sc) 3 times; rep from * across, turn.

Row 3: Ch 4 (counts as dc, ch 1), skip next ch-1 space, dc in next dc, (ch 1, dc) in each of next 2 dc, *ch 4, skip next ch-4 loop, dc in next dc, (ch 1, dc) in each of next 3 dc; rep from * across, ending with last dc in 3rd ch of turning ch, turn.

Row 4: Ch 4 (counts as dc, ch 1), skip next ch-1 space, dc in next dc, (ch 1, dc) in each of next 2 dc, *ch 7, skip next ch-4 loop, dc in next dc, ch 1, turn, 11 sc in next ch-7 loop, ch 1, turn, sl st in space before first sc, ch 3, skip next 2 sc, sl st in next sc, (ch 3, skip next 2 sc, sl st in next sc) twice, ch 3, skip next 2 sc, sl st between last sc and next ch-1 space, (ch 1, dc) in each of next 3 dc; rep from * across, ending with last dc in 3rd ch of turning ch. Fasten off.

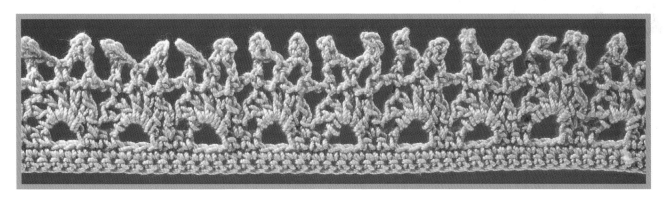

103

Picot: Ch 3, sl st in 3rd ch from hook.

Chain multiples of 5 plus 2.

Row 1 (WS): Sc in 2nd ch from hook, sc in each ch across, turn.

Row 2: Ch 1, sc in each sc across, turn.

Row 3: Ch 1, sc in each of first 2 sc, *ch 5, skip next 2 sc, sc in each of next 3 sc; rep from * across, ending with sc in each of last 2 sc, turn.

Row 4: Ch 1, sc in first sc, *ch 1, (dc, ch 1) 5 times in next ch-5 loop, skip next sc, sc in next sc; rep from * across, turn.

Row 5: Ch 4 (counts as dc, ch 1), skip next 2 ch-1 space, *(sc, ch 2, picot, ch 2) in each of next 3 dc, skip next 4 ch-1 spaces; rep from * across, omitting last (ch 2, picot, ch 2), ch 1, dc in last sc. Fasten off.

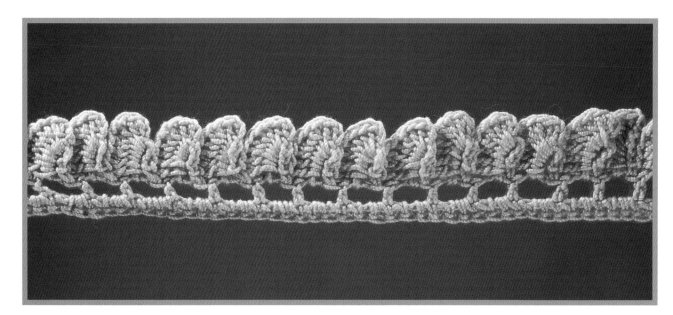

104

Chain multiples of 3 plus 2.

Row 1 (WS): Dc in 8th ch from hook, *ch 2, skip next 2 ch, dc in next ch; rep from * across, turn.

Row 2: Ch 1, sc in first dc, *ch 3, dc in next ch-2 space, ch 3, 7 dc around the post of last dc made, sc in next dc; rep from * across, ending with last sc in 5th ch of turning ch. Fasten off.

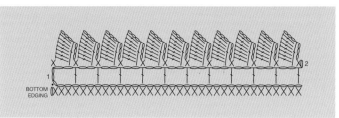

Bottom Edging: With RS facing, working across opposite side of foundation ch, join yarn in first ch, ch 1, sc in first ch, *2 sc in next ch-2 space, sc in next ch; rep from * across. Fasten off.

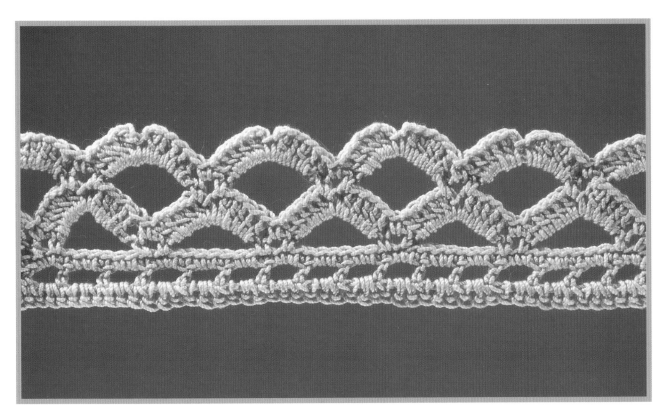

105

Chain multiples of 9 plus 5.

Row 1 (WS): Dc in 8th ch from hook, *ch 2, skip next 2 ch, dc in next ch; rep from * across, turn.

Row 2: Ch 1, sc in first dc, *2 sc in next ch-2 space, sc in next dc; rep from * across, ending with last sc in 5th ch of turning ch, turn.

Row 3: Ch 7 (counts as dc, ch 4), skip first 4 sc, *sc in next sc, ch 3, sc in next sc**, ch 9, skip next 7 sc; rep from * across, ending last rep at **, ch 4, skip next 3 sc, dc in last sc, turn.

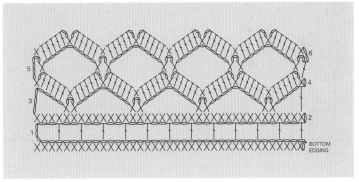

Row 4: Ch 1, sc in first dc, ch 2, 5 dc in next ch-4 loop, sc in next ch-3 loop, *(5 dc, ch 2, sc, ch 2, 5 dc) in next ch-9 loop, sc in next ch-3 loop; rep from * across to last ch-3 loop, 5 dc in next ch-4 loop of turning ch, ch 2, sc in 3rd ch of turning ch, turn.

Row 5: Ch 6 (counts as dc, ch 3), *sc in next ch-2 space, ch 9, skip next 11 sts, sc in next ch-2 space, ch 3; rep from * across to last ch-2 space, dc in last sc, turn.

Row 6: Ch 2, sc in next ch-3 loop, *(5 dc, ch 2, sc, ch 2, 5 dc) in next ch-9 loop, sc in next ch-3 loop; rep from * across. Fasten off.

Bottom Edging: With WS facing, working across opposite side of foundation ch, join yarn in first ch, ch 1, sc in first ch, *2 sc in next ch-2 space, sc in next ch; rep from * across. Fasten off.

106

Chain multiples of 4 plus 3.

Row 1 (RS): Dc in 4th ch from hook, dc in each ch across, turn.

Row 2: Ch 1, sc in first dc, *ch 5, skip next 3 dc, sc in next dc; rep from * across, ending with last sc in 3rd ch of turning ch, turn.

Row 3: Ch 4 (counts as tr), (dc, ch 1, dc, ch 1) in each ch-5 loop across, omitting last ch 1, tr in last sc, turn.

Row 4: Ch 5 (counts as dc, ch 2), sc in next ch-1 space, *ch 5, skip next ch-1 space, sc in next ch-1 space; rep from * across to last ch-1 space, ch 2, dc in 4th ch of turning ch, turn.

Row 5: Ch 1, sc in first dc, skip next ch-2 space, *3 dc in next sc, sc in next ch-5 loop; rep from * across, ending with last sc in 3rd ch of turning ch. Fasten off.

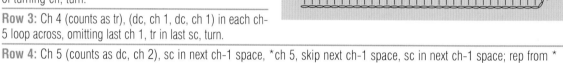

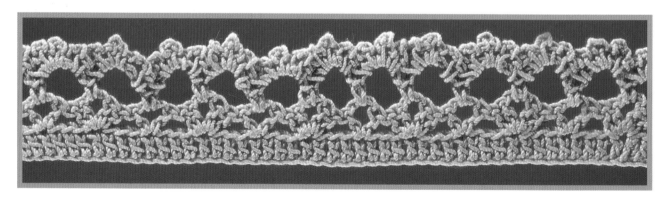

107

Chain multiples of 8 plus 7.

Row 1 (RS): Dc in 4th ch from hook, dc in each ch across, turn.

Row 2: Ch 4 (counts as dc), skip first 4 dc, *(dc, ch 3, dc) in next dc, skip next 3 dc, (2 dc, ch 3, 2 dc) in next dc, skip next 3 dc; rep from * across to turning ch, ch 1, dc in 3rd ch of turning ch, turn.

Row 3: Ch 1, sc in first dc, skip next ch-1 space, (ch 7, sc) in each ch-3 loop across, ending with last sc in 2nd ch of turning ch, turn.

Row 4: Ch 1, sc in first sc, ch 3, (sc, ch 3, sc, ch 3, sc, ch 3, sc) in each ch-7 loop across to last ch-7 loop, ch 3, sc in last sc. Fasten off.

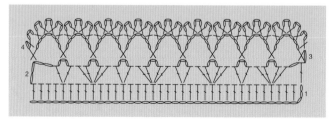

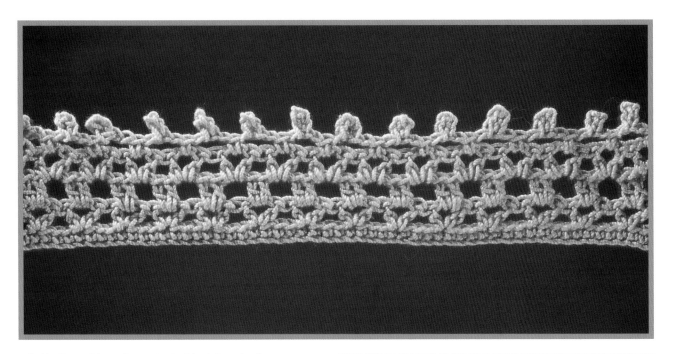

108

Picot: Ch 5, sl st in 5th ch from hook.

Chain multiples of 4.

Row 1 (RS): Sc in 2nd ch from hook, sc in each ch across, turn.

Row 2: Ch 4 (counts as dc, ch 1), *skip next 3 sc, (dc, ch 2, dc) in next sc; rep from * across to within last 3 sc, ch 1, skip next 2 sc, dc in last sc, turn.

Row 3: Ch 5 (counts as dc, ch 2), skip next ch-1 space, (2 dc, ch 2) in each ch-2 space across to turning ch, dc in 3rd ch of turning ch, turn.

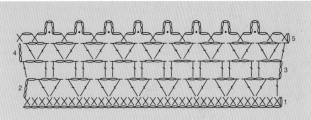

Row 4: Ch 3 (counts as dc), (dc, ch 2, dc) in each ch-2 space across to ch-2 space of turning ch, dc in 3rd ch of turning ch, turn.

Row 5: Ch 1, sc in first dc, ch 1, sc in next ch-2 space, (ch 1, picot, ch 1, sc) in each ch-2 space across to last ch-2 space, ch 1, sc in 3rd ch of turning ch. Fasten off.

109

Picot: Ch 4, sl st in 4th ch from hook.

Chain multiples of 6 plus 2.

Row 1 (RS): Sc in 2nd ch from hook, sc in each ch across, turn.

Row 2: Ch 3 (counts as dc), 3 dc in first sc, *skip next 5 sc, (3 dc, ch 2, 3 dc) in next sc; rep from * across to within last 6 sc, skip next 5 sc, 4 dc in last sc, turn.

Row 3: Ch 3 (counts as dc), 3 dc in first dc, ch 1, (3 dc, ch 2, 3 dc, ch 1) in each ch-2 space across to within last 7 sts, skip next 6 dc, 4 dc in 3rd ch of turning ch, turn.

Row 4: Ch 1, (sc, ch 4, sc) in first dc, *3 dc in next ch-1 space, (sc, ch 4, sc) in next ch-2 space; rep from * across, ending with last (sc, ch 3, sc) in 3rd ch of turning ch, turn.

Row 5: Ch 5 (counts as dc, ch 2), skip next 7 sts, *(2 dc, picot, 2 dc) in next dc**, ch 2, skip next 8 sts; rep from * across, ending last rep at **, ch 1, skip next 6 sts, dc in last sc. Fasten off.

110

Chain multiples of 4.

Row 1 (WS): Dc in 4th ch from hook, *ch 2, skip next 2 ch, dc in each of next 2 ch; rep from * across, turn.

Row 2: Ch 4 (counts as dc, ch 1), (3 dc, ch 1) in each ch-2 space across to last ch-2 space, skip next dc, dc in 3rd ch of turning ch, turn.

Row 3: Ch 1, sc in first dc, ch 1, skip next dc, 3 sc in next dc, *ch 1, skip next 3 sts, 3 sc in next dc; rep from * across to within last 3 sts, ch 1, sc in 3rd ch of turning ch, turn.

Row 4: Ch 3 (counts as dc), sc in first sc, skip next ch-1 space, *sc in next sc, (dc, ch 4, dc) in next sc, sc in next sc, skip next ch-1 space; rep from * across to within last sc, (sc, dc) in last sc. Fasten off.

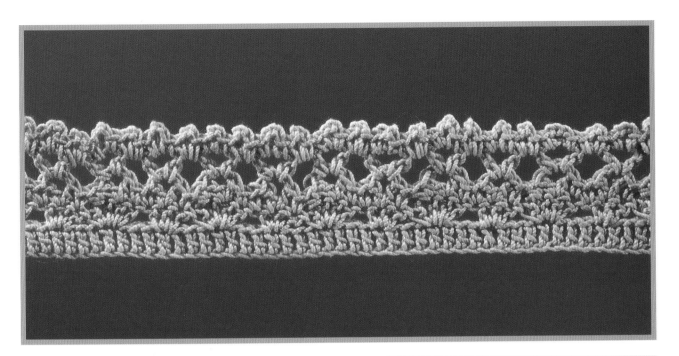

111

Chain multiples of 8 plus 4.

Row 1 (RS): Dc in 4th ch from hook, dc in each ch across, turn.

Row 2: Ch 3 (counts as dc), skip first 2 dc, *3 dc in next dc, skip next 3 dc, (sc, ch 3, 3 dc) in next dc**, skip next 3 dc; rep from * across, ending last rep at ** skip next 2 dc, dc in 3rd ch of turning ch, turn.

Row 3: Ch 2, skip first dc, *sc between next 2 dc, (dc, ch 3, dc) in next dc, sc between same dc and next dc**, skip next 2 dc; rep from * across, ending last rep at **, turn.

Row 4: Ch 6, (dc, ch 3, dc) in each ch-3 loop across, turn.

Row 5: Ch 1, sc in first dc, *(sc, ch 3, sc) in next ch-3 loop**, (sc, ch 3, sc) between next 2 dc; rep from * across, ending last rep at **, sc in last dc. Fasten off.

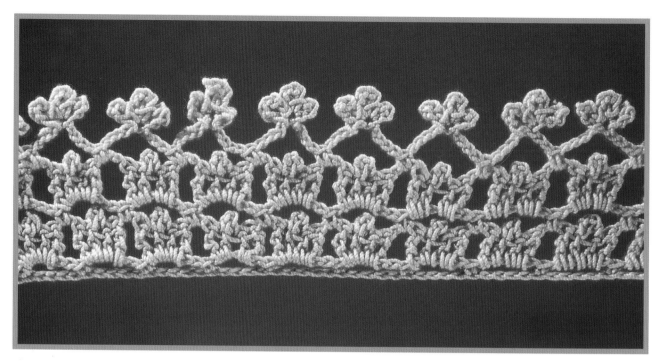

112

Ch-5 Picot: Ch 5, sl st in 5th ch from hook.

Ch-4 Picot: Ch 4, sl st in 4th ch from hook.

Chain multiples of 5 plus 2.

Row 1 (RS): Sc in 2nd ch from hook, *ch 5, skip next 4 ch, sc in next ch; rep from * across, turn.

Row 2: Ch 4 (counts as tr), *(tr, dc, ch-4 picot, dc, tr) in next ch-5 loop**, ch 2; rep from * across, ending last rep at **, tr in last sc, turn.

Row 3: Ch 1, sc in first tr, (ch 6, sc) in each ch-2 space across, ending with last sc in 3rd ch of turning ch, turn.

Row 4: Ch 4 (counts as tr), *(tr, dc, ch-4 picot, dc, tr) in next ch-6 loop**, ch 3; rep from * across, ending last rep at **, tr in last sc, turn.

Row 5: Ch 1, sc in first tr, *ch 4, work 5-ch picot, work 2nd ch-5 picot, sl st in sl st of first picot, work 3rd ch-5 picot, sl st in sl st of first picot, ch 4, skip next picot, sc in next ch-3 loop; rep from * across, ending with last sc in 4th ch of turning ch. Fasten off.

113

Chain multiples of 8 plus 4.

Row 1 (RS): Sc in 2nd ch from hook, sc in each ch across, turn.

Row 2: Ch 4 (counts as dc, ch 1), skip first 2 sc, dc in next sc, *ch 1, skip next sc, dc in next sc; rep from * across, turn.

Row 3: Ch 1, sc in first sc, sc in next ch-1 space, *ch 5, skip next ch-1 space, sc in next ch-1 space; rep from * across, sc in 3rd ch of turning ch, turn.

Row 4: Ch 6 (counts as tr, ch 2), sc in next ch-5 loop, (ch 5, sc) in each ch-5 loop across to last ch-5 loop, ch 2, tr in last sc, turn.

Row 5: Ch 1, sc in first sc, 2 sc in next ch-2 space, *ch 2, sc in next ch-5 loop, ch 5, turn, sl st in next sc forming a ring, turn, ch 4, (dc, ch 1) 5 times in ch-5 ring, dc in same ch-5 ring, ch 1, turn, (sc in next dc, sc in next ch-1 space) 3 times, picot, sc in next dc, (sc in next ch-1 space, sc in next dc) twice, sl st in each of next 4 ch, sl st in next sc, ch 2**, 5 sc in next ch-5 loop in Row 4; rep from * across, ending last rep at **, 2 sc in ch-2 space of turning ch, sc in 4th ch of turning ch, turn.

Row 6: Ch 12 (counts as trtr, ch 4), skip next 6 sc, (sc, ch 7) in each picot across to within last picot, sc in last picot, ch 4, trtr in last sc, turn.

Row 7: Ch 1, (sc, hdc, 2 dc, hdc, sc) in next ch-4 loop, (sc, hdc, dc, 3 tr, dc, hdc, sc) in each ch-7 loop across to turning ch, (sc, hdc, 2 dc, hdc, sc) in ch-4 loop of turning ch. Fasten off.

114

Chain multiples of 12 plus 6.

Row 1 (RS): Dc in 6th ch from hook, *ch 1, skip next ch, dc in next ch; rep from * across, turn.

Row 2: Ch 3 (counts as dc), dc in next ch-1 space, *ch 3, skip next ch-1 space, 2 dc in next ch-1 space; rep from * across, ending with last dc in 4th ch of turning ch, turn.

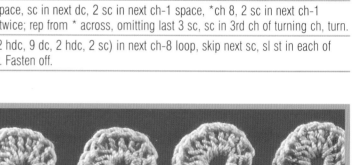

Row 3: Ch 4 (counts as dc, ch 1), (dc, ch 1, dc, ch 1) in each ch-3 loop across to last ch-3 loop, skip next dc, dc in 3rd ch of turning ch, turn.

Row 4: Ch 1, sc in first dc, 2 sc in next ch-1 space, sc in next dc, 2 sc in next ch-1 space, *ch 8, 2 sc in next ch-1 space, (sc in next dc, 2 sc in next ch-1 space) twice; rep from * across, omitting last 3 sc, sc in 3rd ch of turning ch, turn.

Row 5: Ch 1, sl st in each of first 5 sc, (2 sc, 2 hdc, 9 dc, 2 hdc, 2 sc) in next ch-8 loop, skip next sc, sl st in each of next 6 sc; rep from * across, omitting last sl st. Fasten off.

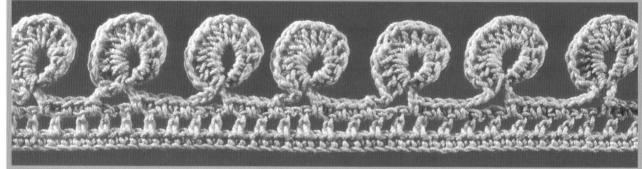

115

Chain multiples of 8.

Row 1 (RS): Sc in 2nd ch from hook, sc in each ch across, turn.

Row 2: Ch 4 (counts as dc, ch 1), skip first 2 sc, dc in next sc, *ch 1, skip next sc, dc in next sc; rep from * across, turn.

Row 3: Ch 1, sc in first dc, sc in next ch-1 space, *ch 10, sl st in 7th ch from hook forming a ring, (sc, hdc, 12 dc, hdc, sc) in ch-7 ring just made, ch 3, skip next ch-1 space, sc in next ch-1 space**, (sc in next dc, sc in next ch-1 space) twice; rep from * across, ending last rep at **, sc in 3rd ch of turning ch. Fasten off.

116

Picot: Ch 4, sl st in 4th ch from hook.

Chain multiples of 6.

Row 1 (RS): Sc in 2nd ch from hook, sc in each ch across, turn.

Row 2: Ch 4 (counts as dc, ch 1), skip first 2 sc, dc in next sc, *ch 1, skip next sc, dc in next sc; rep from * across, turn.

Row 3: Ch 1, sc in first dc, sc in next ch-1 space, *sc in next dc, ch 14, skip next ch-1 space**, (sc in next dc, sc in next ch-1 space) twice; rep from * across, ending last rep at **, sc in 3rd ch of turning ch, turn.

Row 4: Ch 1, *17 sc in next ch-14 loop, skip next 2 sc**, sl st in each of next 2 sc; rep from * across, ending last rep at **, sl st in last sc, turn.

Row 5: Ch 1, skip first sl st, sl st in each of next 4 sc, *sc in each of next 4 sc, picot, sc in each of next 4 sc, skip next 11 sts; rep from * across to within last 5 sc, sl st in each of last 5 sc. Fasten off.

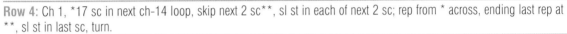

117

Chain multiples of 8 plus 2.

Row 1 (RS): Sc in 2nd ch from hook, sc in each ch across, turn.

Row 2: Ch 1, sc in each of first 4 sc, *(sc, ch 7, sc) in next sc, sc in each of next 7 sc; rep from * across, ending with sc in each of last 4 sc, turn.

Row 3: Ch 4 (counts as dc, ch 1), skip first sc, *sc in next sc, sl st in next sc, skip next 2 sc, 9 sc in next ch-7 loop, skip next 2 sc, sl st in next sc, sc in next sc, dc in next sc; rep from * across, turn.

Row 4: Ch 1, sc in first dc, *ch 4, skip next 5 sc, (sc, ch 5, sc) in next sc, ch 4, skip next 5 sc, sc in next dc; rep from * across, ending with last sc in 3rd ch of turning ch, turn.

Row 5: Ch 1, sc in first sc, *3 sc in next ch-4 loop, 5 sc in next ch-5 loop, 3 sc in next ch-4 loop, sc in next sc; rep from * across. Fasten off.

118

Picot: Ch 3, sl st in 3rd ch from hook.

Chain multiples of 13 plus 3.

Row 1 (WS): Dc in 4th ch from hook, dc in each ch across, turn.

Row 2: Ch 1, sc in first dc, *ch 11, sc in next dc, (ch 5, skip next 2 dc, sc in next dc) 4 times; rep from * across, ending with (sc, ch 6, dtr) in 3rd ch of turning ch, turn.

Row 3: Ch 1, sc in first dtr, 5 sc in next ch-6 loop, *(sc, ch 3) in each of next 3 ch-5 loops, sc in next ch-5 loop, 11 sc in next ch-11 loop; rep from * across, ending with 6 sc in last ch-11 loop, turn.

Row 4: Ch 4 (counts as tr), (picot, ch 1, tr) in each of next 4 sc, *ch 2, skip next ch-3 loop, sc in next ch-3 loop, ch 2, skip next ch-3 loop, skip next 2 sc, tr in next sc**, (picot, ch 1, tr) in each of next 8 sc; rep from * across, ending last rep at **, (picot, ch 1, tr) in each of last 4 sc, turn.

Row 5: Ch 1, sc in first tr, **ch 5, skip next picot, sc in next tr, ch 10, skip next 6 picots, sc in next tr, ch-5, skip next picot, sc in next tr; rep from * across, ending with last sc in 4th ch of turning ch, turn.

Row 6: Ch 6 (counts as tr, ch 2), *sc in next ch-5 loop, ch 5, (sc, ch 5) twice in next ch-10 loop, sc in next ch-5 loop**, ch 5; rep from * across, ending last rep at **, ch 2, tr in last sc, turn.

Row 7: Ch 1, sc in first tr, (ch 5, sc) in each ch-5 loop across, ending with last sc in 4th ch of turning ch, turn.

Row 8: Ch 1, 6 sc in each ch-5 loop across. Fasten off.

.7.

V-Stitches & Small Shells

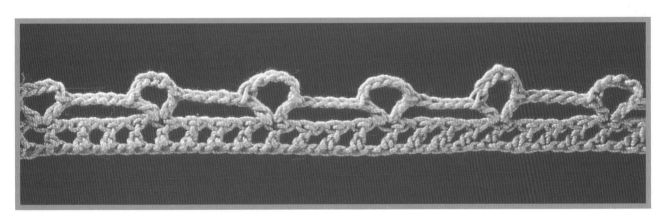

119

Chain multiples of 8 plus 4.

Row 1 (WS): Dc in 6th ch from hook, *ch 1, skip next ch, dc in next ch; rep from * across, turn.

Row 2: Ch 6 (counts as dc, ch 3), dc in first dc, *ch 5, skip next 4 ch-1 spaces**, (dc, ch 5, dc) in next dc; rep from * across, ending last rep at **, (dc, ch 3, dc) in 4th ch of turning ch. Fasten off.

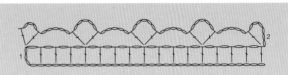

120

Chain multiples of 3.

Row 1 (RS): Dc in 4th ch from hook, dc in each ch across, turn.

Row 2: Ch 1, sc in first dc, *skip next 2 dc, (2 dc, ch 3, sc) in next dc; rep from * across, ending with last (2 dc, ch 3, sc) in 3rd ch of turning ch. Fasten off.

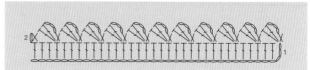

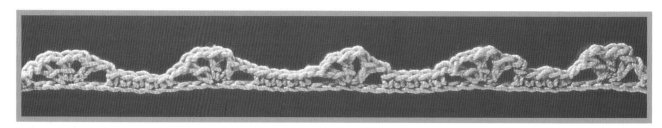

121

Chain multiples of 10 plus 6.

Row 1 (RS): Sc in 2nd ch from hook, sc in each of next 4 ch, *ch 2, skip next 2 ch, (dc, ch 2, dc, ch 2, dc) in next ch, ch 2, skip next 2 ch, sc in each of next 5 ch; rep from * across. Fasten off.

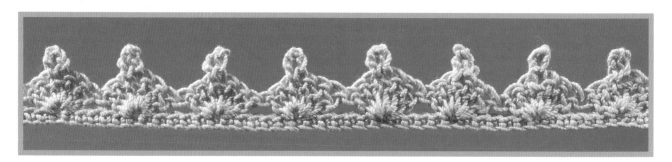

122

Picot: Ch 5, sl st in 5th ch from hook.

Chain multiples of 6 plus 2.

Row 1 (RS): Sc in 2nd ch from hook, sc in each ch across, turn.

Row 2: Ch 3 (counts as dc), picot, 3 dc in first sc, *skip next 5 sc, (3 dc, picot, 3 dc) in next sc; rep from * across to within last 6 sc, skip next 5 sc, (3 dc, picot, dc) in last sc. Fasten off.

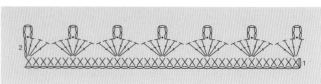

123

Chain multiples of 16 plus 2.

Row 1 (RS): Sc in 2nd ch from hook, sc in each ch across, turn.

Row 2: Ch 1, sc in first sc, *ch 7, skip next 7 sc, (2 dc, ch 2, 2 dc) in next sc, ch 7, skip next 7 sc, sc in next sc; rep from * across, turn.

Row 3: Ch 1 (sc, ch 3, sc) in first sc, *ch 7, skip next ch-7 loop, (2 dc, ch 2, 2 dc) in next next ch-2 space, ch 7, skip next ch-7 loop, (sc, ch 3, sc) in next sc; rep from * across. Fasten off.

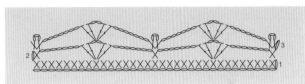

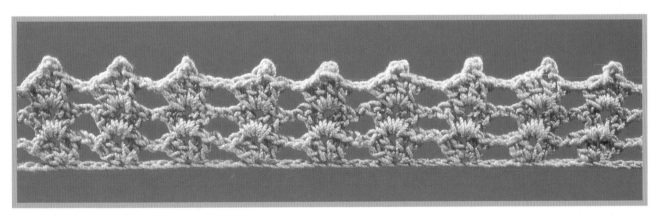

124

Picot: Ch 3, sl st in 3rd ch from hook.

Chain multiples of 5 plus 2.

Row 1 (RS): (2 dc, ch 1, 2 dc) in 5th ch from hook, *ch 2, skip next 4 ch, (2 dc, ch 1, 2 dc) in next ch; rep from * across to within last 2 ch, skip next ch, dc in last ch, turn.

Row 2: Ch 3 (counts as dc), *(2 dc, ch 1, 2 dc) in next ch-1 space**, ch 2, skip next ch-2 space; rep from * across, ending last rep at **, dc in 4th ch of turning ch, turn.

Row 3: Ch 3 (counts as dc), *(2 dc, picot, 2 dc) in next ch-1 space**, ch 2, skip next ch-2 space; rep from * across, ending last rep at **, dc in 3rd ch of turning ch. Fasten off.

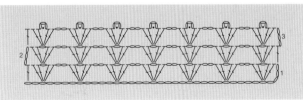

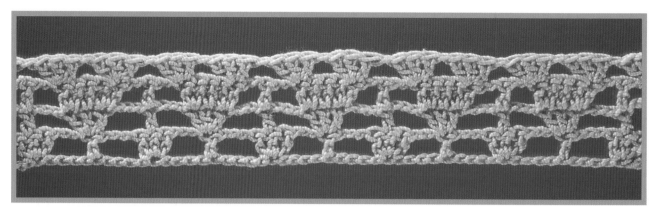

125

Chain multiples of 10 plus 6.

Row 1 (WS): 3 dc in 11th ch from hook, *ch 3, skip next 4 ch, dc in next ch**, ch 3, skip next 4 ch, 3 dc in next ch; rep from * across, ending last rep at **, turn.

Row 2: Ch 3 (counts as dc), dc in first dc, *ch 3, skip next dc, dc in next dc, ch 3, skip next ch-3 loop**, 3 dc in next dc; rep from * across, ending last rep at **, 2 dc in 7th ch of turning ch, turn.

Row 3: Ch 3 (counts as dc), skip first dc, 2 dc in next dc, *ch 2, skip next ch-3 loop, dc in next dc, ch 2, skip next ch-3 loop, 2 dc in next dc**, dc in next dc, 2 dc in next dc; rep from * across, ending last rep at **, dc in 3rd ch of turning ch, turn.

Row 4: Ch 3 (counts as dc), skip first 2 dc, 3 dc in next dc, *ch 1, skip next 2 ch-2 spaces, 3 dc in next dc**, ch 1, skip next 3 dc, 3 dc in next dc; rep from * across, ending last rep at **, skip next dc, dc in 3rd ch of turning ch. Fasten off.

126

Chain multiples of 3 plus 1.

Row 1 (RS): Sc in 2nd ch from hook, sc in each ch across, turn.

Row 2: Ch 4 (counts as dc, ch 1), skip first 2 sc, *dc in each of next 2 sc, ch 1, skip next sc; rep from * across to within last sc, dc in last sc, turn.

Row 3: Ch 1, sc in first dc, ch 3, (2 dc, ch 3, sc) in each ch-1 space across. Fasten off.

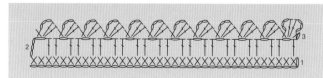

127

Picot: Ch 3, sl st in 3rd ch from hook.

Chain multiples of 5 plus 2.

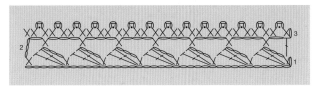

Row 1 (RS): (Sc, ch 3, 2 dc) in 2nd ch from hook, skip next 4 ch, *(sc, ch 3, 2 dc) in next ch, skip next 4 ch; rep from * across to within last ch, sc in last ch, turn.

Row 2: Ch 4 (counts as dc, ch 1), skip first 3 sts, sc in next ch-3 loop, (ch 3, sc) in each ch-3 loop across to last ch-3 loop, ch 1, dc in last sc, turn.

Row 3: Ch 1, sc in first dc, picot, sc in next ch-1 space, *sc in next sc, picot, (2 sc, picot, sc) in next ch-3 loop; rep from * across to last ch-3 loop, sc in next sc, picot, sc in ch-1 space of turning ch, sc in 3rd ch of turning ch. Fasten off.

128

Chain multiples of 4 plus 2.

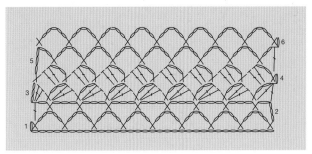

Row 1 (WS): Sc in 2nd ch from hook, *ch 5, skip next 3 ch, sc in next sc; rep from * across, turn.

Row 2: Ch 4 (counts as dc, ch 1), sc in next ch-5 loop, (ch 3, sc) in each ch-5 loop across to last ch-5 loop, ch 1, dc in last sc, turn.

Row 3: Ch 3 (counts as dc), 2 dc in first dc, skip next ch-1 space, *(sc, ch 2, 2 dc) in next sc, skip next ch-3 loop; rep from * across to within last sc, sc in next sc, ch 2, 2-dc cluster, working first half-closed dc in same sc, skip next ch, work 2nd half-closed dc in next ch of turning ch, complete cluster, turn.

Row 4: Ch 1, sc in first st, ch 2, 2 dc in next ch-2 space, (sc, ch 2, 2 dc) in each ch-2 space across to last ch-2 space, sc in 3rd ch of turning ch, turn.

Row 5: Ch 5 (counts as dc, ch 2), sc in next ch-2 space, (ch 5, sc) in each ch-2 space across to last ch-2 space, ch 2, dc in last sc, turn.

Row 6: Ch 1, sc in first dc, (ch 5, sc) in each ch-5 loop across, ending with last sc in 3rd ch of turning ch. Fasten off.

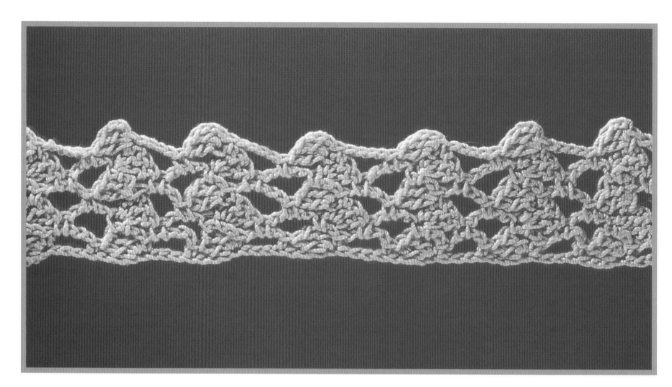

129

Chain multiples of 8 plus 6.

Row 1 (RS): Sc in 2nd ch from hook, *ch 4, skip next 3 ch**, (sc, ch 3, 2 dc) in next ch, skip next 3 ch, sc in next ch; rep from * across, ending last rep at **, sc in last ch, turn.

Row 2: Ch 5 (counts as dc, ch 2), sc in next ch-5 loop, *ch 4, sc in next ch-3 loop, ch 3, 2 dc in last sc made, sc in next ch-4 loop; rep from * across to last ch-4 loop, ch 2, dc in last sc, turn.

Row 3: Ch 1, sc in first dc, ch 4, *sc in next ch-3 loop, ch 3, 2 dc in last sc made, sc in next ch-4 loop, ch 4; rep from * across to turning ch, sc in 3rd ch of turning ch, turn.

Rows 4-5: Rep Rows 2-3. Fasten off.

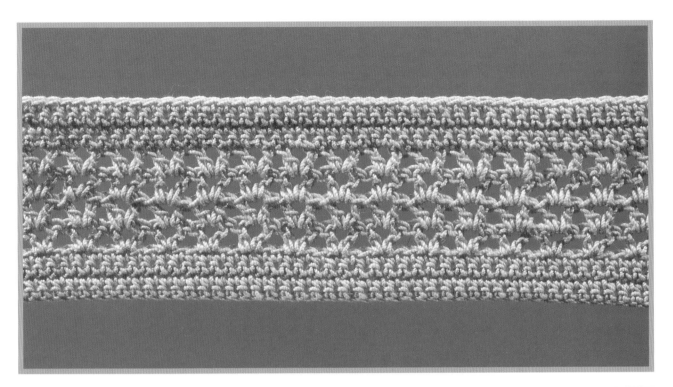

130

Chain multiples of 3 plus 2.

Row 1 (RS): Sc in 2nd ch from hook, sc in each ch across, turn.

Rows 2-4: Ch 1, sc in each sc across, turn.

Row 5: Ch 4 (counts as dc, ch 1), skip first 3 sc, *(dc, ch 2, dc) in next sc, skip next 2 sc; rep from * across to within last sc, ch 1, dc in last sc, turn.

Rows 6-8: Ch 4 (counts as dc, ch 1), skip next ch-1 space, (dc, ch 2, dc) in each ch-2 space across to turning ch, ch 1, dc in 3rd ch of turning ch, turn.

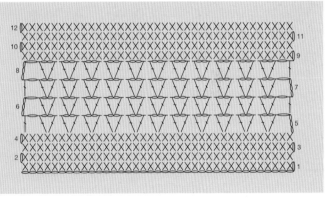

Row 9: Ch 1, sc in first dc, sc in next ch-1 space, *sc in next dc, sc in next ch-2 space, sc in next dc; rep from * across to turning ch, sc in ch-1 space of turning ch, sc in 3rd ch of turning ch, turn.

Rows 10-12: Ch 1, sc in each sc across, turn. Fasten off.

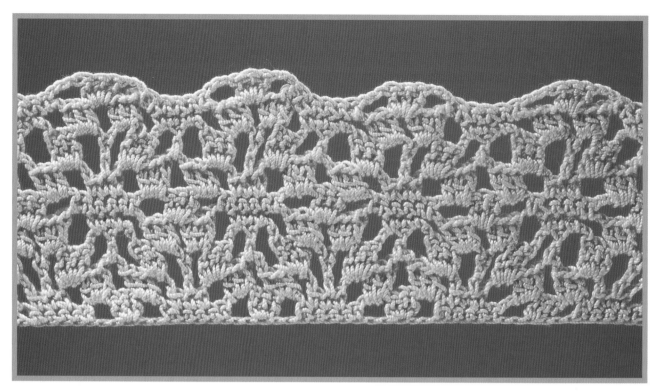

131

Chain multiples of 10 plus 2.

Row 1 (RS): Sc in 2nd ch from hook, sc in each of next 2 ch, *ch 3, skip next 2 ch, 3 dc in next ch, ch 3, skip next 2 ch, sc in each of next 5 ch; rep from * across, ending with sc in each of last 3 ch, turn.

Row 2: Ch 1, sc in each of first 2 sc, *ch 3, 3 dc in next ch-3 loop, ch 3, 3 dc in next ch-3 loop, ch 3, skip next sc, sc in each of next 3 sc; rep from * across, ending with sc in each of last 2 sc, turn.

Row 3: Ch 6 (counts as dc, ch 3), *3 dc in next ch-3 loop, ch 3, dc in next ch-3 loop, ch 3, 3 dc in next ch-3 loop, ch 3, skip next sc, dc in next sc**, ch 3; rep from * across, ending last rep at **, turn.

Row 4: Ch 4 (counts as tr), *3 dc in next ch-3 loop, ch 3, sc in next ch-3 loop, sc in next dc, sc in next ch-3 loop, ch 3, 3 dc in next ch-3 loop**, ch 1; rep from * across, ending last rep at **, tr in 3rd ch of turning ch, turn.

Row 5: Ch 3 (counts as dc), dc in first dc, *ch 3, sc in next ch-3 loop, sc in each of next 3 sc, sc in next ch-3 loop, ch 3**, 3 dc in next ch-1 space; rep from * across, ending last rep at **, skip next 3 dc, 2 dc in 4th ch of turning ch, turn.

Row 6: Ch 3 (counts as dc), *3 dc in next ch-3 loop, ch 3, skip next sc, sc in each of next 3 sc, ch 3, 3 dc in next ch-3 loop**, ch 3; rep from * across, ending last rep at **, skip next dc, dc in 3rd ch of turning ch, turn.

Row 7: Ch 5 (counts as dc, ch 2), *3 dc in next ch-3 loop, ch 3, skip next sc, dc in next sc, ch 3, 3 dc in next ch-3 loop**, ch 3, dc in next ch-3 loop, ch 3; rep from * across, ending last rep at **, ch 2, skip next 3 dc, dc in 3rd ch of turning ch, turn.

Row 8: Ch 1, sc in first dc, *sc in next loop, ch 3, 3 dc in next ch-3 loop, ch 1, 3 dc in next ch-3 loop, ch 3, sc in next loop, sc in next dc; rep from * across, ending with last sc in 3rd ch of turning ch, turn.

Row 9: Ch 1, sc in first 2 sc, *sc in next ch-3 loop, ch 3, 3 dc in next ch-1 space, ch 3, sc in next ch-3 loop, sc in each of next 3 sc; rep from * across, ending with sc in each of last 2 sc. Fasten off.

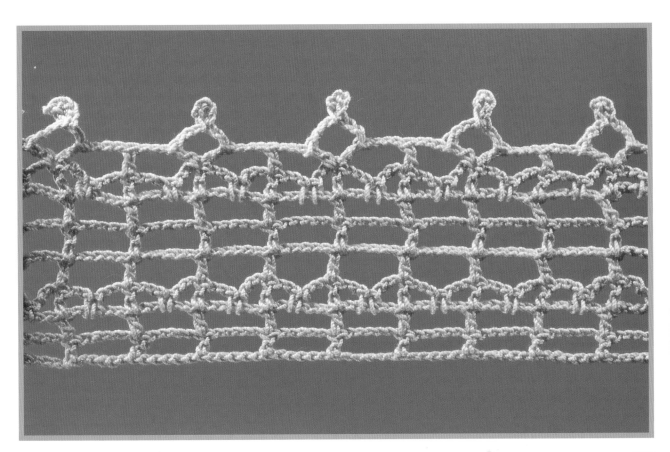

132

Picot: Ch 5, sl st in 5th ch from hook.

Chain multiples of 12 plus 8.

Row 1 (WS): Dc in 14th ch from hook, *ch 5, skip next 5 ch, dc in next ch; rep from * across, turn.

Row 2: Ch 8 (counts as dc, ch 5), skip next ch-5 loop, dc in next dc, *ch 5, skip next ch-5 loop, dc in next dc; rep from * across, ending with last dc in 8th ch of turning ch, turn.

Row 3: Ch 6 (counts as dc, ch 3), sc in next ch-5 loop, ch 3, *dc in next dc, ch 3, sc in next ch-5 loop, ch 3; rep from * across to turning ch, dc in 3rd ch of turning ch, turn.

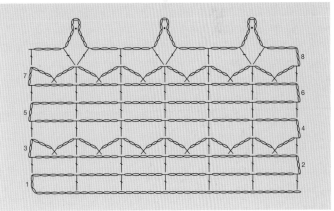

Row 4: Ch 8 (counts as dc, ch 5), skip next 2 ch-3 loops, *dc in next dc, ch 5, skip next 2 ch-3 loops; rep from * across to turning ch, dc in 3rd ch of turning ch, turn.

Rows 5-6: Ch 8 (counts as dc, ch 5), skip next ch-5 loop, dc in next dc, *ch 5, skip next ch-5 loop, dc in next dc; rep from * across, ending with last dc in 3rd ch of turning ch, turn.

Row 7: Rep Row 3.

Row 8: Ch 6 (counts as dc, ch 3), *skip next 2 ch-3 loops, (dc, ch 3, picot, ch 3, dc) in next dc, ch 3, skip next 2 ch-3 loops, dc in next dc**, ch 3; rep from * across, ending last rep at **, with last dc in 3rd ch of turning ch. Fasten off.

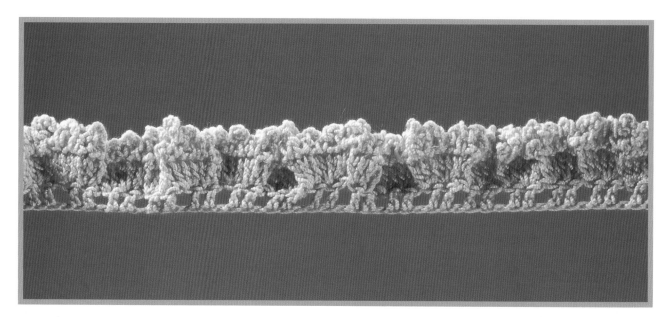

133

Chain multiples of 3 plus 1.

Row 1 (WS): Dc in 4th ch from hook, *ch 1, skip next ch, dc in each of next 2 ch; rep from * across, turn.

Row 2: Ch 3 (counts as dc), 2 dc in first dc, 3 dc in next dc, *ch 3, skip next ch-1 space, 3 dc in each of next 2 dc; rep from * across, ending with last 3 dc in 3rd ch of turning ch, turn.

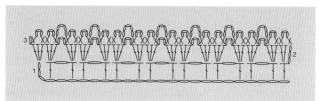

Row 3: Ch 1, sc in first dc, *ch 3, skip next dc, sc in each of next 2 dc, ch 3, skip next dc, sc in next dc**, ch 5, skip next ch-3 loop, sc in next dc; rep from * across, ending last rep at **, with last sc in 3rd ch of turning ch. Fasten off.

134

Picot: Ch 4, sl st in 4th ch from hook.

Chain multiples of 16 plus 2.

Row 1 (RS): Sc in 2nd ch from hook, sc in each of next 2 ch, *ch 7, skip next 5 ch, tr in next ch, ch 7, skip next 5 ch, sc in each of next 5 ch; rep from * across, ending with sc in each of last 3 ch, turn.

Row 2: Ch 1, sc in each of first 2 sc, *ch 7, sc in next ch-7 loop, sc in next dc, sc in next ch-7 loop, ch 7, skip next sc, sc in each of next 3 sc; rep from * across, ending with sc in each of last 2 sc, turn.

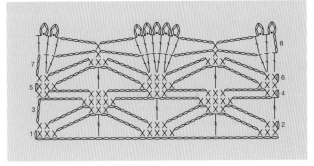

Row 3: Ch 11 (counts as tr, ch 7), *sc in next ch-7 loop, sc in each of next 3 sc, sc in next ch-7 loop, ch 7, skip next sc, tr in next sc**, ch 7; rep from * across, ending last rep at **, turn.

Row 4: Ch 1, sc in first tr, *sc in next ch-7 loop, ch 7, skip next sc, sc in each of next 3 sc, ch 7, sc in next ch-7 loop, sc in next tr; rep from * across, ending with last sc in 4th ch of turning ch, turn.

Row 5: Ch 1, sc in each of first 2 sc, *sc in next ch-7 loop, ch 7, skip next sc, tr in next sc, ch 7, sc in next ch-7 loop, sc in each of next 3 sc; rep from * across, ending with sc in each of last 2 sc, turn.

Row 6: Ch 1, sc in each of first 2 sc, *ch 7, sc in next ch-7 loop, sc in next tr, sc in next ch-7 loop, ch 7, skip next sc, sc in each of next 3 sc; rep from * across, ending with sc in each of last 2 sc, turn.

Row 7: Ch 3 (counts as dc), skip first sc, *2 dc in next sc, ch 7, skip next sc, sc in next sc, ch 7, skip next ch-7 loop**, 2 dc in each of next 3 sc; rep from * across, ending last rep at **, 2 dc in next sc, dc in last sc, turn.

Row 8: Ch 3 (counts as dc), picot, skip first dc, dc in next dc, picot, dc in next dc, ch 6, skip next ch-7 loop, sc in next sc, ch 6, skip next ch-7 loop**, (dc, picot) in each of next 5 dc, dc in next dc; rep from * across, ending last rep at **, (dc, picot) in each of next 2 dc, dc in 3rd ch of turning ch. Fasten off.

135

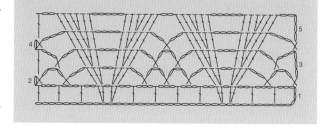

Chain multiples of 16 plus 9.

Row 1 (RS): Dc in 9th ch from hook, ch 3, skip next 2 ch, dc in next ch, *ch 2, skip next 2 ch, 2 dc in next ch, ch 1, 2 dc in next ch, ch 2, skip next 2 ch, dc in next ch**, (ch 3, skip next 2 ch, dc in next ch) 3 times; rep from * across, ending last rep at **, (ch 3, skip next 2 ch, dc in next ch) twice, turn.

Row 2: Ch 1, sc in first dc, ch 3, skip next ch-3 loop, *sc in next ch-3 loop, ch 2, skip next ch-2 space, dc in next dc, 2 dc in next dc, ch 2, skip next ch-1 space, 2 dc in next dc, dc in next dc, ch 2, skip next ch-2 space**, (sc, ch 3) in each of next 2 ch-3 loops; rep from * across, ending last rep at **, sc in next ch-3 loop, ch 3, sc in 5th ch of turning ch, turn.

Row 3: Ch 6 (counts as dc, ch 3), sc in next ch-3 loop, *ch 2, skip next ch-2 space, dc in next dc, 2 dc in next dc, dc in next dc, ch 3, skip next ch-2 space, dc in next dc, 2 dc in next dc, dc in next dc, ch 2, skip next ch-2 space, sc in next ch-3 loop, ch 3**, sc in next ch-3 loop; rep from * across, ending last rep at **, dc in last sc, turn.

Row 4: Ch 1, sc in first dc, ch 3, skip next 2 spaces, *dc in each of next 2 dc, 2 dc in next dc, dc in next dc, ch 4, skip next ch-3 loop, dc in next dc, 2 dc in next dc, dc in each of next 2 dc**, ch 2, skip next ch-2 space, sc in next ch-3 loop, ch 2, skip next ch-2 space; rep from * across, ending last rep at **, ch 3, skip next ch-2 space, skip next 3 ch of turning ch, sc in 3rd ch of turning ch, turn.

Row 5: Ch 5 (counts as dc, ch 2), skip next ch-3 loop, *dc in each of next 2 dc, 2 dc in next dc, dc in each of next 2 dc, ch 5, skip next ch-4 loop, dc in each of next 2 dc, 2 dc in next dc, dc in each of next 2 dc, ch 2**, skip next 2 ch-2 spaces; rep from * across, ending last rep at **, skip next ch-3 loop, dc in last sc. Fasten off.

136

Chain multiples of 2.

Row 1 (WS): Sc in 2nd ch from hook, sc in each ch across, turn.

Row 2: Ch 3 (counts as dc), skip first sc, *2 dc in next sc, dc in next sc; rep from * across, turn.

Row 3: Ch 4 (counts as dc, ch 1), skip first dc, (dc, ch 1) in each dc across to turning ch, dc in 3rd ch of turning ch, turn.

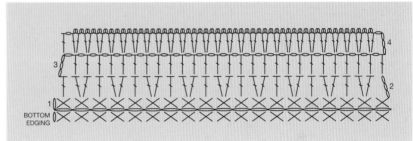

Row 4: Ch 4 (counts as dc, ch 1), skip next ch-1 space, (dc, ch 2, dc) in next dc, (ch 2, dc, ch 2, dc) in each dc across to turning ch, ch 1, dc in 3rd ch of turning ch. Fasten off.

Bottom Edging: With RS facing, working across opposite side of foundation ch, join yarn in first ch, ch 1, sc in each ch across. Fasten off.

.8.
Staggered Squares

137

Chain multiples of 5 plus 1.

Row 1 (WS): Hdc in 3rd ch from hook, hdc in each ch across, turn.

Row 2: Ch 6 (counts as ch 3, dc), skip first 3 ch, work 3 dc around next 3 ch, skip first 3 hdc, hdc in each of next 2 hdc, *sl st in next hdc, ch 6, skip first 3 ch, work 3 dc around next 3 ch, skip next 2 hdc, hdc in each of next 2 hdc; rep from * across, ending with last hdc in 2nd ch of turning ch. Fasten off.

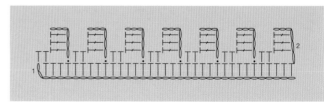

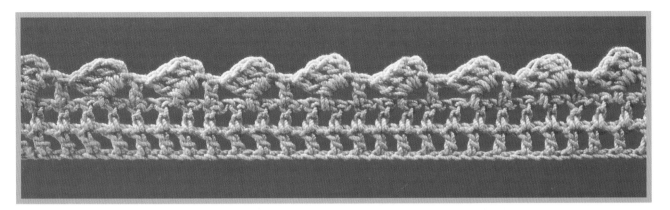

138

Chain multiples of 6 plus 4.

Row 1 (RS): Dc in 6th ch from hook, *ch 1, skip next ch, dc in next ch; rep from * across, turn.

Row 2: Ch 4 (counts as dc, ch 1), skip next ch-1 space, dc in next dc, (ch 1, dc) in each dc across, ending with last dc in 4th ch of turning ch, turn.

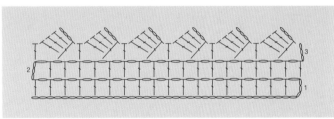

Row 3: Ch 3 (counts as dc), *skip next ch-1 space, dc in next ch-1 space, ch 3, work 3 dc around the post of last dc made, skip next ch-1 space, dc in next ch-1 space; rep from * across, ending with last dc in 3rd ch of turning ch. Fasten off.

139

Chain multiples of 6.

Row 1 (WS): Tr in 9th ch from hook, *ch 2, skip next 2 ch, tr in next ch; rep from * across, turn.

Row 2: Ch 6 (counts as ch 2, tr), skip first 4 ch, work 4 tr around the 2 ch, ch 1, skip next 2 ch-2 spaces, *tr in next tr, ch 4, work 4 tr

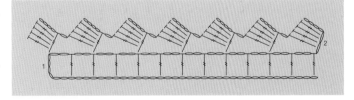

around the post of last tr made, ch 1, skip next 2 ch-2 spaces; rep from * across to turning ch, tr in 6th ch of turning ch, ch 4, work 4 tr around the post of last tr made. Fasten off.

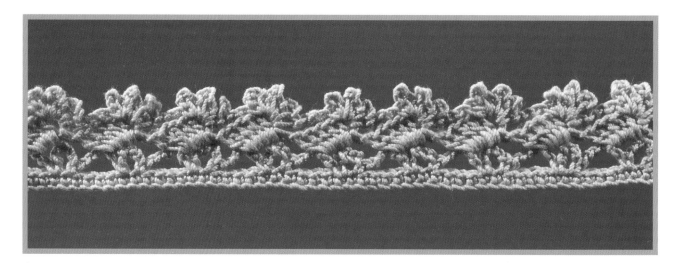

140

Chain multiples of 5 plus 2.

Row 1 (RS): Sc in 2nd ch from hook, sc in each ch across, turn.

Row 2: Ch 1, sc in first sc, *ch 5, skip next 4 sc, (sc, ch 5, sc) in next sc; rep from * across to within last 5 sc, ch 5, skip next 4 sc, sc in last sc, turn.

Row 3: Ch 3 (counts as dc), *dc in next ch-5 loop, ch 3, work 5 dc around the post of last dc made**, skip next ch-5 loop; rep from * across, ending last rep at **, sc in last sc, turn.

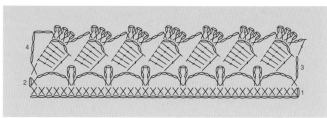

Row 4: Ch 5 (counts as dc, ch 2), (sc, ch 3) 4 times in each ch-3 loop across to within last ch-3 loop, (sc, ch 3) 3 times in last ch-3 loop, sc in same ch-3 loop, ch 2, dc in 3rd ch of turning ch. Fasten off.

141

Chain multiples of 14 plus 4.

Row 1 (WS): Dc in 4th ch from hook, dc in each ch across, turn.

Row 2: Ch 3 (counts as dc), skip first dc, dc in next dc, *skip next 2 dc, tr in next dc, ch 3, work 3 dc around the post of last tr made, skip next 2 dc, dc in each of next 2 dc; rep from * across, ending with last dc in 3rd ch of turning ch, turn.

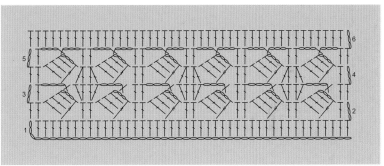

Row 3: Ch 3 (counts as dc), skip first dc, dc in next dc, *ch 3, sc in next ch-3 loop, skip next tr, 2 dc in each of next 2 dc, ch 3, sc in next ch-3 loop, skip next tr, dc in each of next 2 dc; rep from * across, ending with last dc in 3rd ch of turning ch, turn.

Row 4: Ch 3 (counts as dc), skip first dc, dc in next dc, *tr in next ch-3 loop, ch 3, work 3 dc around the post of last tr made, (work 2-dc cluster across next 2 dc) twice, tr in next ch-3 loop, ch 3, work 3 dc around the post of last tr made, dc in each of next 2 dc; rep from * across, ending with last dc in 3rd ch of turning ch.

Row 5: Ch 3 (counts as dc), skip first dc, dc in next dc, *ch 3, sc in next ch-3 loop, skip next tr, ch 3, dc in each of next 2 clusters, ch 3, sc in next ch-3 loop, skip next tr, dc in each of next 2 dc; rep from * across, ending with last dc in 3rd ch of turning ch, turn.

Row 6: Ch 3 (counts as dc), skip first dc, dc in next dc, *2 dc in next ch-3 loop, dc in next sc, 2 dc in next ch-3 loop, dc in each of next 2 dc; rep from * across, ending with last dc in 3rd ch of turning ch. Fasten off.

142

Picot: Ch 5, sl st in 5th ch from hook.

Chain multiples of 30 plus 14.

Row 1 (WS): Sc in 2nd ch from hook, sc in each ch across, turn.

Row 2: Ch 5 (counts as dc, ch 2), skip first 3 sc, dc in next sc, *ch 2, skip next 2 sc, dc in next sc; rep from * across, do not turn. Fasten off.

Row 3: With RS facing, join yarn in 3rd ch of turning ch, ch 6 (counts as tr, ch 2), skip next ch-2 space, tr in next dc,

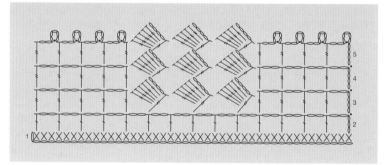

(ch 2, tr) in each of next 3 dc, *skip next ch-2 space, (tr in next dc, ch 4, work 5 tr around the post of last tr made, skip next 2 ch-2 spaces) twice, tr in next dc, ch 4, work 5 tr around the post of last tr made, skip next ch-2 space, tr in next dc, (ch 2, tr) in each of next 4 tr; rep from * across, do not turn. Fasten off.

Row 4: With RS facing, join yarn in 4th ch of turning ch, ch 6 (counts as tr, ch 2), skip next ch-2 space, tr in next tr, (ch 2, tr) in each of next 3 tr, *(tr in next ch-4 loop, ch 4, work 5 tr around the post of last tr made) 3 times, skip next 5 tr, tr in next tr, (ch 2, tr) in each of next 4 tr; rep from * across, do not turn. Fasten off.

Row 5: With RS facing, join yarn in 4th ch of turning ch, ch 4 (counts as tr), (picot, ch 2, tr) in each of next 4 tr, *(tr in next ch-4 loop, ch 4, work 5 tr around the post of last tr made) 3 times, skip next 5 tr, tr in next tr, (picot, ch 2, tr) in each of next 4 tr; rep from * across. Fasten off.

.9.
Dropped Stitches
& Crossed Stitches

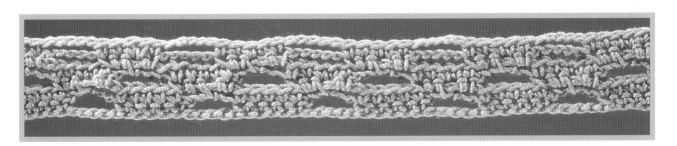

143

Chain multiples of 10 plus 2.

Row 1 (RS): Sc in 2nd ch from hook, ch 2, skip next 2 ch, *sc in each of next 5 ch**, ch 5, skip next 5 ch; rep from * across, ending last rep at **, ch 2, skip next 2 ch, sc in last ch, turn.

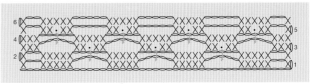

Row 2: Ch 1, sc in first sc, ch 2, skip next ch-2 space, *sc in each of next 5 sc**, ch 5, skip next ch-5 loop; rep from * across, ending last rep at **, ch 2, skip next ch-2 space, sc in last sc, turn.

Row 3: Ch 1, sc in first sc, 2 sc in next ch-2 space, *ch 5, skip next 5 sc**, 2 sc in next ch-5 loop, working over same ch-5 loop, sl st in next corresponding ch-5 loop 2 rows below, 2 sc in same ch-5 loop in row below; rep from * across, ending last rep at **, 2 sc in next ch-2 space, sc in last sc, turn.

Row 4: Ch 1, sc in each of first 3 sc, *ch 5, skip next ch-5 loop**, sc in each of next 5 sts; rep from * across, ending last rep at **, sc in last 3 sc, turn.

Row 5: Ch 1, sc in first sc, ch 2, skip next 2 sc, *2 sc in next ch-5 loop, working over same ch-5 loop, sl st in next corresponding ch-5 loop 2 rows below, 2 sc in same ch-5 loop in row below**, ch 5, skip next 5 sc; rep from * across, ending last rep at **, ch 2, skip next 2 sc, sc in last sc, turn.

Row 6: Ch 1, sc in first sc, ch 2, skip next ch-2 space, *sc in each of next 5 sts**, ch 5, skip next ch-5 loop; rep from * across, ending last rep at **, ch 2, skip next ch-2 space, sc in last sc. Fasten off.

144

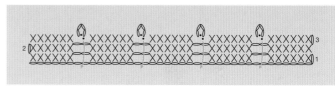

Picot: Ch 4, sl st in 4th ch from hook.

Chain multiples of 8 plus 7.

Row 1 (RS): Sc in 2nd ch from hook, sc in each of next 5 ch, *ch 2, skip next 2 ch, sc in each of next 6 ch; rep from * across, turn.

Row 2: Ch 1, sc in each of first 6 sc, *ch 2, skip next ch-2 space, sc in each of next 6 sc; rep from * across, turn.

Row 3: Ch 1, sc in each of first 6 sc, *sl st over next 3 ch-2 loops in 2 previous rows and foundation ch, picot, sc in each of next 6 sc; rep from * across. Fasten off.

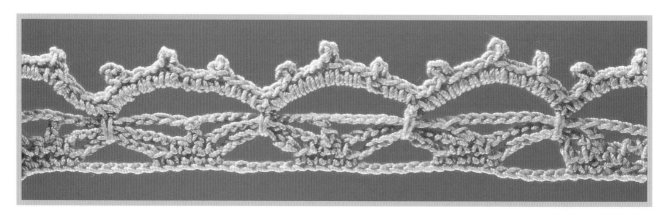

145

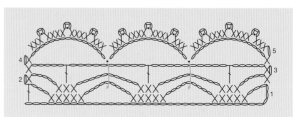

Picot: Ch 3, sl st in 3rd ch from hook.

Chain multiples of 11 plus 5.

Row 1 (RS): Sc in 9th ch from hook, sc in each of next 4 ch, *ch 9, skip next 6 ch, sc in each of next 5 ch; rep from * across to within last 3 ch, ch 3, skip next 2 ch, dc in last ch, turn.

Row 2: Ch 1, sc in first dc, ch 5, skip next sc, sc in each of next 3 sc, *ch 10, skip next (sc, ch 9, sc), sc in each of next 3 sc; rep from * across to turning ch, ch 5, skip next ch-3 loop of turning ch, sc in 5th ch of turning ch, turn.

Row 3: Ch 1, sc in first sc, ch 5, skip next sc, dc in next sc, *ch 10, skip next (sc, ch 10, sc) dc in next sc; rep from * across to within last ch-5 loop, ch 5, skip next ch-5 loop, sc in last sc, turn.

Row 4: Ch 1, sc in first sc, skip next ch-5 loop, *ch 15, sl st over next 3 loops in 3 previous rows; rep from * across, omitting last sl st, sc in last sc, turn.

Row 5: Ch 1, (3 sc, picot, 4 sc, picot, 4 sc, picot, 3 sc) in each ch-5 loop across. Fasten off.

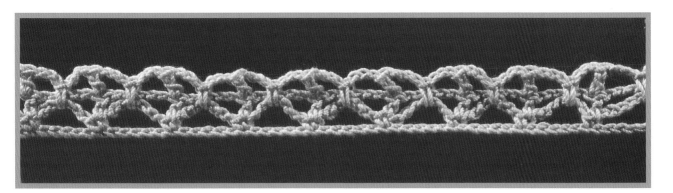

146

Chain multiples of 6 plus 2.

Row 1 (RS): Sc in 2nd ch from hook, *ch 7, skip next 5 ch, sc in next ch; rep from * across, turn.

Row 2: Ch 8 (counts as dc, ch 5), skip next ch-7 loop, dc in next sc, *ch 5, skip next ch-7 loop, dc in next sc; rep from * across, turn.

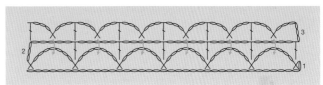

Row 3: Ch 6 (counts as dc, ch 3), *working over next ch-5 loop, sc in next ch-7 loop 2 rows below, ch 3**, dc in next dc, ch 3; rep from * across, ending last rep at **, dc in 3rd ch of turning ch. Fasten off.

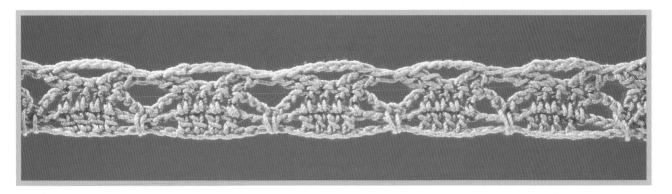

147

Chain multiples of 9 plus 6.

Row 1 (RS): Dc in 4th ch from hook, dc in each of next 2 ch, *ch 5, skip next 5 ch, dc in each of next 4 ch; rep from * across, turn.

Row 2: Ch 3 (counts as dc), skip first dc, dc in each of next 3 dc, *ch 3, sc over next ch-5 loop and over ch-5 loop of foundation ch, ch 3, dc in each of next 4 dc; rep from * across, ending with last dc in 3rd ch of turning ch, turn.

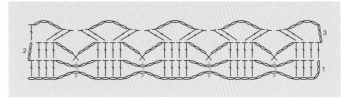

Row 3: Ch 7 (counts as dc, ch 4), skip first 2 dc, *dc in each of next 2 dc, skip next 2 ch-3 loops, dc in each of next 2 dc**, ch 5; rep from * across, ending last rep at **, ch 4, skip next dc, dc in 3rd ch of turning ch. Fasten off.

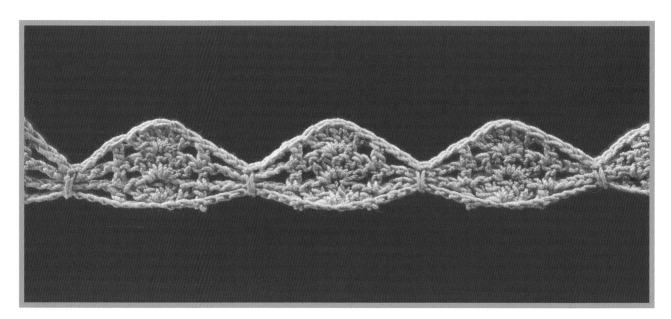

148

Chain multiples of 14 plus 4.

Row 1 (RS): 2 dc in 4th ch from hook, *skip next 2 ch, dc in next ch, ch 7, skip next 7 ch, dc in next ch, skip next 2 ch**, 5 dc in next ch; rep from * across, ending last rep at **, 3 dc in last ch, turn.

Row 2: Ch 3 (counts as dc), 2 dc in first dc, *skip next 2 dc, dc in next dc, ch 7, skip next ch-7 loop, dc in next dc, skip next 2 dc**, 5 dc in next dc; rep from * across, ending last rep at **, 3 dc in 3rd ch of turning ch, turn.

Row 3: Ch 3 (counts as dc), 2 dc in first dc, *skip next 2 dc, dc in next dc, ch 3, sc over next 2 corresponding ch-7 loops and over ch-7 loop of foundation ch, ch 3, dc in next dc, skip next 2 dc**, 5 dc in next dc; rep from * across, ending last rep at **, 3 dc in 3rd ch of turning ch. Fasten off.

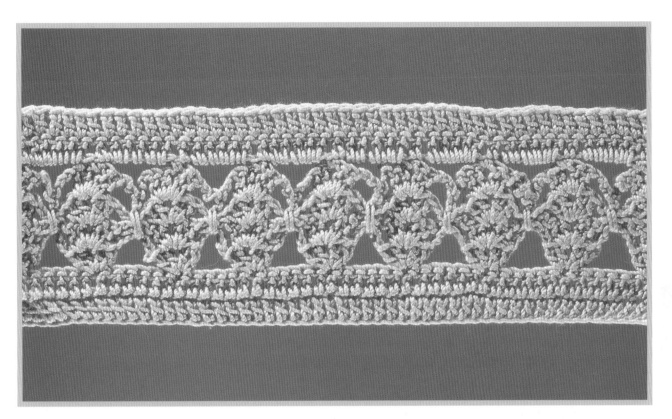

149

Chain multiples of 6 plus 5.

Row 1 (RS): Dc in 4th ch from hook, dc in each ch across, turn.

Row 2: Ch 3 (counts as dc), skip first dc, dc in each dc across, ending with dc in 3rd ch of turning ch across, turn.

Row 3: Ch 5 (counts as dc, ch 2), skip first 4 dc, *(2 dc, ch 1, 2 dc) in next dc**, ch 5, skip next 5 dc; rep from * across, ending last rep at **, ch 2, skip next 3 dc, dc in 3rd ch of turning ch, turn.

Row 4: Ch 5 (counts as dc, ch 2), skip next ch-2 space, *(2 dc, ch 1, 2 dc) in next ch-1 space**, ch 4, skip next loop; rep from * across, ending last rep at **, ch 2, skip next 2 ch of turning ch, dc in 3rd ch of turning ch, turn.

Row 5: Rep Row 4.

Row 6: Ch 5 (counts as dc, ch 2), skip next ch-2 space, *(2 dc, ch 1, 2 dc) in next ch-1 space**, ch 3, sc over next 3 loops in 3 previous rows, ch 3; rep from * across, ending last rep at **, ch 2, skip next 2 ch of turning ch, dc in 3rd ch of turning ch, turn.

Row 7: Ch 1, sc in first dc, ch 3, skip next ch-2 space, sc in next ch-1 space, *ch 5, skip next 2 ch-3 loops, sc in next ch-1 space; rep from * across to last ch-1 space, ch 3, sc in 3rd ch of turning ch, turn.

Row 8: Ch 3 (counts as dc), skip first sc, 3 sc in next ch-3 loop, dc in next sc, *5 dc in next ch-5 loops, dc in next sc; rep from * across to within last ch-3 loop, 3 dc in next ch-3 loop, dc in last sc, turn.

Row 9: Ch 3 (counts as dc), skip first dc, dc in each dc across, ending with dc in 3rd ch of turning ch across. Fasten off.

150

Chain multiples of 5 plus 3.

Row 1 (RS): Sc in 2nd ch from hook, sc in each ch across, turn.

Row 2: Ch 3 (counts as dc), skip first sc, *dc in each of next 2 sc, dc around the posts of last 2 dc made, ch 2, skip next 3 sc; rep from * across to within last sc, dc in last sc, turn.

Row 3: Ch 1, sc in first dc, *2 sc in next ch-2 space, sc in each of next 3 dc; rep from * across to turning ch, sc in 3rd ch of turning ch. Fasten off.

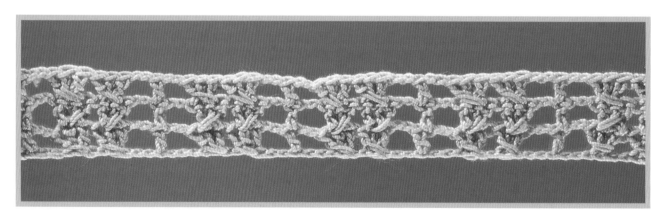

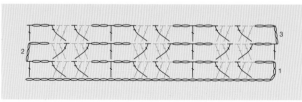

151

Chain multiples of 11 plus 5.

Row 1 (RS): Dc in 9th ch from hook, dc in next ch, working over last 2 dc made, dc in last skipped ch to the right, *skip next ch, dc in each of next 2 ch, working around the posts of last 2 dc made, dc in last skipped ch to the right, ch 2, skip next 2 ch, dc in next ch**, ch 2, skip next 3 ch, dc in each of next 2 dc, working around the posts of last 2 dc made, dc in last skipped ch to the right; rep from * across, ending last rep at **, turn.

Row 2: Ch 5 (counts as dc, ch 2), skip next ch-2 space, *(skip next dc, dc in each of next 2 dc, working around the posts of last 2 dc made, dc in last skipped dc to the right) twice, ch 2, skip next ch-2 space, dc in next dc**, ch 2, skip next ch-2 space; rep from * across, ending last rep at **, with last dc in 3rd ch of turning ch, turn.

Row 3: Rep Row 2. Fasten off.

.10.
Simple Filets
& Shells in Grid

152

Chain multiples of 8.

Row 1 (RS): Dc in 6th ch from hook, *ch 1, skip next ch, dc in next ch; rep from * across, turn.

Row 2: Ch 4 (counts as dc, ch 1), skip next ch-1 space, dc in next dc, ch 1, skip next ch-1 space, *(dc in next dc, dc in next ch-1 space) twice, (dc in next dc, ch 1, skip next ch-1 space) twice; rep from * across to turning ch, dc in 4th ch of turning ch, turn.

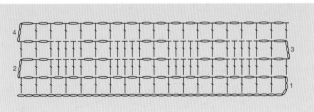

Row 3: Ch 4 (counts as dc, ch 1), skip next ch-1 space, dc in next dc, ch 1, skip next ch-1 space, *dc in each of next 5 dc, ch 1, skip next ch-1 space, dc in next dc, ch 1; rep from * across to turning ch, dc in 3rd ch of turning ch, turn.

Row 4: Ch 4 (counts as dc, ch 1), skip next ch-1 space, dc in next dc, *ch 1, skip next st, dc in next dc; rep from * across, ending with last dc in 3rd ch of turning ch. Fasten off.

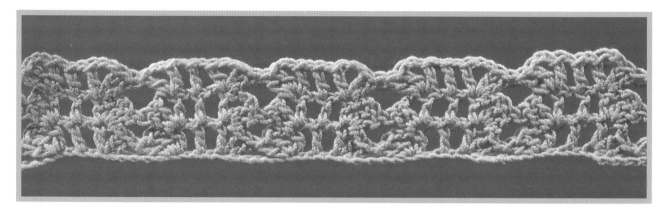

153

Chain multiples of 10 plus 2.

Row 1 (RS): 2 dc in 6th ch from hook, *skip next 5 ch, (2 dc, ch 2, dc) in next ch**, ch 1, skip next ch, dc in next ch, ch 1, skip next ch, (dc, ch 2, 2 dc) in next ch; rep from * across, ending last rep at **, turn.

Row 2: Ch 5 (counts as dc, ch 2), 2 dc in first dc, *skip next 2 ch-2 spaces, (2 dc, ch 2, dc) in next dc**, ch 1, skip next ch-1 space, dc in next dc, ch 1, skip next ch-1 space, (dc, ch 2, 2 dc) in next dc; rep from * across, ending last rep at **, with last (2 dc, ch 2, dc) in 3rd ch of turning ch, turn.

Row 3: Rep Row 2. Fasten off.

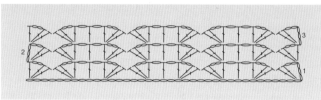

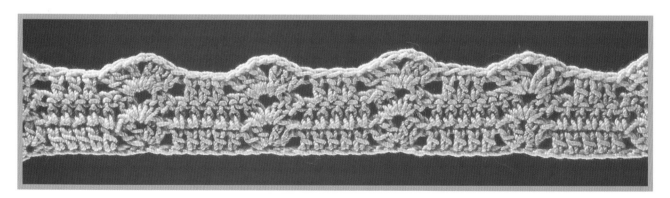

154

Chain multiples of 10 plus 3.

Row 1 (RS): Dc in 4th ch from hook, dc in next ch, *skip next 2 ch, (2 dc, ch 2, 2 dc) in next ch, skip next 2 ch, dc in each of next 5 ch; rep from * across, ending with dc in each of last 3 ch, turn.

Row 2: Ch 3 (counts as dc), skip first dc, dc in each of next 2 dc, *skip next 2 dc, (2 dc, ch 2, 2 dc) in next ch-2 space, skip next 2 dc**, dc in each of next 5 dc; rep from * across, ending last rep at **, dc in each of next 2 dc, dc in 3rd ch of turning ch, turn.

Row 3: Ch 3 (counts as dc), skip first dc, dc in next dc, *skip next 3 dc, (3 dc, ch 2, 3 dc) in next ch-2 space, skip next 3 dc**, dc in each of next 3 dc; rep from * across, ending last rep at **, dc in next dc, dc in 3rd ch of turning ch. Fasten off.

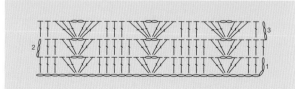

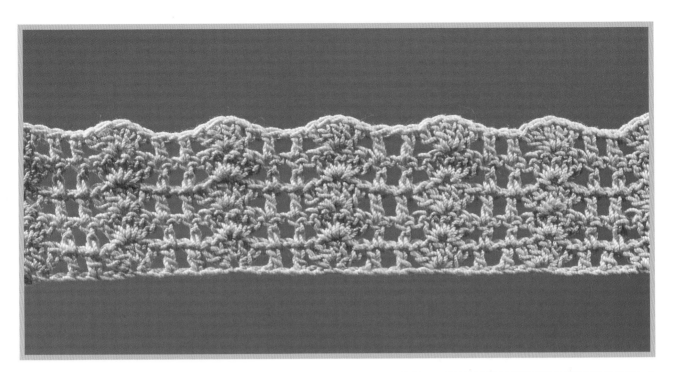

155

Chain multiples of 8 plus 6.

Row 1 (RS): Dc in 6th ch from hook, *skip next 2 ch, 5 dc in next ch, skip next 2 ch, dc in next ch, ch 1, skip next ch, dc in next ch; rep from * across, turn.

Row 2: Ch 4 (counts as dc, ch 1), skip next ch-1 space, dc in next dc, *skip next 2 dc, 5 dc in next dc, skip next 2 dc, dc in next dc, ch 1, skip next ch-1 space, dc in next dc; rep from * across, ending with last dc in 4th ch of turning ch, turn.

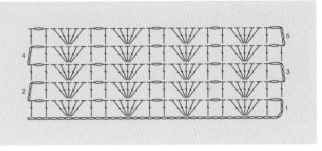

Row 3: Ch 4 (counts as dc, ch 1), skip next ch-1 space, dc in next dc, *skip next 2 dc, 5 dc in next dc, skip next 2 dc, dc in next dc, ch 1, skip next ch-1 space, dc in next dc; rep from * across, ending with last dc in 3rd ch of turning ch, turn.

Rows 4-5: Rep Row 3. Fasten off.

156

Chain multiples of 12 plus 2.

Row 1 (RS): Dc in 6th ch from hook, *skip next 2 ch, 5 dc in next ch, skip next 2 ch**, (dc in next ch, ch 1, skip next ch) 3 times, dc in next ch; rep from * across, ending last rep at **, dc in next ch, ch 1, skip next ch, dc in last ch, turn.

Row 2: Ch 4 (counts as dc, ch 1), skip next ch-1 space, *dc in each of next 6 dc**, (dc, ch 1) in each of next 3 dc; rep from * across, ending last rep at **, dc in next dc, ch 1, dc in 4th ch of turning ch, turn.

Row 3: Ch 5 (counts as dc, ch 2), skip next ch-1 space, skip next dc, * dc in each of next 5 dc, ch 2, skip next ch-1 space**, dc in next dc, ch 1, skip next ch-1 space, dc in next dc, ch 2, skip next dc; rep from * across, ending last rep at **, dc in 3rd ch of turning ch, turn.

Row 4: Ch 6 (counts as dc, ch 3), skip next ch-2 space, *skip next dc, dc in each of next 3 dc, ch 3, skip next ch-2 space**, dc in next dc, ch 1, skip next ch-1 space, dc in next dc, ch 3; rep from * across, ending last rep at **, dc in 3rd ch of turning ch, turn.

Row 5: Ch 7 (counts as dc, ch 4), *skip next ch-3 loop, skip next dc, dc in next dc, ch 4, skip next ch-3 loop**, dc in next dc, ch 1, skip next ch-1 space, dc in next dc, ch 4; rep from * across, ending last rep at **, dc in 3rd ch of turning ch. Fasten off.

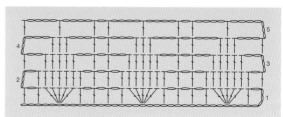

157

Chain multiples of 8 plus 3.

Row 1 (RS): Dc in 4th ch from hook, *skip next 2 ch, (2 dc, ch 1, 2 dc) in next ch, skip next 2 ch, dc in next ch**, ch 1, skip next ch, dc in next ch; rep from * across, ending last rep at **, dc in last ch, turn.

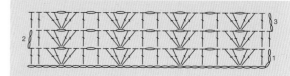

Row 2: Ch 3 (counts as dc), skip first dc, dc in next dc, *skip next 2 dc, (2 dc, ch 1, 2 dc) in next ch-1 space, skip next 2 dc, dc in next dc**, ch 1, skip next ch-1 space, dc in next dc; rep from * across, ending last rep at **, dc in 3rd ch of turning ch, turn.

Row 3: Rep Row 2. Fasten off.

158

Chain multiples of 8 plus 5.

Row 1 (WS): (Dc, ch 1, dc) in 9th ch from hook, *ch 2, skip next 3 ch, dc in next ch**, ch 2, skip next 3 ch, (dc, ch 1, dc) in next ch; rep from * across, ending last rep at **, turn.

Row 2: Ch 5 (counts as dc, ch 2), skip next ch-2 space, *3 dc in next ch-1 space, ch 2, skip next ch-2 space, dc in next dc**, ch 2, skip next ch-2 space; rep from * across, ending last rep at **, with last dc in 6th ch of turning ch, turn.

Row 3: Ch 4 (counts as dc, ch 1), *skip next ch-2 space, skip next dc, 5 dc in next dc, ch 1, skip next ch-2 space, dc in next dc**, ch 1; rep from * across, ending last rep at **, with last dc in 3rd ch of turning ch, turn.

Row 4: Ch 3 (counts as dc), *skip next ch-1 space, skip next 2 dc, 7 dc in next dc, skip next ch-1 space, dc in next dc; rep from * across, ending with last dc in 3rd ch of turning ch. Fasten off.

159

Chain multiples of 12 plus 3.

Row 1 (RS): Dc in 4th ch from hook, dc in each ch across, turn.

Row 2: Ch 5 (counts as dc, ch 2), skip first 3 dc, *dc in next dc, skip next 2 dc, (dc, ch 1, dc, ch 1, dc) in next dc, skip next 2 dc**, (dc in next dc, ch 2, skip next 2 dc) twice; rep from * across, ending last rep at **, dc in next dc, ch 2, skip next 2 dc, dc in 3rd ch of turning ch, turn.

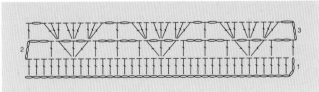

Row 3: Ch 4 (counts as dc, ch 1), *skip next ch-2 space, skip next dc, 3 dc in next dc, (skip next ch-1 space, 3 dc in next dc) twice, ch 1, skip next ch-2 space, dc in next dc**, ch 1; rep from * across, ending last rep at **, with last dc in 3rd ch of turning ch. Fasten off.

160

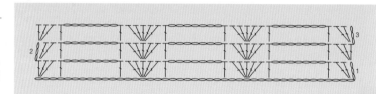

Chain multiples of 14 plus 4.

Row 1 (RS): 2 dc in 4th ch from hook, *skip next 2 ch, dc in next ch, ch 7, skip next 7 ch, dc in next ch, skip next 2 ch**, 5 dc in next ch; rep from * across, ending last rep at **, 3 dc in last ch, turn.

Row 2: Ch 3 (counts as dc), 2 dc in first dc, *skip next 2 dc, dc in next dc, ch 7, skip next ch-7 loop, dc in next dc, skip next 2 dc**, 5 dc in next dc; rep from * across, ending last rep at **, 3 dc in 3rd ch of turning ch, turn.

Row 3: Rep Row 2. Fasten off.

161

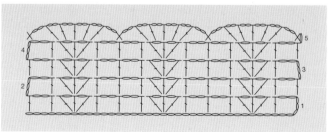

Chain multiples of 12 plus 5.

Row 1 (RS): Dc in 8th ch from hook, *skip next 2 ch, (dc, ch 1, dc, ch 1, dc) in next ch, skip next 2 ch, dc in next ch**, (ch 2, skip next 2 ch, dc in next ch) twice; rep from * across, ending last rep at **, ch 2, skip next 2 ch, dc in last ch, turn.

Row 2: Ch 5 (counts as dc, ch 2), skip next ch-2 space, dc in next dc, *skip next ch-1 space, (dc, ch 1, dc, ch 1, dc) in next dc, skip next ch-1 space, skip next dc, dc in next dc**, (ch 2, skip next ch-2 space, dc in next dc) twice; rep from * across, ending last rep at **, ch 2, skip next 2 ch of turning ch, dc in next ch of turning ch, turn.

Rows 3-4: Rep Row 2.

Row 5: Ch 1, sc in first dc, *ch 2, skip next ch-2 space, skip next dc, dc in next dc, (ch 2, dc in next ch-2 space, ch 2, dc in next dc) twice, ch 2, skip next ch-2 space, sc in next dc; rep from * across, ending with last sc in 3rd ch of turning ch. Fasten off.

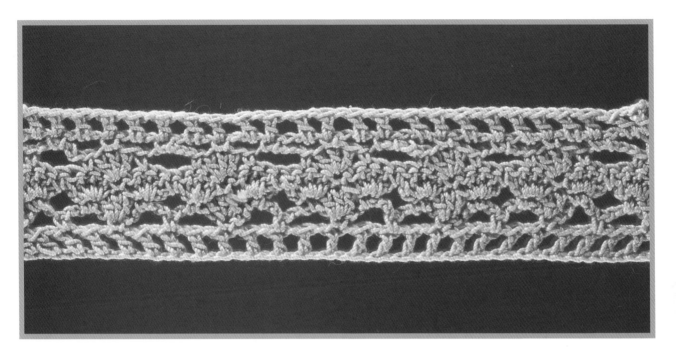

162

Chain multiples of 8 plus 4.

Row 1 (RS): Dc in 6th ch from hook, *ch 1, skip next ch, dc in next ch; rep from * across, turn.

Row 2: Ch 1, sc in first dc, *ch 5, skip next 2 ch-1 spaces, sc in next dc; rep from * across, ending with last sc in 4th ch of turning ch, turn.

Row 3: Ch 5 (counts as dc, ch 2), *sc in next ch-5 loop, 3 dc in next sc, sc in next ch-5 loop**, ch 5; rep from * across, ending last rep at **, ch 2, dc in last sc, turn.

Row 4: Ch 1, sc in first dc, *3 dc in next sc, skip next 2 sts, sc in next dc, skip next dc, 3 dc in next sc, sc in next ch-5 loop; rep from * across, ending with last sc in 3rd ch of turning ch, turn.

Row 5: Ch 3 (counts as dc), dc in first sc, *skip next dc, sc in next dc, ch 5, skip next 3 sts, sc in next dc, skip next dc**, 3 dc in next sc; rep from * across, ending last rep at **, 2 dc in last sc, turn.

Row 6: Ch 1, sc in first dc, *ch 3, sc in next ch-5 loop, ch 3, skip next 2 sts, sc in next dc; rep from * across, ending with last sc in 3rd ch of turning ch, turn.

Row 7: Ch 4 (counts as dc, ch 1), *dc in next ch-3 loop, ch 1, dc in next sc**, ch 1; rep from * across, ending last rep at **. Fasten off.

163

Chain multiples of 17 plus 7.

Row 1 (RS): Sc in 2nd ch from hook, *ch 5, skip next 4 ch, sc in next ch**, skip next 2 ch, ([dc, ch 1, dc, ch 1, dc] in next ch, skip next 2 ch, sc in next ch) twice; rep from * across, ending last rep at **, turn.

Row 2: Ch 5 (counts as dc, ch 2), sc in next ch-5 loop, *ch 5, skip next ch-1 space, sc in next dc, skip next ch-1 space, skip next dc, (dc, ch 1, dc, ch 1, dc) in next sc, skip next ch-1 space, sc in next dc, ch 5, skip next ch-1 space, sc in next ch-5 loop; rep from * across to last ch-5 loop, ch 2, dc in last sc, turn.

Row 3: Ch 1, sc in first dc, ch 5, sc in next ch-5 loop, *(dc, ch 1, dc, ch 1, dc) in next sc, skip next ch-1 space, sc in next dc, skip next ch-1 space, skip next dc, (dc, ch 1, dc, ch 1, dc) in next sc, sc in next ch-5 loop, ch 5, sc in next ch-5 loop; rep from * across, ending with last sc in 3rd ch of turning ch. Fasten off.

164

Chain multiples of 12 plus 2.

Row 1 (WS): Sc in 2nd ch from hook, sc in each ch across, turn.

Row 2: Ch 1, sc in first sc, *ch 5, skip next 3 sc, sc in next sc; rep from * across, turn.

Row 3: Ch 4 (counts as dc, ch 1), dc in first dc, *sc in next ch-5 loop, (ch 5, sc) in each of next 2 ch-5 loops**, (dc, ch 1, dc, ch 1, dc) in next sc; rep from * across, ending last rep at **, (dc, ch 1, dc) in last sc, turn.

Row 4: Ch 1, sc in first dc, * skip next dc, (dc, ch 1, dc, ch 1, dc) in next sc, sc in next ch-5 loop, ch 5, sc in next ch-5 loop, (dc, ch 1, dc, ch 1, dc) in next sc, skip next ch-1 space, sc in next dc; rep from * across, ending with last sc in 3rd ch of turning ch, turn.

Row 5: Ch 5 (counts as dc, ch 2), skip next ch-1 space, sc in next dc, *(dc, ch 1, dc, ch 1, dc) in next sc, sc in next ch-5 loop, (dc, ch 1, dc, ch 1, dc) in next sc, skip next ch-1 space, sc in next dc**, ch 5, skip next 5 sts, sc in next dc; rep from * across, ending last rep at **, ch 2, skip next 2 sts, dc in last sc, turn.

Row 6: Ch 1, sc in first dc, *ch 5, skip next ch-1 space, sc in next dc, (dc, ch 1, dc, ch 1, dc) in next sc, skip next ch-1 space, sc in next dc, ch 5, sc in next ch-5 loop; rep from * across, ending with last sc in 3rd ch of turning ch. Fasten off.

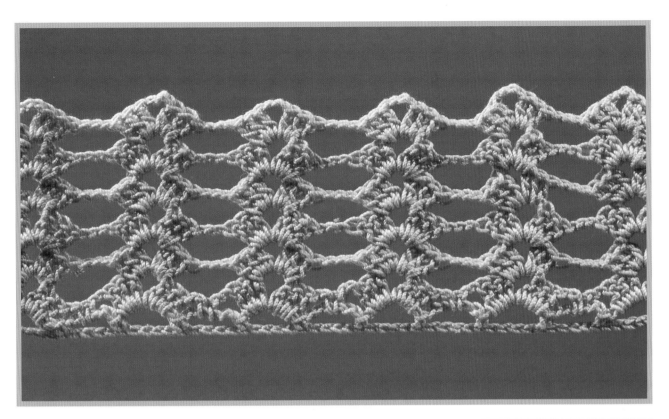

165

Chain multiples of 10 plus 7.

Row 1 (RS): Sc in 2nd ch from hook, *ch 6, skip next 4 ch, sc in next ch; rep from * across, turn.

Row 2: Ch 3 (counts as dc), *(3 dc, ch 3, 3 dc) in next ch-5 loop**, ch 2, sc in next ch-5 loop, ch 2; rep from * across, ending last rep at **, dc in last sc, turn.

Row 3: Ch 3 (counts as dc), skip first 4 dc, *(3 dc, ch 3, 3 dc) in next ch-3 loop**, ch 3, skip next 2 ch-2 spaces; rep from * across, ending last rep at **, skip next 3 dc, dc in 3rd ch of turning ch, turn.

Row 4-7: Rep Row 3. Fasten off.

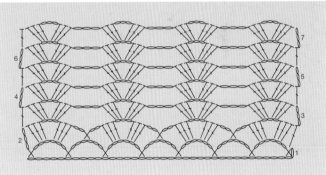

166

Chain multiples of 14 plus 8.

Row 1 (RS): Dc in 6th ch from hook, *ch 1, skip next ch, dc in next ch; rep from * across, turn.

Row 2: Ch 1, sc in first dc, *sc in next ch-1 space, sc in next dc, sc in next ch-1 space**, ch 4, skip next 2 ch-1 spaces, (2 dc, ch 3, 2 dc) in next ch-1 space, ch 4,

skip next 2 ch-1 spaces; rep from * across, ending last rep at **, sc in 4th ch of turning ch, turn.

Row 3: Ch 1, sc in each of first 4 sc, *sc in next ch-4 loop, ch 3, (3 dc, ch 4, 3 dc) in next ch-3 loop, ch 3, sc in next ch-4 loop, sc in each of next 3 sc; rep from * across to within last sc, sc in last sc, turn.

Row 4: Ch 1, sc in each of first 4 sc, *ch 4, skip next ch-3 loop, (dc, ch 1) 6 times in next ch-4 loop, dc in same ch-4 loop, ch 4, skip next ch-3 loop, skip next sc, sc in each of next 3 sc; rep from * across to within last sc, sc in last sc, turn.

Row 5: Ch 1, sc in each of first 3 sc, *ch 4, skip next ch-4 loop, (sc, ch 3) in each of next 5 ch-1 spaces, sc in next ch-1 space, ch 4, skip next ch-4 loop, skip next sc, sc in next sc; rep from * across to within last 2 sc, sc in each of last 2 sc. Fasten off.

167

Chain multiples of 12 plus 6.

Row 1 (RS): Dc in 6th ch from hook, *ch 1, skip next ch, dc in next ch; rep from * across, turn.

Row 2: Ch 1, sc in first dc, *sc in next ch-1 space, ch 4, skip next 2 ch-1 spaces, (dc, ch 5, dc) in next ch-1 space, ch 4, skip next 2 ch-1 spaces, sc in next ch-1 space; rep from * across to turning ch, sc in 4th ch of turning ch, turn.

Row 3: Ch 1, sc in each of first 2 sc, *ch 5, skip next ch-4 loop, (2 dc, ch 5, 2 dc) in next ch-5 loop, ch 5, skip next ch-4 loop, sc in next sc; rep from * across to within last sc, sc in last sc, turn.

Row 4: Ch 1, sc in each of first 2 sc, *ch 6, skip next ch-5 loop, (2 dc, ch 5, 2 dc) in next ch-5 loop, ch 6, skip next ch-5 loop, sc in next sc; rep from * across to within last sc, sc in last sc, turn.

Row 5: Ch 1, sc in each of first 2 sc, *ch 7, skip next ch-6 loop, (2 dc, ch 5, 2 dc) in next ch-5 loop, ch 7, skip next ch-6 loop, sc in next sc; rep from * across to within last sc, sc in last sc. Fasten off.

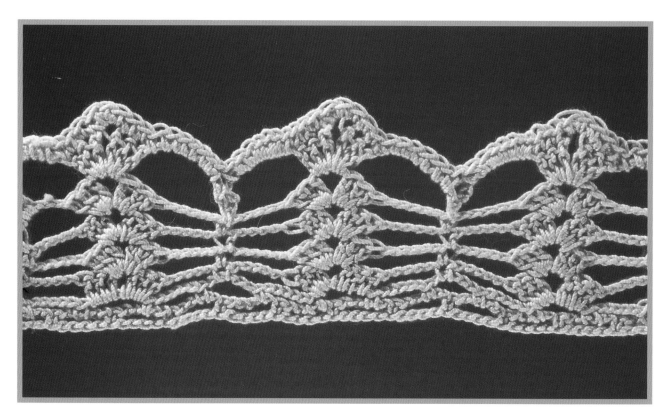

168

Chain multiples of 20 plus 2.

Row 1 (WS): Sc in 2nd ch from hook, *ch 5, skip next 4 ch, sc in next ch; rep from * across, turn.

Row 2: Ch 5 (counts as dc, ch 2), sc in next ch-5 loop, (ch 5, sc) in each ch-5 loop across to last ch-5 loop, ch 2, dc in last sc, turn.

Row 3: Ch 1, sc in first dc, *ch 5, skip next ch-5 loop, (3 dc, ch 2, 3 dc) in next ch-5 loop, ch 5, skip next ch-5 loop, sc in next ch-5 loop; rep from * across, ending with last sc in 3rd ch of turning ch, turn.

Row 4: Ch 1, sc in first sc, *ch 5, skip next ch-5 loop, (3 dc, ch 2, 3 dc) in next ch-2 space, ch 5, skip next ch-5 loop, sc in next sc; rep from * across, turn.

Rows 5-6: Rep Row 4.

Row 7: Ch 1, sc in first sc, *ch 7, skip next ch-5 loop, (3 dc, ch 3, 3 dc) in next ch-2 space, ch 7, skip next ch-5 loop, sc in next sc; rep from * across, turn.

Row 8: Ch 1, sc in first sc, *7 sc in next ch-7 loop, sc in each of next 3 dc, 2 sc in next ch-3 loop, sc in each of next 3 dc, 7 sc in next ch-7 loop, sc in next sc; rep from * across. Fasten off.

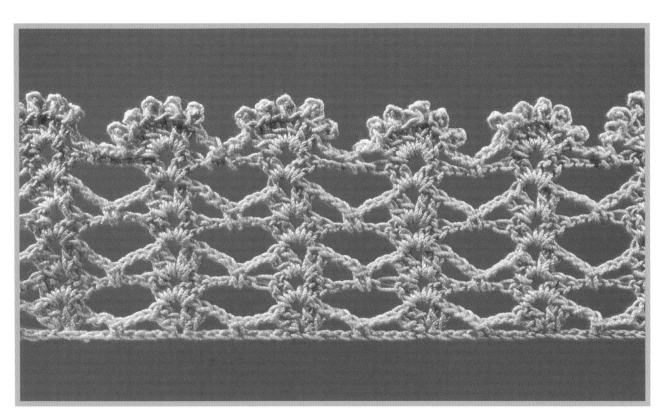

169

Picot: Ch 3, sl st in 3rd ch from hook.

Chain multiples of 10 plus 2.

Row 1 (RS): Sc in 2nd ch from hook, *ch 3, skip next 4 ch, (2 dc, ch 2, 2 dc) in next ch, ch 3, skip next 4 ch, sc in next ch; rep from * across, turn.

Row 2: Ch 6 (counts as tr, ch 2), skip next ch-3 loop, *(2 dc, ch 2, 2 dc) in next ch-2 space**, ch 4, skip next 2 ch-3 loops; rep from * across, ending last rep at **, ch 2, skip next ch-3 loop, tr in last sc, turn.

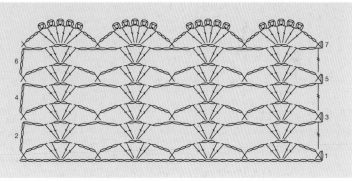

Row 3: Ch 1, sc in first tr, ch 3, skip next ch-2 space, *(2 dc, ch 2, 2 dc) in next ch-2 space, ch 3**, sc in next ch-4 loop, ch 3; rep from * across, ending last rep at **, sc in 4th ch of turning ch, turn.

Rows 4-5: Rep Rows 2-3.

Row 6: Rep Row 2.

Row 7: Ch 1, sc in first tr, skip next ch 2 space, *ch 3, (dc, picot) 5 times in next ch-2 space, dc in same ch-2 space, ch 3**, sc in next ch-4 loop, ch 3; rep from * across, ending last rep at **, sc in 4th ch of turning ch. Fasten off.

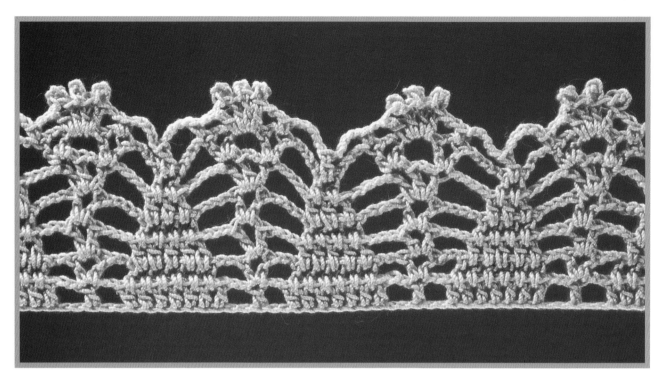

170

Picot: Ch 4, sl st in 4th ch from hook.

Chain multiples of 12 plus 5.

Row 1 (RS): Dc in 8th ch from hook, dc in each of next 6 ch, *ch 2, skip next 2 ch, dc in next ch**, ch 2, skip next 2 ch, dc in each of next 7 ch; rep from * across, ending last rep at **, turn.

Row 2: Ch 4 (counts as dc, ch 1), dc in first dc, *ch 2, skip next dc (dc between next 2 dc) 6 times, ch 2, skip next ch-2 space**, (dc, ch 2, dc) in next dc; rep from * across, ending last rep at **, (dc, ch 1, dc) in 5th ch of turning ch, turn.

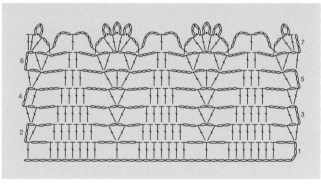

Row 3: Ch 4 (counts as dc, ch 1), dc in next ch-1 space, *ch 3, skip next dc, (dc between next 2 dc) 5 times, ch 3, skip next ch-2 space**, (dc, ch 2, dc) in next ch-2 space; rep from * across, ending last rep at **, (dc, ch 1, dc) in ch-1 space of turning ch, turn.

Row 4: Ch 4 (counts as dc, ch 1), dc in next ch-1 space, *ch 4, skip next ch-3 loop, skip next dc, (dc between next 2 dc) 4 times, ch 4, skip next ch-3 loop**, (dc, ch 2, dc) in next ch-2 space; rep from * across, ending last rep at **, (dc, ch 1, dc) in ch-1 space of turning ch, turn.

Row 5: Ch 5 (counts as dc, ch 2), dc in next ch-1 space, *ch 4, skip next ch-4 loop, skip next dc, (dc between next 2 dc) 3 times, ch 4, skip next ch-4 loop**, (dc, ch 2, dc, ch 2, dc) in next ch-2 space; rep from * across, ending last rep at **, (dc, ch 1, dc) in ch-1 space of turning ch, turn.

Row 6: Ch 4 (counts as dc, ch 1), skip next ch-2 space, *(dc, ch 2, dc) in next dc, ch 4, skip next ch-4 loop, skip next dc, (dc between next 2 dc) twice, ch 4, skip next ch-4 loop, (dc, ch 2, dc) in next dc**, ch 2, skip next 2 ch-2 spaces; rep from * across, ending last rep at **, ch 1, dc in 3rd ch of turning ch, turn.

Row 7: Ch 3 (counts as dc), (dc, picot, dc) in next ch-1 space, *ch 2, skip next ch-2 space, sc in next dc, ch 5, skip next ch-4 loop, dc between next 2 dc, ch 5, skip next ch-4 loop, sc in next dc, ch 2**, (dc, picot) 3 times in next ch-2 space, dc in same ch-2 space; rep from * across, ending last rep at **, (dc, picot, dc) in next ch-1 space of turning ch, dc in 3rd ch of turning ch. Fasten off.

.11.
Clusters & Inverted Shells

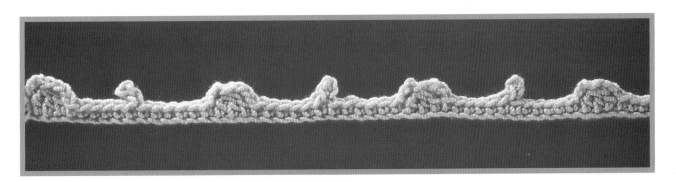

171

Picot: Ch 4, sl st in 4th ch from hook.

Chain multiples of 15 plus 13.

Row 1 (RS): Sc in 2nd ch from hook, sc in each of next 5 ch, *picot, sc in each of next 6 ch**, ch 3, 3-dc cluster worked across next 3 ch, ch 3, sc in each of next 6 ch; rep from * across, ending last rep at **. Fasten off.

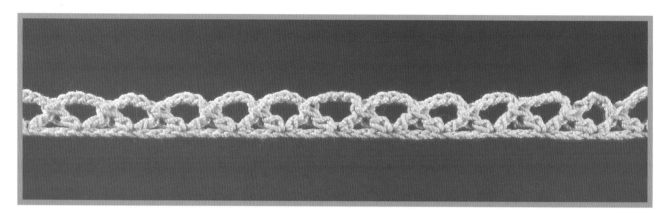

172

Chain multiples of 4 plus 3.

Row 1 (RS): Work 2-dc cluster, working first half-closed dc in 7th ch from hook, skip next 3 ch, work 2nd half-closed dc in next ch, complete cluster, *ch 5, work 2-dc cluster, working first half closed dc in same ch holding last dc of last cluster, skip next 3 ch, work 2nd half-closed dc in next ch, complete cluster; rep from * across to last ch, ch 3, dc in same ch holding last dc of last cluster. Fasten off.

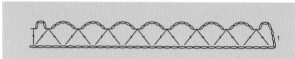

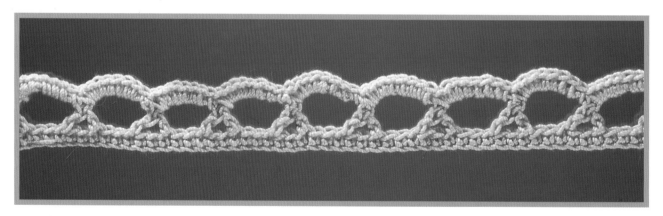

173

Chain multiples of 6 plus 1.

Row 1 (RS): Sc in 2nd ch from hook, sc in each ch across, turn.

Row 2: Ch 6 (counts as dc, ch 3), skip first sc, *work 2-dc cluster, working first half closed dc in next sc, skip next 2 sc, work 2nd half-closed dc in next sc, complete cluster**, ch 7, skip next 2 sc; rep from * across, ending last rep at **, ch 3, dc in last sc, turn.

Row 3: Ch 1, sc in first dc, 3 sc in next ch-3 loop, 8 sc in each ch-7 loop across to turning ch, 3 sc in ch-3 loop of ch of turning ch, sc in 3rd ch of turning ch. Fasten off.

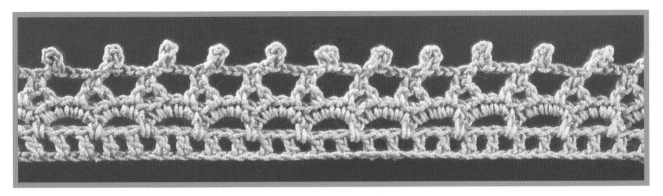

174

Picot: Ch 5, sl st in 5th ch from hook.

Chain multiples of 4 plus 3.

Row 1 (RS): Dc in 4th ch from hook, *ch 1, skip next ch, dc in next ch; rep from * across to within last ch, dc in last ch, turn.

Row 2: Ch 1, sc in first dc, *ch 5, skip next ch-1 space, sc in next ch-1 space; rep from * across, ending with last sc in 3rd ch of turning ch, turn.

Row 3: Ch 1, sc in first dc, 5 sc in each ch-5 loop across, sc in last sc, turn.

Row 4: Ch 3 (counts as dc), skip first 2 sc, dc in next sc, *picot, ch 3, skip next sc**, work 2-dc cluster, working first half closed dc in next sc, skip next 2 sc, work 2nd half-closed dc in next sc, complete cluster; rep from * across, ending last rep at **, work 2-dc cluster, working first half closed dc in next sc, skip next sc, work 2nd half-closed dc in last sc, complete cluster, work picot. Fasten off.

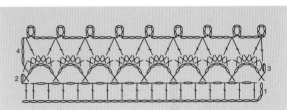

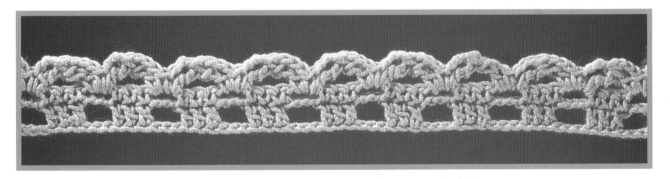

175

Chain multiples of 6 plus 3.

Row 1 (RS): Dc in 4th ch from hook, *ch 3, skip next 3 ch, dc in each of next 3 ch; rep from * across, ending with dc in each of last 2 ch, turn.

Row 2: Ch 1, sc in first 2 dc, *ch 3, skip next ch-3 loop, sc in each of next 3 dc; rep from * across to within last ch-3 loop, ch 3, skip next ch-3 loop, sc in next dc, sc in 3rd ch of turning ch, turn.

Row 3: Ch 3 (counts as dc), tr in next ch-3 loop, *ch 3, sc in same ch-3 loop, ch 3**, work 2-tr cluster, working first half-closed tr in same ch-3 loop holding last sc, skip next 3 sc, work 2nd half-closed tr in next ch-3 loop; rep from * across, ending last rep at **, work tr-dc cluster, working first half closed tr in same ch-3 loop holding last sc, skip next sc, work a half-closed dc in last sc, complete cluster. Fasten off.

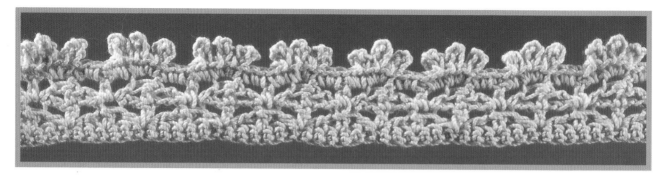

176

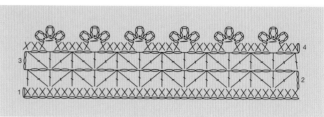

Picot: Ch 5, sl st in 5th ch from hook.

Chain multiples of 6 plus 2.

Row 1 (RS): Sc in 2nd ch from hook, sc in each ch across, turn.

Row 2: Ch 3 (counts as dc), skip first 3 sc, dc in next sc, *ch 2, dc in same sc holding last dc made, ch 2**, work 3-dc cluster, working first half-closed dc in same sc holding last dc made, skip next 2 sc, work 2nd half-closed dc in next sc, skip next 2 sc, work 3rd half-closed dc in next sc, complete cluster; rep from * across, ending last rep at **, work 2-dc cluster, working first half-closed dc in same sc holding last dc made, skip next 2 sc, work 2nd half-closed dc in last sc, complete cluster, turn.

Row 3: Ch 3 (counts as dc), skip next ch-2 space, dc in next dc, *ch 2, dc in same dc holding last dc made, ch 2**, work 3-dc cluster, working first half-closed dc in same dc holding last dc made, skip next ch-2 space, work 2nd half-closed dc in next cluster, skip next ch-2 space, work 3rd half-closed dc in next dc, complete cluster; rep from * across, ending last rep at **, work 2-dc cluster, working first half-closed dc in same dc holding last dc made, skip next ch-2 space, work 2nd half-closed dc in 3rd ch of turning ch, complete cluster, turn.

Row 4: Ch 1, sc in first cluster, *2 sc in next ch-2 space, work first picot, work 2nd picot, sl st in base of first picot, work 3rd picot, sl st in base of first picot, 2 sc in next ch-2 space, sc in next cluster; rep from * across, ending with last sc in 3rd ch of turning ch. Fasten off.

177

Chain multiples of 4 plus 2.

Row 1 (WS): Sc in 2nd ch from hook, *ch 3, work 2-dc cluster, working first half-closed dc in same ch holding last sc, skip next 3 ch, work 2nd half-closed dc in next ch, complete cluster, ch 3, sc in same ch holding last dc made; rep from * across, turn.

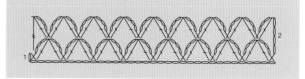

Row 2: Ch 4 (counts as tr), skip next ch-3 loop, dc in next cluster, *ch 3, sc in same cluster holding last dc, ch 3**, work 2-dc cluster, working first half-closed dc in same cluster holding last sc, skip next 2 ch-3 loops, work 2nd half-closed dc in next cluster, complete cluster; rep from * across, ending last rep at **, work a dc-tr cluster, working a half-closed dc in same cluster holding last sc, skip next ch-3 loop, work a half-closed tr in last sc, complete cluster. Fasten off.

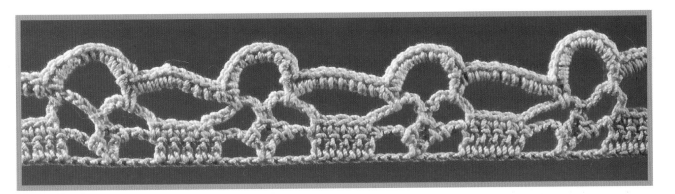

178

Chain multiples of 12 plus 2.

Row 1 (WS): Sc in 2nd ch from hook, *ch 5, skip next 3 ch, dc in each of next 5 ch, ch 5, skip next 3 ch, sc in next ch; rep from * across, turn.

Row 2: Ch 3 (counts as dc), dc in next ch-5 loop, *ch 7, sc in each of next 5 dc, ch 7**, work 2-dc cluster over next 2 ch-5 loops; rep from * across, ending last rep at **, work 2-dc cluster, working first half-closed dc in next ch-5 loop, work 2nd half-closed dc in last sc, complete cluster, turn.

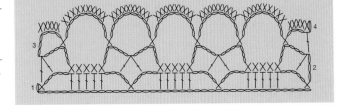

Row 3: Ch 6 (counts as dc, ch 3), sc in next ch-7 loop, (ch 10, sc) in each ch-7 loop across to last ch-7 loop, ch 3, dc in 3rd ch of turning ch, turn.

Row 4: Ch 1, sc in first dc, 4 sc in next ch-3 loop, 10 sc in each ch-10 loop across to turning ch, 4 sc in ch-3 loop of turning ch, sc in 3rd ch of turning ch. Fasten off.

179

Cluster: Work half-closed tr in next sc, work half-closed dc in next ch-5 loop, work half-closed tr in next sc, yo, draw yarn through 4 loops on hook to complete cluster.

Chain multiples of 4 plus 2.

Row 1 (WS): Sc in 2nd ch from hook, *ch 5, skip next 3 ch, sc in next ch; rep from * across, turn.

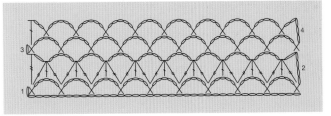

Row 2: Ch 5 (counts as tr, ch 1), work cluster across next (sc, ch-5 loop, sc), *ch 5, work cluster across (same sc holding last tr made, next ch-5 loop, and next sc); rep from * across to last sc, ch 1, tr in last sc already holding last tr made, turn.

Row 3: Ch 1, sc in first tr, (ch 5, sc) in each ch-5 loop across, ending with last sc in 4th ch of turning ch, turn.

Row 4: Ch 5 (counts as dc, ch 2), sc in next ch-5 loop, (ch 5, sc) in each ch-5 loop across to last ch-5 loop, ch 2, dc in last sc. Fasten off.

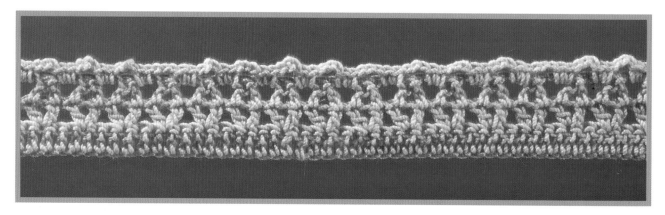

180

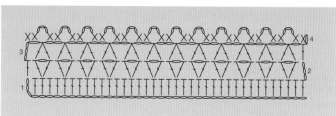

Chain multiples of 3 plus 1.

Row 1 (WS): Dc in 4th ch from hook, dc in each ch across, turn.

Row 2: Ch 3 (counts as dc), skip first 2 dc, *(dc, ch 1, dc) in next dc, skip next 2 dc; rep from * across to within last 2 sts, skip next dc, dc 3rd ch of turning ch, turn.

Row 3: Ch 4 (counts as dc, ch 1), *work 2-dc cluster over next 2 dc**, ch 2; rep from * across, ending last rep at **, ch 1, dc in 3rd ch of turning ch, turn.

Row 4: Ch 1, sc in first dc, sc in next ch-1 space, (ch 2, 2 sc) in each ch-2 space across, ending with last sc in 3rd ch of turning ch. Fasten off.

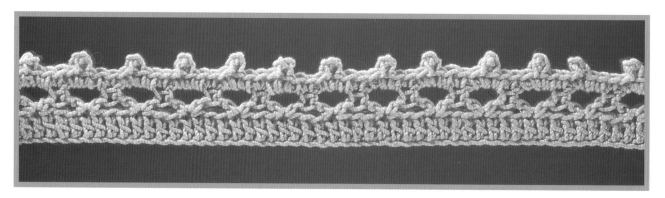

181

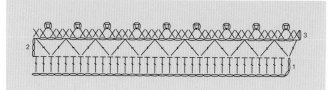

Picot: Ch 3, sl st in 3rd ch from hook.

Chain multiples of 4 plus 1.

Row 1 (RS): Dc in 4th ch from hook, dc in each ch across, turn.

Row 2: Ch 3 (counts as dc), skip first 2 dc, dc in next dc, *ch 3, work 2-dc cluster, working first half-closed dc in same dc holding last dc made, skip next 3 dc, work 2nd half-closed dc in next dc, complete cluster; rep from * across, ending with last half-closed dc in 3rd ch of turning ch, ch 2, dc in 3rd ch of turning ch holding last dc made, turn.

Row 3: Ch 1, sc in first dc, (sc, picot, sc) in next ch-2 space, *sc in next cluster, (2 sc, picot, sc) in next ch-3 loop; rep from * across to turning ch, sc in 3rd ch of turning ch. Fasten off.

182

Chain multiples of 14 plus 6.

Row 1 (RS): Dc in 4th ch from hook, dc in each of next 2 ch, *ch 5, skip next 4 ch, dc in each of next 2 ch, ch 5, skip next 4 ch, dc in each of next 4 ch; rep from * across, turn.

Row 2: Ch 4 (counts as dc, ch 1), work 2-dc cluster, working first half-closed dc in first dc, skip next 2 dc, work 2nd half-closed dc in next dc, complete cluster, *ch 5, skip next ch-5 loop, (dc, ch 3, dc) between next 2 dc, ch 5, skip next ch-5 loop, work 2-dc cluster, working first half-closed dc in next dc, skip next 2 dc, work 2nd half-closed dc in next dc, complete cluster; rep from * across, ending with last half-closed dc in 3rd ch of turning ch, ch 1, dc in 3rd ch of turning ch holding last dc made, turn.

Row 3: Ch 1, sc in first dc, ch 1, skip next ch-1 space, sc in next cluster, *ch 5, skip next ch-5 loop, (tr, ch 3, dtr, ch 3, tr) in next ch-3 loop, ch 5, skip next ch-5 loop, sc in next cluster; rep from * across to turning ch, ch 1, sc in 3rd ch of turning ch. Fasten off.

183

Chain multiples of 4 plus 2.

Row 1 (WS): Sc in 2nd ch from hook, sc in each ch across, turn.

Row 2: Ch 5 (counts as tr, ch 1), skip first sc, *work 3-tr cluster over next 3 sc**, ch 3, skip next sc; rep from * across, ending last rep at **, ch 1, tr in last sc, turn.

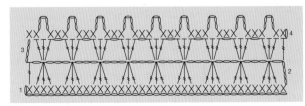

Row 3: Ch 4 (counts as tr), skip next ch-1 space, 3 tr in next cluster, (ch 1, 3 tr) in each cluster across to turning ch, tr in 4th ch of turning ch, turn.

Row 4: Ch 1, sc in first tr, *sc in next tr, ch 5, skip next tr, sc in next tr**, sc in next ch-1 space; rep from * across, ending last rep at **, sc in 4th ch of turning ch. Fasten off

184

Chain multiples of 9 plus 1.

Row 1 (RS): Dc in 4th ch from hook, dc in each of next 5 ch, *ch 3, skip next 3 ch, dc in each of next 6 ch; rep from * across to within last ch, dc in last ch, turn.

Row 2: Ch 5 (counts as tr, ch 1), *work 3-tr cluster over next 3 dc, ch 5, work 3-tr cluster over next 3 dc**, ch 5, sc in next ch-3 loop, ch 5; rep from * across, ending last rep at **, ch 1, tr in 3rd ch of turning ch, turn.

Row 3: Ch 3 (counts as dc), *12 tr in next ch-5 loop**, skip next 2 ch-5 loops; rep from * across, ending last rep at **, dc in 4th ch of turning ch. Fasten off.

185

Chain multiples of 8 plus 5.

Row 1 (WS): Work 2-dc cluster, working first half-closed dc in 5th ch from hook, skip next 3 ch, work 2nd half-closed dc in next ch, complete cluster, *ch 3, work 2-dc cluster, working first half-closed dc in same ch as last dc worked, skip next 3 ch, work 2nd half-closed dc in next ch, complete cluster; rep from * across to last ch, ch 1, dc in last ch, turn.

Row 2: Ch 3 (counts as dc), skip next ch-1 space, dc in next cluster, *ch 3, work 2-dc cluster, working first half-closed dc in last cluster holding last dc made, work 2nd half-closed dc in next cluster, complete cluster; rep from * across to last cluster, ch 3, work 2-dc cluster, working first half-closed dc in last cluster holding last dc made, work 2nd half-closed dc in 3rd ch of turning ch, complete cluster, turn.

Row 3: Ch 1, sc in first cluster, ch 2, *sc in next ch-3 loop, ch 8, sc in next ch-3 loop**, ch 5, sc in next ch-3 loop; rep from * across, ending last rep at **, ch 2, sc in 3rd ch of turning ch, turn.

Row 4: Ch 1, sc in first sc, skip next ch-2 space, *19 dc in next ch-8 loop, sc in next ch-5 loop; rep from * across, ending with last sc in last sc. Fasten off.

186

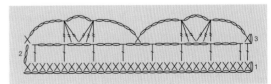

Chain multiples of 16.

Row 1 (RS): Sc in 2nd ch from hook, sc in each ch across, turn.

Row 2: Ch 3 (counts as dc), skip first sc, dc in next sc, *ch 3, skip next 3 sc, dc in next sc; rep from * across to within last sc, dc in last sc, turn.

Row 3: Ch 1, sc in first dc, *ch 6, skip next ch-3 loop, work 3-tr cluster, working first half-closed tr in next dc, work 2nd half-closed in next ch, work 3rd half-closed in next ch, complete cluster, ch 4, work 3-tr cluster, working first half-closed tr in same ch that holds last tr made, work 2nd half-closed tr in next ch, work 3rd half-closed tr in next dc, complete cluster, ch 6, skip next ch-3 loop, sc in next ch-3 loop; rep from * across, ending with last sc in 3rd ch of turning ch. Fasten off.

187

Picot: Ch 4, sl st in 4th ch from hook.

Chain multiples of 8 plus 5.

Row 1 (WS): 2 dc in 5th ch from hook, *skip next 3 ch, sc in next ch, skip next 3 ch**, (3 dc, ch 3, 3 dc) in next ch; rep from * across, ending last rep at **, (2 dc, ch 1, dc) in last ch, turn.

Row 2: Ch 1, sc in first dc, *ch 4, picot, skip next ch-1 space, work 4-dc cluster, working first 2 half-closed dc in next 2 dc, skip next sc, work next 2 half-closed dc in next 2 dc, complete cluster, ch 4, picot, sc in next ch-3 loop; rep from * across, ending with last sc in 3rd ch of turning ch. Fasten off.

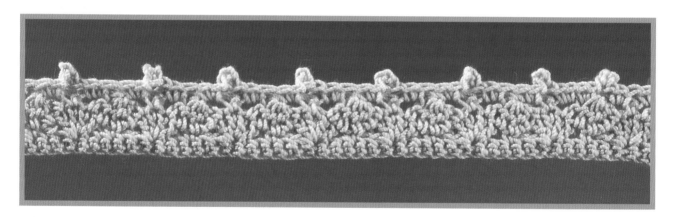

188

Picot: Ch 5, sl st in 5th ch from hook.

Chain multiples of 6 plus 2.

Row 1 (WS): Sc in 2nd ch from hook, sc in each ch across, turn.

Row 2: Ch 3 (counts as dc), 2 dc in first sc, *skip next 2 sc, sc in next sc, skip next 2 sc**, 5 dc in next sc; rep from * across, ending last rep at **, 3 dc in last sc, turn.

Row 3: Ch 1, sc in first dc, *ch 2, work 5-dc cluster over next 5 sts, ch 2, sc in next dc; rep from * across, ending with last sc in 3rd ch of turning ch, turn.

Row 4: Ch 1, sc in first sc, *2 sc in next ch-2 space, picot, 2 sc in next ch-2 space; rep from * across to last ch-2 space, sc in last sc. Fasten off.

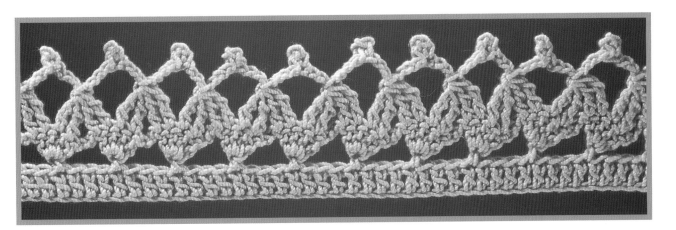

189

Picot: Ch 3, sl st in 3rd ch from hook.

Y-st: Tr in next st, 3 dc in center of last tr made.

Chain multiples of 4 plus 3.

Row 1 (RS): Dc in 4th ch from hook, dc in each ch across, turn.

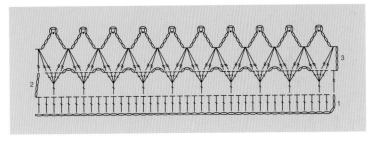

Row 2: Ch 4 (counts as tr), skip first 2 dc, *Y-st in next dc**, ch 3, skip next 3 dc; rep from * across, ending last rep at **, skip next dc, tr in 3rd ch of turning ch, turn.

Row 3: Ch 4 (counts as tr), skip first tr, 2-tr cluster worked over next 2 sts, *ch 3, picot, ch 3**, work 4-tr cluster, working first 2 half-closed tr in next 2 sts, skip next ch-3 loop, work next 2 half-closed tr in next 2 sts, complete cluster; rep from * across, ending last rep at **, work 3-tr cluster over last 3 sts. Fasten off.

190

Chain multiples of 11 plus 4.

Row 1 (RS): Dc in 4th ch from hook, *ch 3, skip next 4 ch, 5 dc in next ch, ch 3, skip next 4 ch, work 2-dc cluster over next 2 ch; rep from * across, turn.

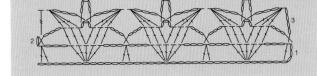

Row 2: Ch 1, sc in first dc, *ch 3, skip next ch-3 loop, dc in each of next 2 dc, (dc, ch 3, dc) in next dc, dc in each of next 2 dc, ch 3, skip next ch-3 loop, sc in next cluster; rep from * across, ending with last sc in 3rd ch of turning ch, turn.

Row 3: Ch 4 (counts as tr), skip next ch-3 loop, *work 3-dc cluster over next 3 dc, ch 3, (sc, ch 5, sc) in next ch-3 loop, ch 3, work 3-dc cluster over next 3 dc**, skip next 2 ch-3 loops; rep from * across, ending last rep at **, skip next ch-3 loop, tr in last sc. Fasten off.

191

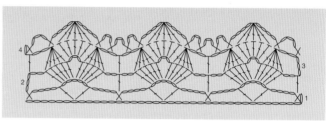

Chain multiples of 12 plus 2.

Row 1 (RS): Sc in 2nd ch from hook, *ch 4, skip next 5 ch, (dc, ch 5, dc) in next ch, ch 4, skip next 5 ch, sc in next ch; rep from * across, turn.

Row 2: Ch 5 (counts as dc, ch 2), *skip next ch-4 loop, (5 dc, ch 3, 5 dc) in next ch-5 loop, ch 2, skip next ch-4 loop, dc in next sc**, ch 2; rep from * across, ending last rep at **, turn.

Row 3: Ch 5 (counts as dc, ch 2), skip next ch-2 space, *work 5-dc cluster over next 5 dc, 5 dc in next ch-3 loop, work 5-dc cluster over next 5 dc, ch 2, skip next ch-2 space**, dc in next dc, ch 2; rep from * across, ending last rep at **, dc in 3rd ch of turning ch, turn.

Row 4: Ch 1, sc in first dc, ch 3, skip next ch-2 space, *sc in next cluster, ch 4, work 5-dc cluster over next 5 dc, ch 4, sc in next cluster, ch 3**, (sc, ch 3) in each of next 2 ch-2 spaces; rep from * across, ending last rep at **, sc in 3rd ch of turning ch. Fasten off.

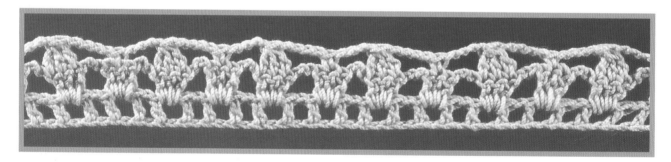

192

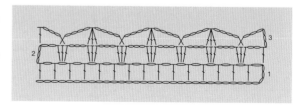

Chain multiples of 8 plus 2.

Row 1 (RS): Dc in 6th ch from hook, *ch 1, skip next ch, dc in next ch; rep from * across, turn.

Row 2: Ch 5 (counts as dc, ch 2), skip next ch-1 space, 3 dc in next ch-1 space, *ch 3, skip next ch-1 space, 3 dc in next ch-1 space; rep from * across to turning ch, ch 2, skip next ch of turning ch, dc in next ch of turning ch, turn.

Row 3: Ch 6 (counts as dc, ch 3), skip next ch-2 space, skip next dc, sc in next dc, *ch 4, skip next ch-3 loop, work 3-dc cluster over next 3 dc, ch 4, skip next ch-3 loop, skip next dc, sc in next dc; rep from * across to turning ch, ch 3, dc in 3rd ch of turning ch. Fasten off.

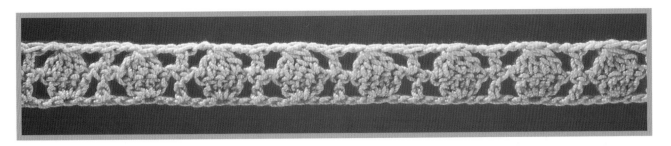

193

Chain multiples of 6 plus 4.

Row 1 (WS): 4 dc in 7th ch from hook, *ch 1, skip next 2 ch, dc in next ch**, ch 1, skip next 2 ch, 4 dc in next ch; rep from * across, ending last rep at **, turn.

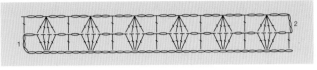

Row 2: Ch 5 (counts as dc, ch 2), skip next ch-1 space, *work 4-dc cluster over next 4 dc, ch 2, skip next ch-1 space**, dc in next dc, ch 2, skip next ch-1 space; rep from * across, ending last rep at **, dc in next ch of turning ch. Fasten off.

194

Chain multiples of 6 plus 4.

Row 1 (WS): 4 dc in 7th ch from hook, *ch 1, skip next 2 ch, dc in next ch**, ch 1, skip next 2 ch, 4 dc in next ch; rep from * across, ending last rep at **, turn.

Row 2: Ch 5 (counts as dc, ch 2), skip next ch-1 space, *work 4-dc cluster over next 4 dc, ch 2, skip next ch-1 space**, dc in next dc, ch 2, skip next ch-1 space; rep from * across, ending last rep at **, dc in next ch of turning ch, turn.

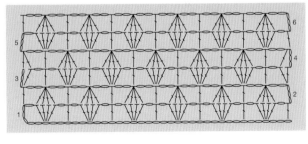

Row 3: Ch 3 (counts as dc), dc in first dc, *ch 1, skip next ch-2 space, dc in next cluster, ch 1, skip next ch-2 space**, 4 dc in next dc; rep from * across, ending last rep at **, 2 dc in 3rd ch of turning ch, turn.

Row 4: Ch 3 (counts as dc), skip first dc, dc in next dc, *ch 2, skip next ch-1 space, dc in next dc, ch 2, skip next ch-1 space**, work 4-dc cluster over next 4 dc; rep from * across, ending last rep at **, work 2-dc cluster of over last 2 sts, turn.

Row 5: Ch 4 (counts as dc, ch 1), skip next ch-2 space, *4 dc in next dc, ch 1, skip next ch-2 space**, dc in next cluster, ch 1, skip next ch-2 space; rep from * across, ending last rep at **, dc in 3rd ch of turning ch, turn.

Row 6: Rep Row 2. Fasten off.

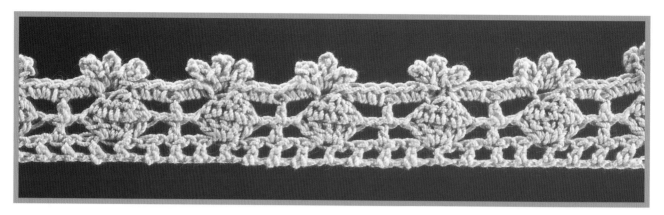

195

Picot: Ch 5, sl st in 5th ch from hook.

Chain multiples of 8 plus 4.

Row 1 (WS): Dc in 6th ch from hook, *ch 1, skip next ch, dc in next ch; rep from * across, turn.

Row 2: Ch 4 (counts as dc, ch 1), *skip next 2 ch-1 spaces, 5 dc in next dc, ch 1, skip next 2 ch-1 space**, dc in next dc, ch 1; rep from * across, ending last rep at **, dc in 4th ch of turning ch, turn.

Row 3: Ch 6 (counts as dc, ch 3), skip next ch-1 space, *work 5-dc cluster over next 5 dc, ch 3, skip next ch-1 space**, dc in next dc, ch 3, skip next ch-1 space; rep from * across, ending last rep at **, dc in 3rd ch of turning ch, turn.

Row 4: Ch 1, sc in first dc, *3 sc in next ch-3 loop, sc in next cluster, work picot, work 2nd picot, sl st in base of first picot, work 3rd picot, sl st in base of first picot, 3 sc in next ch-3 loop; rep from * across, sc in 3rd ch of turning ch. Fasten off.

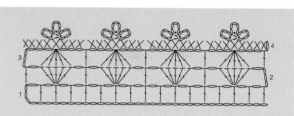

196

Picot: Ch 3, sl st in 3rd ch from hook.

Chain multiples of 10 plus 4.

Row 1 (WS): Dc in 4th ch from hook, *skip next 4 ch, (4 dc, picot, 4 dc) in next ch, skip next 4 ch**, (dc, ch 1, dc) in next ch; rep from * across, ending last rep at **, 2 dc in last ch, turn.

Row 2: Ch 3 (counts as dc), dc in first dc, *ch 3, skip next dc, work 8-dc cluster, working first 4 half-closed dc in next 4 dc, skip next picot, work last 4 half-closed dc in next 4 dc, complete cluster, ch 5**, (dc, ch 1, dc) in next ch-1 space, skip next dc; rep from * across, ending last rep at **, skip next dc, 2 dc in 3rd ch of turning ch. Fasten off.

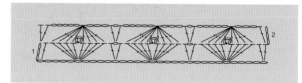

197

Picot: Ch 3, sl st in 3rd ch from hook.

Chain multiples of 9 plus 4.

Row 1 (RS): 3 dc in 4th ch from hook, *ch 6, skip next 8 ch, 4 dc in each of next ch; rep from * across, turn.

Row 2: Ch 3 (counts as dc), dc in first dc, *dc in next dc, picot, dc in next dc**, 2 dc in next dc, ch 5, skip next ch-6 loop, 2 dc in next dc; rep from * across, ending last rep at **, 2 dc in 3rd ch of turning ch, turn.

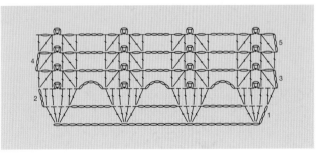

Row 3: Ch 4 (counts as dc, ch 1), work 2-dc cluster, working first half-closed dc in first dc, skip next dc, work 2nd half-closed dc in next dc, complete cluster, *picot, skip next picot, work 2-dc cluster, working first half-closed dc in next dc, skip next dc, work 2nd half-closed dc in next dc, complete cluster, ch 1, dc in same dc holding last dc made**, ch 4, skip next ch-5 loop, dc in next dc, ch 1, work 2-dc cluster, working first half-closed dc in same dc holding last dc made, skip next dc, work 2nd half-closed dc in next dc, complete cluster; rep from * across, ending last rep at **, working last dc in 3rd ch of turning ch, turn.

Rows 4-5: Ch 4 (counts as dc, ch 1), work 2-dc cluster, working first half-closed dc in first dc, work 2nd half-closed dc in next cluster, complete cluster, *picot, skip next picot, work 2-dc cluster, working first half-closed dc in next cluster, skip next ch-1 space, work 2nd half-closed dc in next dc, complete cluster, ch 1, dc in same dc holding last dc made**, ch 4, skip next ch-4 loop, dc in next dc, ch 1, work 2-dc cluster, working first half-closed dc in same dc holding last dc made, skip next ch-1 space, work 2nd half-closed dc in next cluster, complete cluster; rep from * across, ending last rep at **, working last dc in 3rd ch of turning ch, turn. Fasten off.

.12.
Small Shells

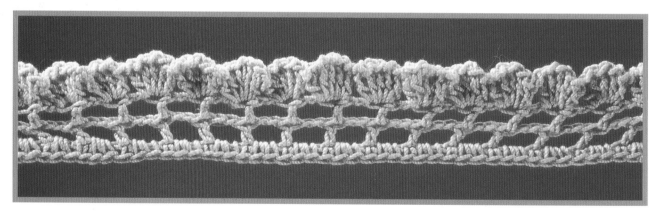

198

Chain multiples of 3 plus 2.

Row 1 (RS): Dc in 8th ch from hook, *ch 2, skip next 2 ch, dc in next ch; rep from * across, turn.

Row 2: Ch 5 (counts as dc, ch 2), skip next ch-2 space, (dc, ch 2) in each dc across to turning ch, skip next 2 ch of turning ch, dc in next ch of turning ch, turn.

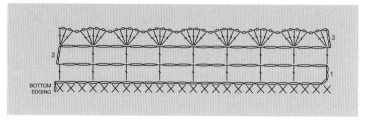

Row 3: Ch 4 (counts as dc, ch 1), (dc, ch 1, dc) in first dc, ch 1, skip next ch-2 space, *(dc, ch 1, dc, ch 1, dc, ch 1, dc, ch 1, dc) in next dc, ch 1, skip next ch-2 space; rep from * across to turning ch, (dc, ch 1, dc, ch 1, dc) in 3rd ch of turning ch. Fasten off.

Bottom Edging: With RS facing, working across opposite side of foundation ch, join yarn in first ch, ch 1, sc in first ch, *2 sc in next ch-2 space, sc in next ch; rep from * across. Fasten off.

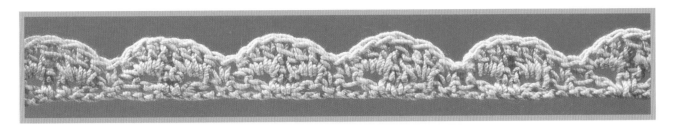

199

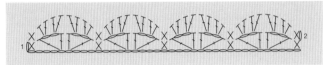

Chain multiples of 9 plus 2.

Row 1 (WS): Sc in 2nd ch from hook, *skip next 3 ch, (dc, ch 2, dc) in each of next 2 ch, skip next 3 ch, sc in next ch; rep from * across, turn.

Row 2: Ch 1, *(hdc, dc) in next ch, 2 dc in next ch, skip next 2 dc, 2 dc in next ch, (dc, hdc) in next ch, skip next dc, sc in next sc; rep from * across. Fasten off.

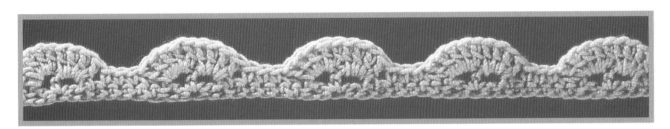

200

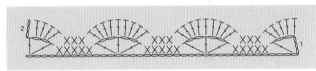

Chain multiples of 12 plus 6.

Row 1 (RS): Dc in 6th ch from hook, *skip next 3 ch, sc in each of next 5 ch, skip next 3 ch**, (dc, ch 2, dc, ch 2, dc) in next ch; rep from * across, ending last rep at **, (dc, ch 2, dc) in last ch, turn.

Row 2: Ch 3 (counts as dc), *4 dc in next ch-2 space, skip next dc and sc, sc in each of next 3 sc, 4 dc in next ch-2 space, dc in next dc; rep from * across, ending with last dc in 3rd ch of turning ch. Fasten off.

201

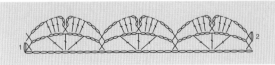

Chain multiples of 10 plus 2.

Row 1 (WS): Sc in 2nd ch from hook, *ch 3, skip next 4 ch, (dc, ch 3, dc, ch 3, dc) in next ch, ch 3, skip next 4 ch, sc in next ch; rep from * across, turn.

Row 2: Ch 1, sc in first sc, *ch 3, skip next ch-3 loop, 3 dc in next ch-3 loop, ch 3, sc in next dc, ch 3, 3 dc in next ch-3 loop, ch 3, skip next ch-3 loop, sc in next sc; rep from * across. Fasten off.

202

Chain multiples of 12 plus 5.

Row 1 (WS): Sc in 7th ch from hook, *skip next 3 ch, (dc, ch 2, dc, ch 2, dc, ch 2, dc) in next ch, skip next 3 ch, sc in next ch**, ch 5, skip next 3 ch, sc in next ch; rep from * across, ending last rep at **, ch 2, skip next ch, dc in last ch, turn.

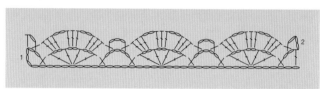

Row 2: Ch 3 (counts as hdc, ch 1), sc in next ch-2 space, *(3 dc, ch 2) in each of next 2 ch-2 spaces, 3 dc in next ch-2 space**, (sc, ch 3, sc) in next ch-5 loop; rep from * across, ending last rep at **, sc in next ch-2 space of turning ch, hdc in 2nd ch of turning ch. Fasten off.

203

Chain multiples of 10 plus 2.

Row 1 (WS): Sc in 2nd ch from hook, *ch 2, skip next 4 ch, (dc, ch 3, dc, ch 3, dc) in next ch, ch 2, skip next 4 ch, sc in next ch; rep from * across, turn.

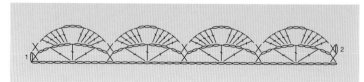

Row 2: Ch 1, sc in first sc, *skip next ch-2 space, 5 dc in next ch-3 loop, ch 3, 5 dc in next ch-3 loop, skip next ch-2 space, sc in next sc; rep from * across. Fasten off.

204

Chain multiples of 6 plus 4.

Row 1 (RS): Dc in 4th ch from hook, *ch 1, skip next ch, dc in each of next 2 ch; rep from * across, turn.

Row 2: Ch 5 (counts as dc, ch 2), sc in next ch-1 space, (ch 5, sc) in each ch-1 space across to within last 2 sts, ch 2, skip next dc, dc in 3rd ch of turning ch, turn.

Row 3: Ch 1, sc in first dc, (dc, ch 1) 4 times in next ch-5 loop, dc in same ch-5 loop, sc in next ch-5 loop; rep from * across, ending with last sc in 3rd ch of turning ch. Fasten off.

Bottom Edging: With RS facing, working across opposite side of foundation ch, join yarn in first ch, ch 1, sc in each of first 2 ch, *sc in next ch-1 space, sc in each of next 2 ch; rep from * across. Fasten off.

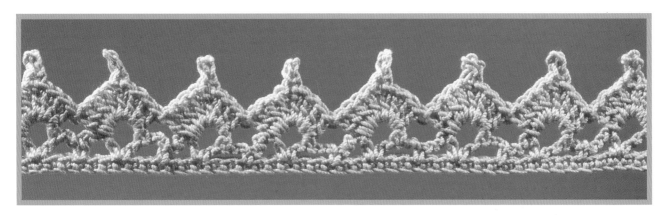

205

Picot: Ch 4, sl st in 4th ch from hook.

Chain multiples of 6 plus 2.

Row 1 (RS): Sc in 2nd ch from hook, sc in each ch across, turn.

Row 2: Ch 1, sc in first sc, *ch 3, skip next 2 sc, (dc, ch 4, dc) in next sc, ch 3, skip next 2 sc, sc in next sc; rep from * across, turn.

Row 3: Ch 3 (counts as dc), skip next ch-3 loop, *(4 dc, ch 1, picot, sc in next ch before picot, 4 dc) in next ch-4 loop**, skip next 2 ch-3 loops; rep from * across, ending last rep at **, skip next ch-3 loop, dc in last sc. Fasten off.

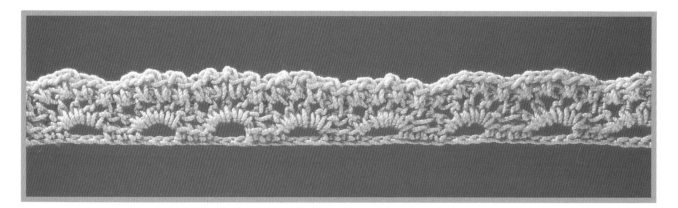

206

Chain multiples of 6 plus 4.

Row 1 (RS): Sc in 2nd ch from hook, sc in each of next 2 ch, *ch 4, skip next 3 ch, sc in each of next 3 ch; rep from * across, turn.

Row 2: Ch 3 (counts as dc), (dc, ch 1) 4 times in next ch-4 loop, *work 2-dc cluster, working first half-closed dc in same ch-4 loop holding last dc made, work 2nd half-closed dc in next ch-4 loop, complete cluster, ch 1, (dc, ch 1) 3 times in same ch-4 loop; rep from * across to last ch-4 loop, dc in same ch-4 loop, skip next 2 sc, dc in last sc, turn.

Row 3: Ch 1, sc in first dc, ch 1, *(sc, ch 2) in each of next 3 ch-1 spaces, sc in next ch-1 space; rep from * across, ch 1, skip next dc, sc in 3rd ch of turning ch. Fasten off.

207

Chain multiples of 9 plus 3.

Row 1 (RS): Dc in 4th ch from hook, dc in each ch across, turn.

Row 2: Ch 1, sc in first dc, *ch 2, skip next 2 dc, sc in next dc; rep from * across, ending with last sc in 3rd ch of turning ch, turn.

Row 3: Ch 5 (counts as dc, ch 2), sc in next ch-2 space, *(dc, ch 1) 4 times in next ch-2 space, dc in same ch-2 space, sc in next ch-2 space**, ch 5, sc in next ch-2 space; rep from * across, ending last rep at **, ch 2, dc in last sc, turn.

Row 4: Ch 1, sc in first dc, *ch 3, skip next sc, (sc, ch 2) in each of next 4 dc, sc in next dc, ch 3, sc in next ch-5 loop; rep from * across, ending with last sc in 3rd ch of turning ch. Fasten off.

208

Chain multiples of 11 plus 3.

Row 1 (RS): Sc in 2nd ch from hook, sc in each ch across, turn.

Row 2: Ch 1, sc in each of first 2 sc, *ch 3, skip next 4 sc, (tr, ch 1) 4 times in next sc, tr in same sc, ch 3, skip next 4 sc, sc in each of next 2 sc; rep from * across, turn.

Row 3: Ch 1, sc in first sc, *4 sc in next ch-3 loop, ch 3, (sc, ch 3) in each of next 4 ch-1 spaces, 4 sc in next ch-3 loop**, skip next 2 sc; rep from * across, ending last rep at **, skip next sc, sc in last sc. Fasten off.

209

Chain multiples of 8 plus 2.

Row 1 (RS): Dc in 4th ch from hook, dc in each of next 2 ch, *ch 3, dc in each of next 8 ch; rep from * across to within last 4 ch, ch 3, dc in each of last 4 ch, turn.

Row 2: Ch 1, sc in first dc, *tr in next ch-3 loop, (ch 2, tr) 6 times in same ch-3 loop**, skip next 8 dc; rep from * across, ending last rep at **, skip next 3 dc, sc in 3rd ch of turning ch, turn.

Row 3: Ch 1, sl st in first sc, *(sc, ch 3) in each of next 5 ch-2 spaces, sc in next ch-2 space; rep from * across to last ch-2 space, sl st in last sc. Fasten off.

210

Picot: Ch 5, sl st in 5th ch from hook.

Chain multiples of 6 plus 4.

Row 1 (RS): Dc in 6th ch from hook, *ch 1, skip next ch, dc in next ch; rep from * across, turn.

Row 2: Ch 1, sl st in first dc, sl st in each of next 2 sts, *ch 5, skip next ch-1 space**, sl st in each of next 5 sts; rep from * across, ending last rep at **, sl st in next dc, sl st in each of next 2 ch of turning ch, turn.

Row 3: Ch 1, (5 dc, picot, 5 dc) in each ch-5 loop across to last ch-5 loop, ch 1, skip next 2 sl sts, sl st in last sl st. Fasten off.

211

Chain multiples of 8 plus 4.

Row 1 (RS): Dc in 6th ch from hook, *ch 1, skip next ch, dc in next ch; rep from * across, turn.

Row 2: Ch 3 (counts as hdc, ch 1), sc in next ch-1 space, (ch 3, sc) in each ch-1 space across to ch-1 space of turning ch, ch 1, hdc in 4th ch of turning ch, turn.

Row 3: Ch 1, sc in first hdc, skip next ch-1 space, *ch 1, skip next ch-3 loop, (dc, ch 1) 5 times in next ch-3 loop, skip next ch-3 loop, sc in next ch-3 loop; rep from * across, ending with last sc in 2nd ch of turning ch, turn.

Row 4: Ch 5 (counts as dc, ch 2), skip next ch-1 space, *(sc, ch 3) in each of next 3 ch-1 spaces, sc in next ch-1 space**, ch 3, skip next 2 ch-1 spaces; rep from * across, ending last rep at **, ch 2, skip next ch-1 space, dc in last sc, turn

Row 5: Ch 5 (counts as dc, ch 2), skip next ch-2 space, *(sc, ch 3) in each of next 2 ch-3 loops, sc in next ch-3 loop**, ch 5, skip next ch-3 loop; rep from * across, ending last rep at **, ch 2, dc in 3rd ch of turning ch. Fasten off.

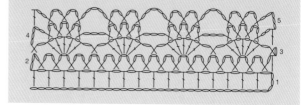

212

Picot: Ch 5, sl st in 5th ch from hook.

Chain multiples of 8 plus 3.

Row 1 (WS): Dc in 4th ch from hook, dc in each ch across, turn.

Row 2: Ch 1, sc in first dc, *skip next 2 dc, 2 dc in next dc, ch 3, sc in next dc; rep from * across, ending with last sc in 3rd ch of turning ch, turn.

Row 3: Ch 6 (counts as tr, ch 2), *sc in next ch-3 loop, skip next 2 dc, (dc, ch 3, dc) in next sc, sc in next ch-3 loop**, ch 5, skip next 3 sts; rep from * across, ending last rep at **, ch 2, skip next 2 dc, tr in last sc, turn.

Row 4: Ch 3 (counts as dc), picot, dc in first dc, 4 dc in next ch-2 space, sc in next ch-3 loop, *(5 dc, picot, 5 dc) in next ch-5 loop, sc in next ch-3 loop; rep from * across to last ch-3 loop, 5 dc in next ch-2 space of turning ch, picot, dc in 4th ch of turning ch. Fasten off.

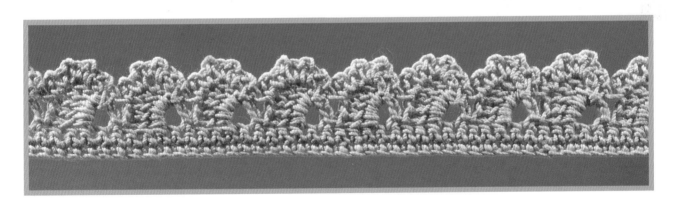

213

Chain multiples of 5 plus 2.

Row 1 (RS): Sc in 2nd ch from hook, sc in each ch across, turn.

Row 2: Ch 1, sc in each sc across, turn.

Row 3: Ch 1, sc in first sc, *ch 2, dc in next sc, ch 3, work 5 dc around the post of last dc made, skip next 3 sc, sc in next sc; rep from * across, turn.

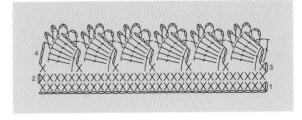

Row 4: Ch 3, *skip next 3 sts, (sc, ch 2) in each of next 3 dc, (sc, ch 2, sc) in next ch-3 loop, skip next ch-2 space; rep from * across to last ch-3 loop, dc in last sc. Fasten off.

214

Chain multiples of 10 plus 3.

Row 1 (WS): Dc in 4th ch from hook, dc in each ch across, turn.

Row 2: Ch 1, sc in each of first 3 dc, *ch 3, skip next 2 dc, (2 dc, ch 2, 2 dc) in next dc, ch 3, skip next 2 dc**, sc in each of next 5 dc; rep from * across, ending last rep at **, sc in each of next 2 dc, sc in 3rd ch of turning ch, turn.

Row 3: Ch 1, sc in each of first 2 sc, *ch 3, skip next ch-3 loop, (3 dc, ch 2, 3 dc) in next ch-2 space, ch 3, skip next sc**, sc in each of next 3 sc; rep from * across, ending last rep at **, sc in each of last 2 sc, turn.

Row 4: Ch 1, sc in first sc, *ch 3, skip next ch-3 loop, (4 dc, ch 2, 4 dc) in next ch-2 space, ch 3, skip next sc, sc in next sc; rep from * across. Fasten off.

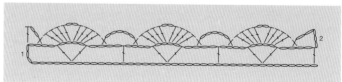

215

Chain multiples of 13 plus 7.

Row 1 (WS): (Dc, ch 4, dc) in 13th ch from hook, *ch 4, skip next 6 ch, dc in next ch**, ch 4, skip next 5 ch, (dc, ch 4, dc) in next ch; rep from * across, ending last rep at **, turn.

Row 2: Ch 5 (counts as dc, ch 2), sc in next ch-4 loop, *(4 dc, ch 2, 4 dc) in next ch-4 loop, sc in next ch-4 loop**, ch 5, sc in next ch-4 loop; rep from * across, ending last rep at **, ch 2, dc in 8th ch of turning ch. Fasten off.

216

Chain multiples of 10 plus 7.

Row 1 (RS): Sc in 2nd ch from hook, *ch 1, skip next 4 ch, (dc, ch 1) 7 times in next ch, skip next 4 ch, sc in next ch; rep from * across to within last 5 ch, ch 1, skip next 4 ch, (dc, ch 1) 3 times in last ch, dc in same ch, turn.

Rows 2-3: Ch 1, sc in first dc, *ch 1, skip next 4 ch-1 spaces, (dc, ch 1) 7 times in next sc, skip next 4 ch-1 spaces, sc in next dc; rep from * across to within last 4 ch-1 spaces, ch 1, skip next 4 ch-1 spaces, (dc, ch 1) 3 times in last sc, dc in same sc, turn. Fasten off.

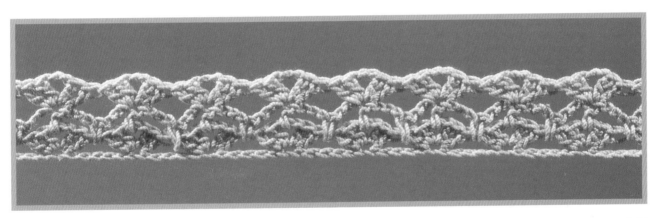

217

Chain multiples of 6 plus 3.

Row 1 (RS): (2 dc, ch 2, 2 dc) in 6th ch from hook, *skip next 5 ch, (2 dc, ch 2, 2 dc) in next ch; rep from * across to within last 3 ch, skip next 2 ch, dc in last ch, turn.

Row 2: Ch 1, sc in first dc, *ch 3, dc in next ch-2 space, ch 3, skip next 2 dc, sc between last skipped and next dc; rep from * across, ending with last sc in 5th ch of turning ch, turn.

Row 3: Ch 4 (counts as tr), skip next ch-3 loop, *(2 dc, ch 2, 2 dc) in next dc**, skip next 2 ch-3 loops; rep from * across, ending last rep at **, skip next ch-3 loop, tr in last sc. Fasten off.

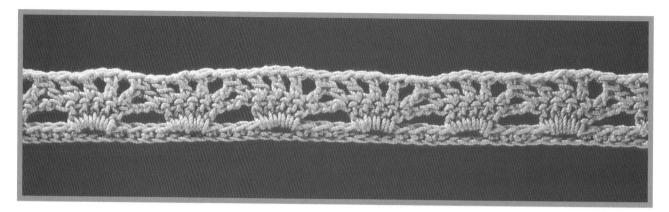

218

Chain multiples of 6 plus 4.

Row 1 (RS): Sc in 2nd ch from hook, sc in each of next 2 ch, *ch 3, skip next 3 ch, sc in each of next 3 ch; rep from * across, turn.

Row 2: Ch 4 (counts as dc, ch 1), *5 dc in next ch-3 loop**, ch 3; rep from * across, ending last rep at **, ch 1, skip next 2 sc, dc in last sc, turn.

Row 3: Ch 3 (counts as dc), skip next ch-1 space, *(dc, ch 1) in each of next 4 dc, dc in next dc**, skip next ch-3 loop; rep from * across, ending last rep at **, dc in 3rd ch of turning ch. Fasten off.

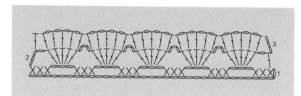

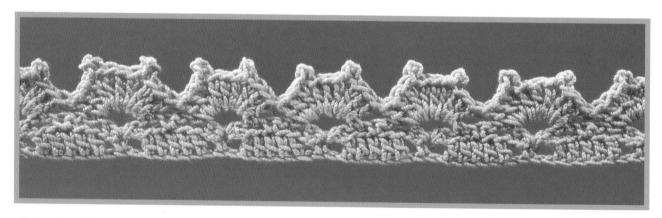

219

Picot: Ch 3, sl st in 3rd ch from hook.

Chain multiples of 8 plus 3.

Row 1 (RS): Dc in 4th ch from hook, dc in next ch, *ch 2, skip next ch, sc in next ch, ch 2, skip next ch, dc in each of next 5 ch; rep from * across, ending with dc in each of last 3 ch, turn.

Row 2: Ch 1, sc in first dc, *ch 1, skip next ch-2 space, (dc, ch 3, dc) in next sc, ch 1, skip next 2 dc, sc in next dc; rep from * across, ending with last sc in 3rd ch of turning ch, turn.

Row 3: Ch 3 (counts as dc), skip next ch-1 space, *(3 dc, picot, 3 dc, picot, 3 dc) in next ch-3 loop**, skip next 2 ch-1 spaces; rep from * across, ending last rep at **, skip next ch-1 space, dc in last sc. Fasten off.

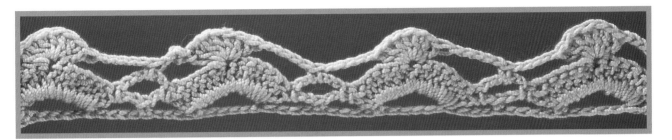

220

Chain multiples of 15 plus 2.

Row 1 (RS): Sc in 2nd ch from hook, *ch 5, skip next 4 ch, sc in next ch; rep from * across, turn.

Row 2: Ch 5 (counts as dc, ch 2), *sc in next ch-5 loop, 13 dc in next ch-5 loop, sc in next ch-5 loop**, ch 5; rep from * across, ending last rep at **, ch 2, dc in last sc, turn.

Row 3: Ch 1, sc in first dc, *ch 5, skip next sc and 3 dc, sc in next dc, skip next 2 dc, 7 dc in next dc, skip next 2 dc, sc in next dc, ch 5, sc in next ch-5 loop; rep from * across, ending with last sc in 3rd ch of turning ch. Fasten off.

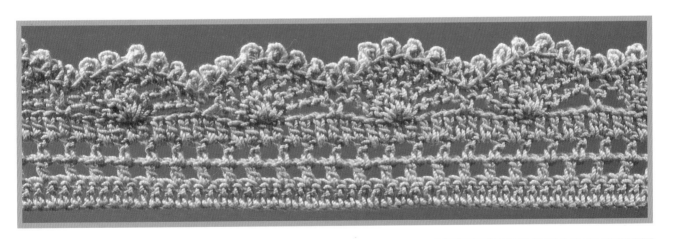

221

Chain multiples of 10 plus 3.

Row 1 (WS): Dc in 4th ch from hook, dc in each ch across, turn.

Row 2: Ch 4 (counts as dc, ch 1), skip first 2 dc, *dc in next dc, ch 1, skip next dc; rep from * across to turning ch, dc in 3rd ch of turning ch, turn.

Row 3: Ch 4 (counts as dc, ch 1), skip next ch-1 space, (dc, ch 1) in each dc across to turning ch, dc in 3rd ch of turning ch, turn.

Row 4: Ch 3 (counts as dc), *dc in next ch-1 space, dc in next dc; rep from * across, ending with last dc in 3rd ch of turning ch, turn.

Row 5: Ch 1, sl st in first dc, *ch 1, skip next 4 dc, (dtr, ch 1) 7 times in next dc, skip next 4 dc, sl st in next dc; rep from * across, ending with last sl st in 3rd ch of turning ch, turn.

Row 6: Ch 1, *sl st in next ch-1 space, (picot, sc) in each of next 6 ch-1 spaces, picot, sl st in next ch-1 space; rep from * across. Fasten off.

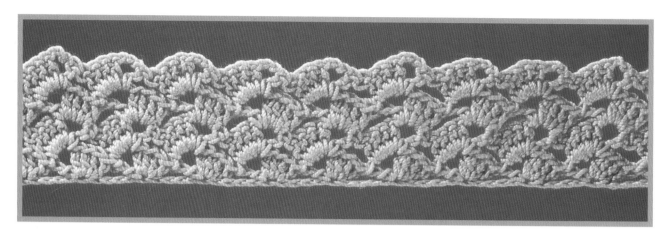

222

Chain multiples of 5 plus 4.

Row 1 (RS): (4 dc, ch 3, dc) in 6th ch from hook, *skip next 4 ch, (4 dc, ch 3, dc) in next ch; rep from * across to within last 3 ch, skip next 2 ch, dc in last ch, turn.

Rows 2-4: Ch 3 (counts as dc), (4 dc, ch 3, dc) in each ch-3 loop across to last ch-3 loop, skip next 4 dc, dc in top of turning ch, turn. Fasten off.

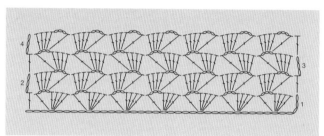

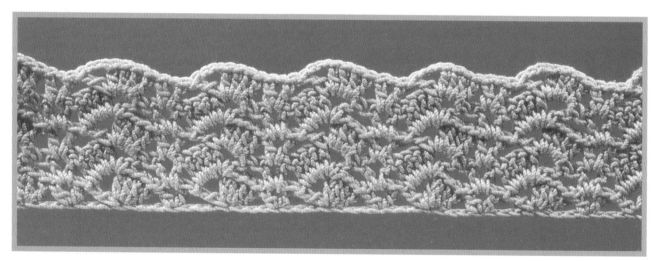

223

Chain multiples of 8 plus 4.

Row 1 (RS): Dc in 4th ch from hook, *skip next 3 ch, (4 dc, ch 3, dc) in next ch, skip next 3 ch**, (dc, ch 1, dc) in next ch; rep from * across, ending last rep at **, 2 dc in last ch, turn.

Rows 2-5: Ch 3 (counts as dc), dc in first dc, *(4 dc, ch 3, dc) in next ch-3 loop**, (dc, ch 1, dc) in next ch-1 space; rep from * across, ending last rep at **, skip next 5 dc, 2 dc in 3rd ch of turning ch, turn. Fasten off.

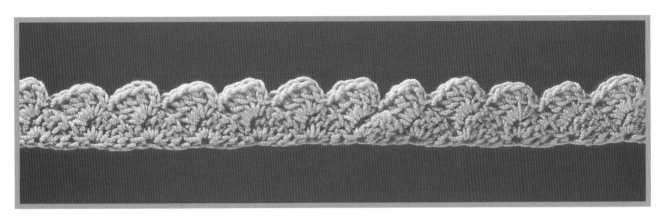

224

Chain multiples of 4 plus 2.

Row 1 (WS): (Sc, ch 2, 4 dc) in 2nd ch from hook, *skip next 3 ch, (sc, ch 2, 4 dc) in next ch; rep from * across to within last 4 ch, skip next 3 ch, sc in last ch, turn.

Row 2: Ch 3 (counts as dc), 2 dc in first dc, *(sc, ch 2, 4 dc) in each ch-2 space across to within last ch-2 space, sc in last ch-2 space, 2 dc in last sc. Fasten off.

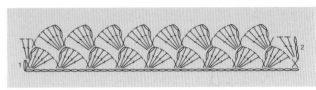

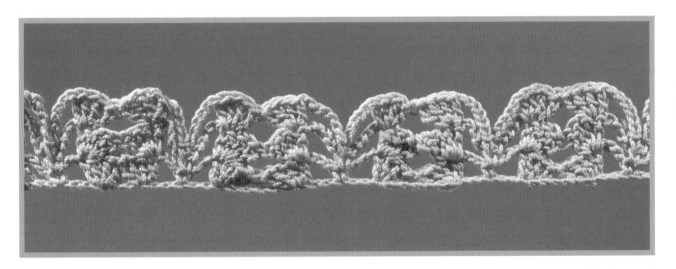

225

Chain multiples of 12 plus 10.

Row 1 (RS): 3 dc in 4th ch from hook, *skip next 5 ch, 4 dc in next ch**, ch 4, skip next 2 ch, sc in next ch, ch 4, skip next 2 ch, 4 dc in next ch; rep from * across, ending last rep at **, turn.

Row 2: Ch 3 (counts as dc), 3 dc in first dc, *skip next 6 dc, 4 dc in next dc, ch 5, skip next ch-4 loop, sc in next sc, ch 5, skip next ch-4 loop, 4 dc in next dc; rep from * across to within last 7 sts, skip next 6 dc, 4 dc in 3rd ch of turning ch, turn.

Row 3: Ch 3 (counts as dc), 3 dc in first dc, *skip next 6 dc, 4 dc in next dc, ch 6, skip next ch-5 loop, sc in next sc, ch 6, skip next ch-5 loop, 4 dc in next dc; rep from * across to within last 7 sts, skip next 6 dc, 4 dc in 3rd ch of turning ch, turn. Fasten off.

226

Chain multiples of 6 plus 3.

Row 1 (RS): Dc in 4th ch from hook, *ch 1, skip next ch, dc in next ch; rep from * across to within last ch, dc in last ch, turn.

Row 2: Ch 3 (counts as hdc, ch 1), skip first dc, *sc in next dc, (sc in next ch-1 space, sc in next dc) twice**, ch 3, skip next ch-1 space; rep from * across, ending last rep at **, ch 1, hdc in 3rd ch of turning ch, turn.

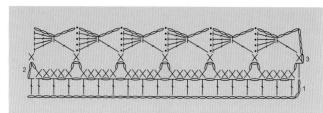

Row 3: Ch 1, sc in first hdc, ch 7, dc in last sc made, *ch 3, 4 dc in last dc made**, sc in next ch-3 loop, turn, sl st in each of last 4 dc made, sl st in top of ch-3, turn, ch 3, skip next 5 sl sts, dc in next sc; rep from * across, ending last rep at **, sc in 2nd ch of turning ch, turn. Fasten off.

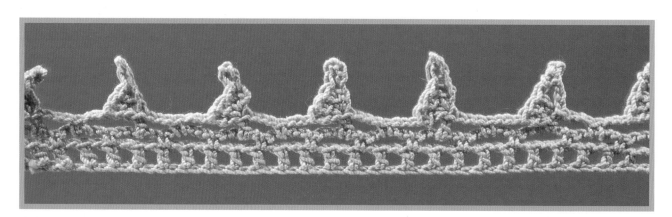

227

Picot: Ch 4, sl st in 4th ch from hook.

Chain multiples of 8 plus 4.

Row 1 (RS): Dc in 4th ch from hook, *ch 1, skip next ch, dc in next ch; rep from * across, turn.

Row 2: Ch 5 (counts as dc, ch 2), skip next ch-1 space, sc in next dc, *ch 5, skip next 2 ch-1 spaces, sc in next dc; rep from * across to turning ch, ch 2, dc in 4th ch of turning ch, turn.

Row 3: Ch 1, sc in first dc, *ch 3, dc in next ch-5 loop, ch 4, picot, 3 dc in last dc made, ch 3, sc in next ch-5 loop; rep from * across, ending with last sc in 3rd ch of turning ch. Fasten off.

.13.
Shells—Large Patterns

228

Chain multiples of 11 plus 2.

Row 1 (RS): Sc in 2nd ch from hook, sc in each of next 4 ch, *ch 3, skip next 2 ch, sc in each of next 9 ch; rep from * across, ending with sc in each of last 5 ch, turn.

Row 2: Ch 1, sc in first sc, *ch 4, 9 dc in next ch-3 loop, ch 4, skip next 4 sc, sc in next sc; rep from * across, turn.

Row 3: Ch 1, sc in first sc, *ch 4, skip next ch-4 loop, dc in each of next 9 dc, ch 4, skip next ch-4 loop, sc in next sc; rep from * across, turn.

Row 4: Ch 1, sc in first sc, *ch 4, skip next ch-4 loop, (dc, ch 1) in each of next 8 dc, dc in next dc, ch 4, skip next ch-4 loop, sc in next sc; rep from * across, turn.

Row 5: Ch 7 (counts as dtr, ch 2), skip next ch-4 loop, (sc in next dc, sc in next ch-1 space) 8 times, sc in next dc**, ch 3, skip next 2 ch-4 loops; rep from * across, ending last rep at **, ch 2, skip next ch-4 loop, dtr in last sc. Fasten off.

229

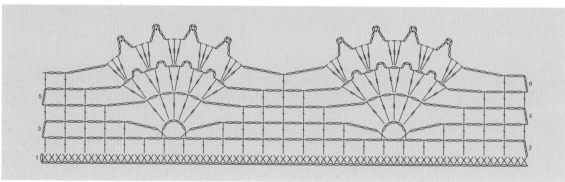

Picot: Ch 3, sl st in 3rd ch from hook.

Chain multiples of 33 plus 8.

Row 1 (WS): Sc in 2nd ch from hook, sc in each ch across, turn.

Row 2: Ch 5 (counts as dc, ch 2), skip first 3 sc, dc in next sc, *ch 2, skip next 2 sc, dc in next sc; rep from * across, turn.

Row 3: Ch 5 (counts as dc, ch 2), skip next ch-2 space, dc in next dc, (ch 2, dc) in each of next 3 dc, *ch 4, skip next 2 ch-2 spaces, sc in next dc, ch 5, sc in next dc, ch 4, skip next 2 ch-2 spaces, dc in next dc**, (ch 2, dc) in each of next 6 dc; rep from * across, ending last rep at **, (ch 2, dc) in each of next 3 dc, ch 2, dc in 3rd ch of turning ch, turn.

Row 4: Ch 5 (counts as dc, ch 2), skip next ch-2 space, dc in next dc, (ch 2, dc) in each of next 2 dc, *ch 5, skip next 2 loops, (tr, ch 1) 4 times in next ch-5 loop, tr in same ch-5 loop, ch 5, skip next 2 loops, dc in next dc**, (ch 2, dc) in each of next 4 dc; rep from * across, ending last rep at **, (ch 2, dc) in each of next 2 dc, ch 2, dc in 3rd ch of turning ch, turn.

Row 5: Ch 5 (counts as dc, ch 2), skip next ch-2 space, dc in next dc, ch 2, dc in next dc, *ch 5, skip next 2 loops, (tr, ch 1, tr, ch 3) in each of next 4 tr, (tr, ch 3, tr) in next tr, ch 5, skip next 2 loops, dc in next dc, (ch 2, dc) in each of next 2 dc; rep from * across, ending with last dc in 3rd ch of turning ch, turn.

Row 6: Ch 5 (counts as dc, ch 2), skip next ch-2 space, dc in next dc, **ch 5, skip next 2 loops, *3 tr in next ch-1 space, ch 2, picot, ch 2, skip next ch-3 loop; rep from 3 times, 3 tr in next ch-1 space, ch 5, skip next 2 loops, dc in next dc; rep from ** across to turning ch, ch 2, dc in 3rd ch of turning ch. Fasten off.

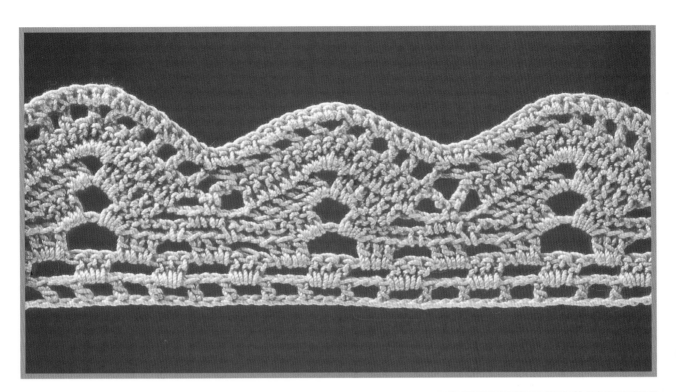

230

Chain multiples of 18 plus 2.

Row 1 (RS): Dc in 4th ch from hook, *ch 2, skip next 2 ch, dc in next ch; rep from * across to within last ch, dc in last ch, turn.

Row 2: Ch 4 (counts as dc, ch 1), 3 dc in next ch-2 space, *ch 3, skip next ch-2 space, 3 dc in next ch-2 space; rep from * across to last ch-2 space, ch 1, skip next dc, dc in 3rd ch of turning ch, turn.

Row 3: Ch 3 (counts as dc), dc in next ch-1 space, *ch 3, 3 dc in next ch-3 loop, ch 5, 3 dc in next ch-3 loop, ch 3**, 3 dc in next ch-3 loop; rep from * across, ending last rep at **, dc in ch-1 space of turning ch, dc in 3rd ch of turning ch, turn.

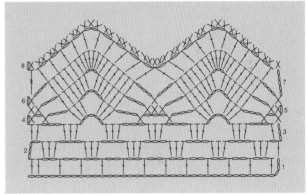

Row 4: Ch 1, sc in first dc, ch 1, sc in next ch-3 loop, *ch 3, (3 dc, ch 5, 3 dc) in next ch-5 loop, ch 3, sc in next ch-3 loop**, ch 3, sc in next ch-3 loop; rep from * across, ending last rep at **, ch 1, skip next dc, sc in 3rd ch of turning ch, turn.

Row 5: Ch 1, sc in first sc, sc in next ch-1 space, *ch 2, skip next ch-3 loop, dc in each of next 3 dc, (3 dc, ch 3, 3 dc) in next ch-5 loop, dc in each of next 3 dc, ch 2, skip next ch-3 loop**, 3 sc in next ch-3 loop; rep from * across, ending last rep at **, sc in next ch-1 space, sc in last sc, turn.

Row 6: Ch 1, sc in first sc, *ch 3, skip next ch-2 space, dc in each of next 6 dc, 5 dc in next ch-3 loop, dc in each of next 6 dc, ch 3, skip next sc, sc in next sc; rep from * across, turn.

Row 7: Ch 5 (counts as dtr), skip next ch-3 loop, *(dc in next dc, ch 1, skip next dc) 4 times, dc in next dc, ch 2, (dc in next dc, ch 1, skip next dc) 4 times**, 2-dc cluster worked across next 2 dc, skipping 2 ch-3 loops in the middle, ch 1; rep from * across, ending last rep at **, skip next ch-3 loop, dtr in last sc, turn.

Row 8: Ch 1, sc in first dtr, *2 sc in each of next 4 ch-1 spaces, 3 sc in next ch-2 space, 2 sc in each of next 4 ch-1 spaces**, sc in next cluster; rep from * across, ending last rep at **, skip next dc, sc in 4th ch of turning ch. Fasten off.

231

Bobble: (Yo, insert hook in next st, yo, draw yarn through st and up to level of work) 3 times in same st, yo, draw yarn through 7 loops on hook.

Chain multiples of 14 plus 2.

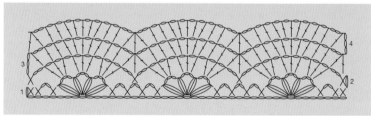

Row 1 (WS): Sc in 2nd ch from hook, sc in next ch, ch 2, skip next ch, sc in next ch, *skip next 3 ch, (bobble, ch 3) 3 times in next ch, bobble in same ch, skip next 3 ch**, (sc in next ch, ch 2, skip next ch) 3 times, sc in next ch; rep from * across, ending last rep at **, sc in next ch, ch 2, skip next ch, sc in each of last 2 ch, turn.

Row 2: Ch 1, sc in first sc, *ch 2, skip next ch-2 space, (dc, ch 1, dc , ch 1, dc, ch 1) in each of next 2 ch-3 loops, (dc, ch 1, dc , ch 1, dc) in next ch-3 loop, ch 2, skip next ch-2 space, sc in next ch-2 space; rep from * across, ending with last sc in last sc, turn.

Row 3: Ch 3 (counts as dc), skip next ch-2 space, dc in next dc, *ch 2, (dc, ch 1) in each of next 3 dc, dc in next ch-1 space, ch 1, dc in next dc, ch 1, dc in next ch-1 space, ch 1, (dc, ch 1) in each of next 2 dc, dc in next dc, ch 2**, 3-dc cluster worked across next (dc, sc, dc); rep from * across, ending last rep at **, 2-dc cluster worked across next dc and last sc, turn.

Row 4: Ch 3 (counts as dc), skip next ch-2 space, dc in next dc, *ch 2, (dc, ch 1) in each of next 3 dc, dc in next ch-1 space, ch 1, dc in next dc, ch 1, dc in next ch-1 space, ch 1, (dc, ch 1) in each of next 2 dc, dc in next dc, ch 2**, 3-dc cluster worked across next (dc, cluster, dc); rep from * across, ending last rep at **, 2-dc cluster worked across next dc and in 3rd ch of turning ch. Fasten off.

232

Picot: Ch 3, sl st in 3rd ch from hook.

Chain multiples of 15 plus 3.

Row 1 (WS): Dc in 4th ch from hook, dc in each ch across, turn.

Row 2: Ch 1, sc in first dc, *ch 5, skip next 4 dc, dc in each of next 6 dc, ch 5, skip next 4 dc, sc in next dc; rep from * across, ending with last sc in 3rd ch of turning ch, turn.

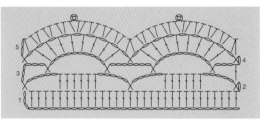

Row 3: Ch 6 (counts as dc, ch 3), *sc in next ch-5 loop, ch 10, sc in next ch-5 loop**, ch 7; rep from * across, ending last rep at **, ch 3, dc in last sc, turn.

Row 4: Ch 1, sc in first dc, skip next ch-3 loop, *ch 1, (dc, ch 1) 8 times in next ch-10 loop, sc in next ch-7 loop; rep from * across, ending with last sc in 3rd ch of turning ch, turn.

Row 5: Ch 2 (counts as hdc), hdc in next ch-1 space, *2 hdc in each of next 3 ch-1 spaces, (hdc, picot, 2 hdc) in next ch-1 space, 2 hdc in each of next 3 ch-1 spaces**, 2-hdc cluster worked across next 2 ch-1 spaces; rep from * across, ending last rep at **, 2-hdc cluster worked across next ch-1 space and last sc. Fasten off.

233

Picot: Ch 5, sl st in 4th ch from hook.

Chain multiples of 10 plus 2.

Row 1 (RS): Sc in 2nd ch from hook, *ch 5, skip next 4 ch, (dc, ch 3, dc) in next ch, ch 5, skip next 4 ch, sc in next ch; rep from * across, turn.

Row 2: Ch 6 (counts as tr, ch 2), *sc in next ch-5 loop, (3 dc, ch 3, 3 dc) in next ch-3 loop, sc in next ch-5 loop**, ch 5; rep from * across, ending last rep at **, ch 2, tr in last sc, turn.

Row 3: Ch 1, sc in first tr, *skip next sc, dc in next dc, picot, dc in each of next 2 dc, picot, (2 dc, picot, 2 dc) in next ch-3 loop, picot, dc in each of next 2 dc, picot, dc in next dc, sc in next ch-5 loop; rep from * across, ending with last sc in 4th ch of turning ch. Fasten off.

234

Picot: Ch 4, sl st in 4th ch from hook.

Chain multiples of 20 plus 6.

Row 1 (RS): Dc in 6th ch from hook, *ch 1, skip next ch, dc in next ch; rep from * across, turn.

Row 2: Ch 1, sc in first dc, (sc in next ch-1 space, sc in next dc) 3 times, *ch 3, skip next 2 ch-1 spaces, (dc, ch 2, dc) in next ch-1 space, ch 3, skip next 2 ch-1 spaces, sc in next dc**, (sc in next ch-1 space, sc in next dc) 5 times; rep from * across, ending last rep at **, (sc in next ch-1 space, sc in next dc) twice, sc in ch-1 space of turning ch, sc in 4th ch of turning ch, turn.

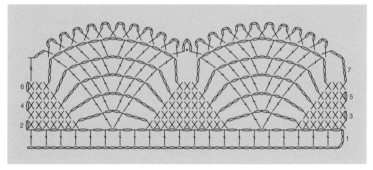

Row 3: Ch 1, sc in each of first 6 sc, *ch 3, skip next ch-3 loop, dc in next dc, ch 1, (dc, ch 3, dc) in next ch-2 space, ch 1, dc in next dc, ch 3, skip next sc**, sc in each of next 9 sc; rep from * across, ending last rep at **, sc in each of last 6 sc, turn.

Row 4: Ch 1, sc in each of first 5 sc, *ch 3, skip next ch-3 loop, (dc, ch 1) in each of next 2 dc, (dc, ch 3, dc) in next ch-3 loop, (ch 1, dc) in each of next 2 dc, ch 3, skip next sc**, sc in each of next 7 sc; rep from * across, ending last rep at **, sc in each of last 5 sc, turn.

Row 5: Ch 1, sc in each of first 4 sc, *ch 3, skip next ch-3 loop, (dc, ch 1) in each of next 3 dc, (dc, ch 3, dc) in next ch-3 loop, (ch 1, dc) in each of next 3 dc, ch 3, skip next sc**, sc in each of next 5 sc; rep from * across, ending last rep at **, sc in each of last 4 sc, turn.

Row 6: Ch 1, sc in each of first 3 sc, *ch 3, skip next ch-3 loop, (dc, ch 1) in each of next 4 dc, (dc, ch 3, dc) in next ch-3 loop, (ch 1, dc) in each of next 4 dc, ch 3, skip next sc, sc in each of next 3 sc; rep from * across, turn.

Row 7: Ch 6 (counts as tr, ch 2), skip next ch-3 loop, *(sc, ch 3) in each of next 5 dc, sc in next ch-3 loop, (ch 3, sc) in each of next 5 dc**, picot, skip next 2 ch-3 loops; rep from * across, ending last rep at **, ch 2, skip next 2 sc, tr in last sc. Fasten off.

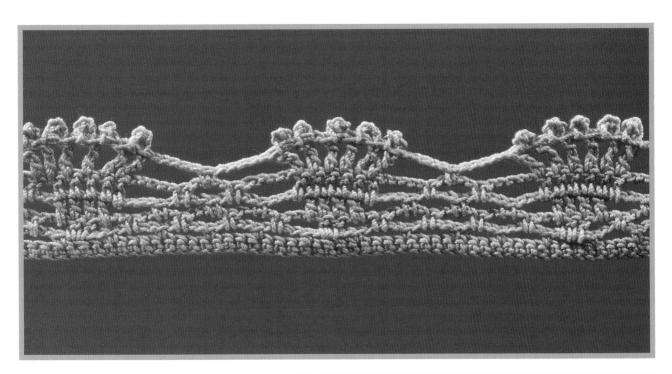

235

Picot: Ch 4, sl st in 4th ch from hook.

Chain multiples of 20 plus 2.

Row 1 (WS): Sc in 2nd ch from hook, sc in each ch across, turn.

Row 2: Ch 1, sc in first sc, *ch 4, skip next 3 sc, sc in next sc; rep from * across, turn.

Row 3: Ch 6 (counts as tr, ch 2), sc in next ch-4 loop, ch 4, *sc in next ch-4 loop, ch 3, 2 dc in next ch-4 loop, ch 3**, (sc, ch 4) in each of next 3 ch-4

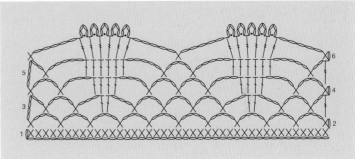

loops; rep from * across, ending last rep at **, sc in next ch-4 loop, ch 4, sc in next ch-4 loop, ch 2, tr in last sc, turn.

Row 4: Ch 1, sc in first tr, skip next ch-2 space, *ch 4, sc in next ch-4 loop, ch 4, dc in next ch-3 loop, dc in each of next 2 dc, dc in next ch-3 loop, ch 4, sc in next ch-4 loop, ch 4, sc in next ch-4 loop; rep from * across, ending with last sc in 4th ch of turning ch, turn.

Row 5: Ch 6 (counts as tr, ch 2), sc in next ch-4 loop, *ch 5, dc in next ch-4 loop, dc in each of next 4 dc, dc in next ch-4 loop, ch 5, sc in next ch-4 loop**, ch 4, sc in next ch-4 loop; rep from * across, ending last rep at **, ch 2, tr in last sc, turn.

Row 6: Ch 1, sc in first tr, *ch 5, skip next ch-5 loop, (tr, picot) in each of next 5 dc, tr in next dc, ch 5, skip next ch-5 loop, sc in next ch-5 loop; rep from ** across, ending with last sc in 4th ch of turning ch. Fasten off.

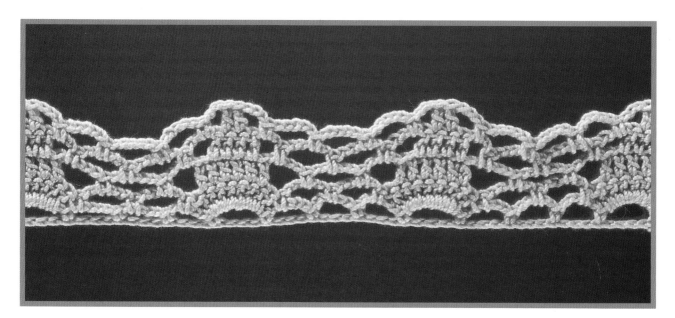

236

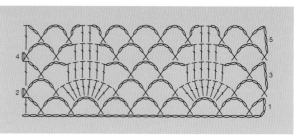

Chain multiples of 16 plus 5.

Row 1 (RS): Sc in 7th ch from hook,*ch 4, skip next 3 ch, sc in next ch; rep from * across to within last 2 ch, ch 2, skip next ch, dc in last ch, turn.

Row 2: Ch 1, sc in first dc, ch 5, sc in next ch-5 loop, *8 dc in next ch-5 loop**, (sc, ch 5) in each of next 2 ch-5 loops, sc in next ch-5 loop; rep from * across, ending last rep at **, sc in next ch-5 loop, ch 5, sc in 4th ch of turning ch, turn.

Row 3: Ch 5 (counts as dc, ch 2), sc in next ch-5 loop, *ch 4, skip next (sc, dc), dc in each of next 6 dc, ch 4, sc in next ch-5 loop**, ch 5, sc in next ch-5 loop; rep from * across, ending last rep at **, ch 2, dc in last sc, turn.

Row 4: Ch 1, sc in first dc, ch 5, *sc in next ch-4 loop, ch 3, skip next dc, dc in each of next 4 dc, ch 3**, (sc, ch 5) in each of next 2 ch-5 loops; rep from * across, ending last rep at **, sc in next ch-5 loop, ch 5, sc in 3rd ch of turning ch, turn.

Row 5: Ch 5 (counts as dc, ch 2), sc in next ch-5 loop, ch 5, *sc in next ch-3 loop, ch 3, skip next dc, dc in each of next 2 dc, ch 3, sc in next ch-3 loop**, (ch 5, sc) in each of next 3 loops; rep from * across, ending last rep at **, ch 5, sc in next ch-5 loop, ch 2, dc in last sc. Fasten off.

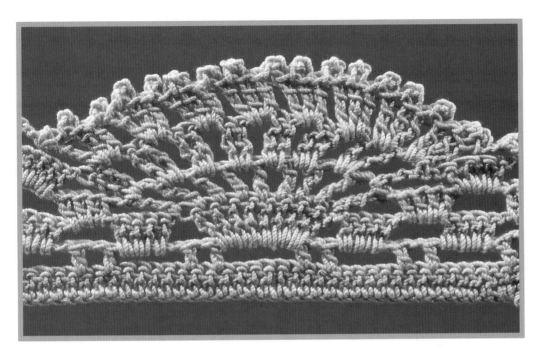

237

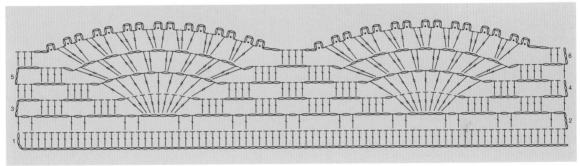

Picot: Ch 3, sl st in 3rd ch from hook.

Chain multiples of 40 plus 5.

Row 1 (WS): Dc in 4th ch from hook, dc in each ch across, turn.

Row 2: Ch 4 (counts as dc, ch 1), skip first 2 dc, *dc in next dc, ch 4, skip next 5 dc, dc in next dc, ch 1, skip next dc; rep from * across to turning ch, dc in 3rd ch of turning ch, turn.

Row 3: Ch 6 (counts as dc, ch 3), skip next ch-1 space, 4 dc in next ch-4 loop, ch 4, skip next ch-1 space, *4 dc in next ch-4 loop, ch 1, skip next ch-1 space, 9 tr in next ch-4 loop, ch 1, skip next ch-1 space**, (4 dc in next ch-4 loop, ch 4, skip next ch-1 space) 3 times; rep from * across, ending last rep at **, 4 dc in next ch-4 loop, ch 4, skip next ch-1 space, 4 dc in next ch-4 loop, ch 3, skip next ch-1 space of turning ch, dc in 3rd ch of turning ch, turn.

Row 4: Ch 3 (counts as dc), 2 dc in next ch-3 loop, ch 4, *4 dc in next ch-4 loop, ch 1, skip next ch-1 space, (tr, ch 1) in each of next 9 tr, skip next ch-1 space**, (4 dc, ch 4) in each of next 2 ch-4 loops; rep from * across, ending last rep at **, 4 dc in next ch-4 loop, ch 4, 2 dc in ch-3 loop of turning ch, dc in 3rd ch of turning ch, turn.

Row 5: Ch 6 (counts as dc, ch 3), *4 dc in next ch-4 loop, ch 1, skip next ch-1 space, (2 tr, ch 2) in each of next 7 ch-1 space, 2 tr in next ch-1 space, ch 1, skip next ch-1 space, 4 dc in next ch-4 loop**, ch 4; rep from * across, ending last rep at **, ch 3, skip next 2 dc, dc in 3rd ch of turning ch, turn.

Row 6: Ch 3 (counts as dc), 2 dc in next ch-3 loop, *ch 2, picot, skip next ch-1 space, (tr, picot, 2 tr, picot) in each of next 7 ch-2 space, ch 2, skip next ch-1 space**, 4 dc in next ch-4 loop; rep from * across, ending last rep at **, 2 dc in ch-3 loop of turning ch, dc in 3rd ch of turning ch. Fasten off.

238

Picot: Ch 3, sl st in 3rd ch from hook.

Chain multiples of 21 plus 2.

Row 1 (RS): Sc in 2nd ch from hook, sc in each ch across, turn.

Row 2: Ch 1, sc in each of first 3 sc, *2 sc in next sc, ch 6, skip next 5 sc, dc in each of next 4 sc, ch 6, skip next 5 sc, 2 sc in next sc**, sc in each of next 5 sc; rep from * across, ending last rep at **, sc in each of last 3 sc, turn.

Row 3: Ch 1, sc in each of first 4 sc, *ch 6, skip next ch-6 loop, 2 dc in next dc, dc in next dc, ch 3, dc in next dc, 2 dc in next dc, ch 6, skip next sc**, sc in each of next 7 sc; rep from * across, ending last rep at **, sc in each of last 4 sc, turn.

Row 4: Ch 1, sc in each of first 3 sc, *ch 6, skip next ch-6 loop, dc in each of next 3 dc, ch 3, (dc, ch 3, dc) in next ch-3 loop, ch 3, dc in each of next 3 dc, ch 6, skip next sc**, sc in each of next 5 sc; rep from * across, ending last rep at **, sc in each of last 3 sc, turn.

Row 5: Ch 1, sc in each of first 2 sc, ch 6, skip next ch-6 loop, dc in each of next 3 dc, ch 3, dc in next dc, ch 3, (dc, ch 3, dc) in next ch-3 loop, ch 3, dc in next dc, ch 3, dc in each of next 3 dc, ch 6, skip next sc**, sc in each of next 3 sc; rep from * across, ending last rep at **, sc in each of last 2 sc, turn.

Row 6: Ch 1, sc in first sc, *ch 6, skip next ch-6 loop, dc in each of next 3 dc, (ch 3, dc) in each of next 2 dc, ch 3, (dc, ch 3, dc) in next ch-3 loop, ch 3, (dc, ch 3) in each of next 2 dc, dc in each of next 3 dc, ch 6, skip next sc, sc in next sc; rep from * across, turn.

Row 7: Ch 8 (counts as dtr, ch 3), skip next ch-6 loop, *dc in each of next 3 dc, (ch 3, dc) in each of next 3 dc, ch 3, (dc, ch 3, dc) in next ch-3 loop, ch 3, (dc, ch 3) in each of next 3 dc, dc in each of next 3 dc, ch 3**, skip next 2 ch-6 loops; rep from * across, ending last rep at **, skip next ch-6 loop, dtr in last sc, turn.

Row 8: Ch 5 (counts as dtr), skip next ch-3 loop, dc in each of next 3 dc, *(ch 3, dc) in each of next 4 dc, ch 3, (dc, ch 3, dc) in next ch-3 loop, ch 3, (dc, ch 3) in each of next 4 dc, dc in each of next 2 dc**, 3-dc cluster worked across next (dc, ch-3 loop, dc), dc in each of next 2 dc; rep from * across, ending last rep at **, dc in next dc, dtr in 5th ch of turning ch, turn.

Row 9: Ch 1, sc in first 4 sts, *(2 sc, picot, 2 sc) in each of next 11 ch-3 loops**, sc in each of next 5 sts; rep from * across, ending last rep at **, sc in each of next 3 dc, sc in 5th ch of turning ch. Fasten off.

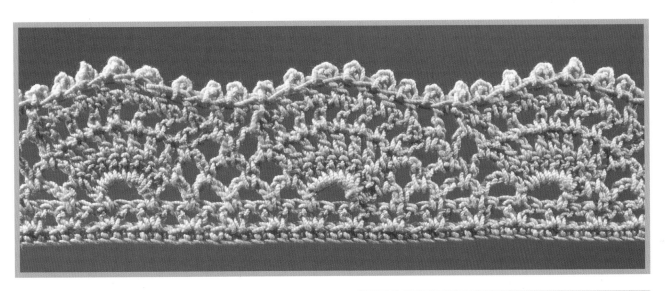

239

Picot: Ch 3, sl st in 3rd ch from hook.

Chain multiples of 15 plus 3.

Row 1 (RS): Sc in 2nd ch from hook, sc in each ch across, turn.

Row 2: Ch 3 (counts as dc), skip first 2 sc, (dc, ch 1, dc) in next sc, *skip next 2 sc, (dc, ch 1, dc) in next sc; rep from * across to within last 2 sc, skip next sc, dc in last sc, turn.

Row 3: Ch 5 (counts as dc, ch 2), sc in next ch-1 space, (ch 5, sc) in each ch-1 space across to last ch-1 space, ch 2, skip next dc, dc in 3rd ch of turning ch, turn.

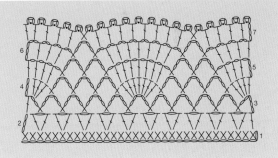

Row 4: Ch 3 (counts as dc), 3 dc in next ch-2 space, *(sc, ch 5) in each of next 3 ch-5 loops, sc in next ch-5 loop**, 7 dc in next ch-5 loop; rep from * across, ending last rep at **, 3 dc in next ch-2 space of turning ch, dc in 3rd ch of turning ch, turn.

Row 5: Ch 4 (counts as dc, ch 1), skip first dc, (dc, ch 1) in each of next 3 dc, *(sc, ch 5) in each of next 2 ch-5 loops, sc in next ch-5 loop, ch 1**, (dc, ch 1) in each of next 7 dc; rep from * across, ending last rep at **, (dc, ch 1) in each of next 3 dc, dc in 3rd ch of turning ch, turn.

Row 6: Ch 5 (counts as dc, ch 2), skip next ch-1 space, (dc, ch 2) in each of next 3 dc, *sc in next ch-5 loop, ch 5, sc in next ch-5 loop, ch 2, skip next ch-1 space**, (dc, ch 2) in each of next 7 dc; rep from * across, ending last rep at **, (dc, ch 2) in each of next 3 dc, dc in 3rd ch of turning ch, turn.

Row 7: Ch 3 (counts as dc), picot, (dc, picot) in each of next 4 ch-2 spaces, *sc in next ch-5 loop, picot**, (dc, picot) in each of next 8 ch-2 spaces; rep from * across, ending last rep at **, (dc, picot) in each of next 4 ch-2 spaces, dc in 3rd ch of turning ch. Fasten off.

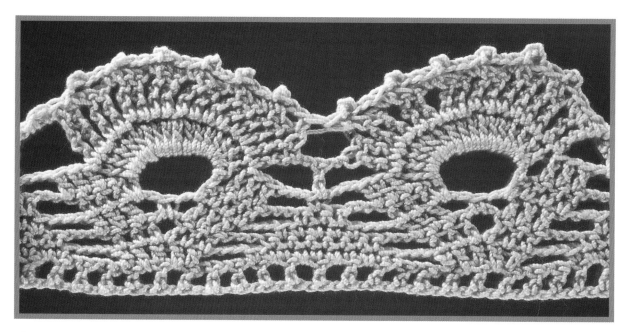

240

Picot: Ch 4, sl st in 4th ch from hook.

Chain multiples of 24 plus 4.

Row 1 (WS): Dc in 6th ch from hook, *ch 1, skip next ch, dc in next ch; rep from * across, turn.

Row 2: Ch 1, sc in first dc, (sc in next ch-1 space, sc in next dc) twice, *ch 3, skip next 3 ch-1 spaces, dc in next dc, (dc in next ch-1 space, dc in next dc) twice, ch 3, skip next 3 ch-1 spaces, sc in next dc**, (sc in next ch-1 space, sc in next dc) 4 times; rep from * across, ending last rep at **, sc in next ch-1 space, sc in next dc, sc in ch-1 space of turning ch, sc in 4th ch of turning ch, turn.

Row 3: Ch 1, sc in each of first 4 sc, *ch 3, skip next ch-3 loop, dc in each of next 2 dc, (dc, ch 2, dc) in next dc, dc in each of next 2 dc, ch 3, skip next sc**, sc in each of next 7 sc; rep from * across, ending last rep at **, sc in each of last 4 sc, turn.

Row 4: Ch 1, sc in each of first 3 sc, *ch 3, skip next ch-3 loop, dc in each of next 3 dc, ch 2, sc in next ch-2 space, ch 2, dc in each of next 3 dc, ch 3, skip next sc**, sc in each of next 5 sc; rep from * across, ending last rep at **, sc in each of last 3 sc, turn.

Row 5: Ch 1, sc in each of first 2 sc, *ch 3, skip next ch-3 loop, dc in each of next 3 dc, ch 2, sc in next ch-2 space, ch 10, sc in next ch-2 space, ch 2, dc in each of next 3 dc, ch 3, skip next sc**, sc in each of next 3 sc; rep from * across, ending last rep at **, sc in each of last 2 sc, turn.

Row 6: Ch 1, sc in first sc, *ch 3, skip next ch-3 loop, dc in each of next 3 dc, skip next ch-2 space, 16 dc in next ch-10 loop, skip next ch-2 space, dc in each of next 3 dc, ch 3, skip next sc, sc in next sc; rep from * across, turn.

Row 7: Ch 5 (counts as dc, ch 2), *skip next ch-3 loop, skip next 3 dc, (tr in each of next 2 dc, ch 2) 8 times, skip next ch-3 loop, dc in next sc**, ch 2; rep from * across, ending last rep at **, turn.

Row 8: Ch 1, sl st in each of first 5 sts, *(sc, picot) in each of next 6 ch-2 spaces, sc in next ch-2 space**, skip next 2 ch-2 spaces; rep from * across, ending last rep at **, sl st in each of next 5 sts. Fasten off.

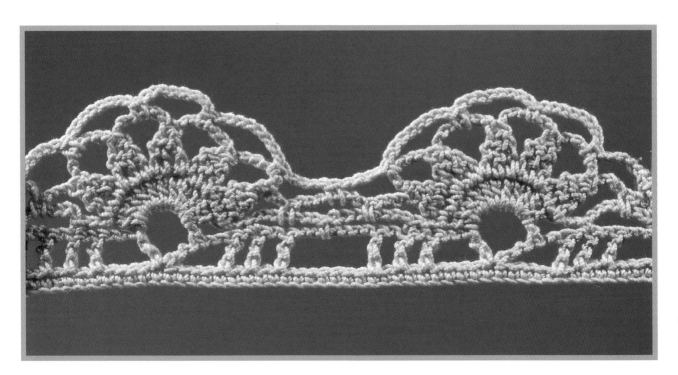

241

Chain multiples of 26 plus 2.

Row 1 (RS): Sc in 2nd ch from hook, sc in each ch across, turn.

Row 2: Ch 7 (counts as tr, ch 3), skip first 4 sc, *(tr in next sc, ch 1, skip next sc) twice, tr in next sc, ch 2, skip next 4 sc, (tr, ch 7, tr) in next sc, ch 2, (tr in next sc, ch 1, skip next sc) twice, tr in next sc**, ch 7, skip next 7 sc; rep from * across, ending last rep at **, ch 3, skip next 3 sc, tr in last sc, turn.

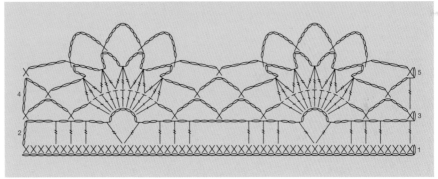

Row 3: Ch 1, sc in first tr, ch 7, skip next 2 spaces, *sc in next tr, ch 2, skip next ch-2 space, 11 dc in next ch-7 loop, ch 2, skip next 2 spaces, sc in next tr, ch 7**, skip next ch-1 space, sc in next ch-7 loop, ch 7, skip next ch-1 space; rep from * across, ending last rep at **, sc in 4th ch of turning ch, turn.

Row 4: Ch 7 (counts as tr, ch 3), sc in next ch-7 loop, *ch 3, skip next ch-2 space, 3-tr cluster worked across next 3 dc, (ch 7, starting in same dc holding last tr made, work 3-tr cluster across next 3 dc) 4 times, ch 4, skip next ch-2 space, sc in next ch-7 loop**, ch 7, sc in next ch-7 loop; rep from * across, ending last rep at **, ch 3, tr in last sc, turn.

Row 5: Ch 1, sc in first tr, skip next ch-3 loop, *ch 4, skip next ch-4 loop, sc in next ch-7 loop, (ch 9, sc) in each of next 3 ch-7 loops, ch 4, skip next ch-3 loop, sc in next ch-7 loop; rep from * across, ending with last sc in 4th ch of turning ch. Fasten off.

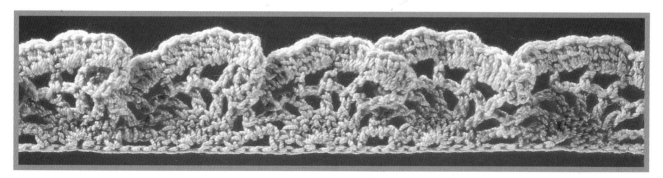

242

Chain multiples of 9 plus 6.

Row 1 (WS): Sc in 7th ch from hook, *skip next 2 ch, 6 dc in next ch, skip next 2 ch, sc in next ch**, ch 5, skip next 2 ch, sc in next ch; rep from * across, ending last rep at **, ch 2, skip next ch, dc in last ch, turn.

Row 2: Ch 1, sc in first dc, *ch 2, skip next sc, (dc, ch 2) in each of next 6 dc, sc in next ch-5 loop; rep from * across, ending with last sc in 4th ch of turning ch, turn.

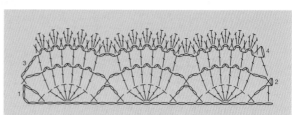

Row 3: Ch 4 (counts as dc), skip next ch-2 space, *dc in next dc, (ch 3, dc) in each of next 5 dc**, ch 3, skip next 2 ch-2 spaces; rep from * across, ending last rep at **, skip next ch-2 space, dc in last sc, turn.

Row 4: Ch 1, skip first dc, sc in next dc, *3 dc in next ch-3 loop, sc in next dc; rep from * across. Fasten off.

243

Chain multiples of 8 plus 3.

Row 1 (WS): Sc in 4th ch from hook, *ch 3, skip next ch, sc in next ch; rep from * across to within last ch, ch 1, hdc in last ch, turn.

Row 2: Ch 1, sc in first hdc, skip next ch-1 space, *ch 3, sc in next ch-3 loop, 7 tr in next ch-3 loop, sc in next ch-3 loop, ch 3, sc in next ch-3 loop; rep from * across, ending with last sc in 2nd ch of turning ch, turn.

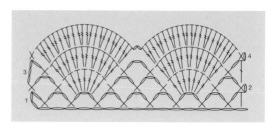

Row 3: Ch 4 (counts as dc, ch 1), *sc in next ch-3 loop, skip next sc, 2 tr in each of next 7 tr, sc in next ch-3 loop**, ch 3; rep from * across, ending last rep at **, ch 1, dc in last sc, turn.

Row 4: Ch 1, sc in first dc, *skip next sc, (2 tr in next tr, tr in next tr) 3 times, 2 tr in each of next 2 tr, (tr in next tr, 2 tr in next tr) 3 times**, ch 2, skip next (sc, ch 3, sc); rep from * across, ending last rep at **, sc in 3rd ch of turning ch. Fasten off.

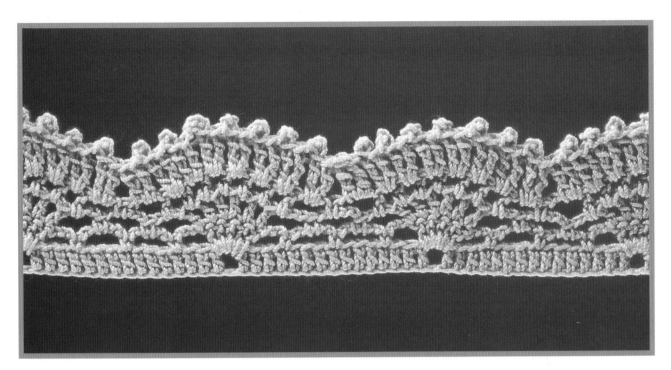

244

Picot: Ch 3, sl st in 3rd ch from hook.

Chain multiples of 16 plus 3.

Row 1 (RS): Dc in 4th ch from hook, dc in each of next 6 ch, *ch 1, skip next ch, dc in each of next 15 ch; rep from * across, ending with dc in each of last 8 ch, turn.

Row 2: Ch 1, sc in first dc, *ch 5, skip next 3 dc, sc in next dc, ch 3, 5 dc in next ch-1 space, ch 3, skip next 3 dc, sc in next dc, ch 5, skip next 3 dc**, sc in next dc; rep from * across, ending last rep at **, sc in 3rd ch of turning ch, turn.

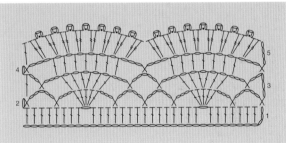

Row 3: Ch 5 (counts as dc, ch 2), *sc in next ch-5 loop, ch 3, skip next ch-3 loop, (dc, ch 1) in each of next 2 dc, (dc, ch 1, dc) in next dc, (ch 1, dc) in each of next 2 dc, ch 3, skip next ch-3 loop, sc in next ch-5 loop**, ch 5; rep from * across, ending last rep at **, ch 2, dc in last sc, turn.

Row 4: Ch 1, sc in first dc, *ch 3, dc in next ch-3 loop, ch 1, (dc, ch 1) in each of next 5 ch-1 spaces, dc in next ch-3 loop, ch 3, sc in next ch-5 loop; rep from * across, ending with last sc in 3rd ch of turning ch, turn.

Row 5: Ch 4 (counts as dc), *2 tr in next ch-3 loop, picot, (2 tr, picot) in each of next 6 ch-1 spaces, 2 tr in next ch-3 loop; rep from * across to last ch-3 loop, dc in last sc. Fasten off.

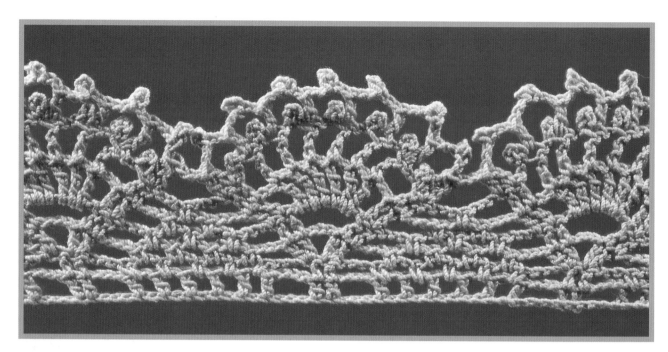

245

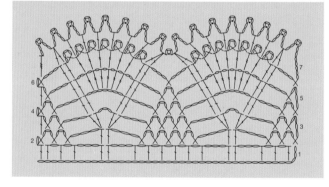

Picot: Ch 3, sl st in 3rd ch from hook.

Chain multiples of 19 plus 3.

Row 1 (RS): Dc in 4th ch from hook, (ch 1, skip next ch, dc in next ch) twice, *ch 3, skip next 3 ch, dc in each of next 2 ch, ch 3, skip next 3 ch, dc in next ch**, (ch 1, skip next ch, dc in next ch) 5 times; rep from * across, ending last rep at **, (ch 1, skip next ch, dc in next ch) twice, dc in last ch, turn.

Row 2: Ch 1, sc in first dc, *(ch 3, sc) in each of next 2 ch-1 space, *ch 3, skip next ch-3 loop, dc in each of next 2 dc, ch 3, skip next ch-3 loop, sc in next ch-1 space**, (ch 3, sc) in each of next 4 ch-1 spaces; rep from * across, ending last rep at **, ch 3, sc in next ch-1 space, ch 3, sc in 3rd ch of turning ch, turn.

Row 3: Ch 4 (counts as dc, ch 1), sc in next ch-3 loop, ch 3, sc in next ch-3 loop, *ch 3, skip next ch-3 loop, (2 dc, ch 3) in each of next 2 dc, skip next ch-3 loop, sc in next ch-3 loop**, (ch 3, sc) in each of next 3 ch-3 loops; rep from * across, ending last rep at **, ch 3, sc in next ch-3 loop, ch 1, dc in last sc, turn.

Row 4: Ch 1, sc in first dc, ch 3, sc in next ch-3 loop, *ch 3, skip next ch-3 loop, dc in each of next 2 dc, ch 7, skip next ch-3 loop, dc in each of next 2 dc, ch 3, skip next ch-3 loop, sc in next ch-3 loop**, (ch 3, sc) in each of next 2 ch-3 loops; rep from * across, ending last rep at **, ch 3, sc in 3rd ch of turning ch, turn.

Row 5: Ch 4 (counts as dc, ch 1), sc in next ch-3 loop, *ch 3, skip next ch-3 loop, dc in each of next 2 dc, ch 2, (tr, ch 1) 5 times in next ch-7 loop, tr in same loop, ch 2, dc in each of next 2 dc, ch 3, skip next ch-3 loop, sc in next ch-3 loop**, ch 3, sc in next ch-3 loop; rep from * across, ending last rep at **, ch 1, dc in last sc, turn.

Row 6: Ch 1, sc in first dc, *ch 3, skip next ch-3 loop, dc in each of next 2 dc, (ch 4, sc in 4th ch from hook, skip next space, tr in next tr) 6 times, ch 4, sc in 4th ch from hook, skip next ch-2 space, dc in each of next 2 dc, ch 3, skip next ch-3 loop, sc in next ch-3 loop; rep from * across, ending with last sc in 3rd ch of turning ch, turn.

Row 7: Ch 7 (counts as dtr, ch 2), picot, ch 2, skip next ch-3 loop, *2-dc cluster worked across next 2 dc, (ch 2, picot, ch 2, dc in next tr) 6 times, ch 2, picot, ch 2, 2-dc cluster worked across next 2 dc**, picot, skip next 2 ch-3 loops; rep from * across, ending last rep at **, ch 2, picot, ch 2, skip next ch-3 loop, dtr in last sc. Fasten off.

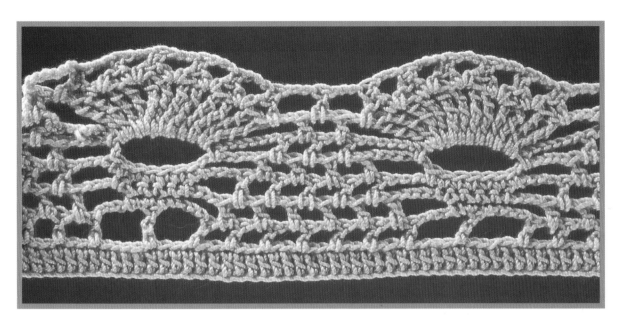

246

Chain multiples of 28 plus 3.

Row 1 (RS): Dc in 4th ch from hook, dc in each ch across, turn.

Row 2: Ch 5 (counts as dc, ch 2), skip first 3 dc, dc in next dc, (ch 2, skip next 2 dc, dc in next dc) twice, *ch 5, skip next 4 dc, tr in next dc, ch 5, skip next 4 dc, dc in next dc**, (ch 2, skip next 2 dc, dc in next dc) 6 times; rep from * across, ending last rep at **, (ch 2, skip next 2 dc, dc in next dc) twice, ch 2, skip next 2 dc, dc in 3rd ch of turning ch, turn.

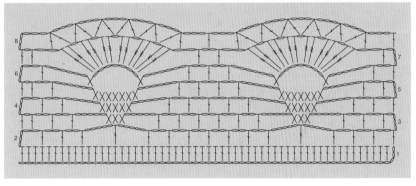

Row 3: Ch 4 (counts as dc, ch 3), dc in next ch-2 space, (ch 2, dc) in each of next 2 ch-2 spaces, *ch 5, sc in next ch-5 loop, sc in next tr, sc in next ch-5 loop, ch 5, dc in next ch-2 space**, (ch 2, dc) in each of next 5 ch-2 spaces; rep from * across, ending last rep at **, (ch 2, dc) in each of next 2 ch-2 spaces, ch 1, dc in 3rd ch of turning ch, turn.

Row 4: Ch 5 (counts as dc, ch 2), skip next ch-1 space, dc in next ch-2 space, ch 2, dc in next ch-2 space, *ch 5, sc in next ch-5 loop, sc in each of next 3 sc, sc in next ch-5 loop, ch 5, dc in next ch-2 space**, (ch 2, dc) in each of next 4 ch-2 spaces; rep from * across, ending last rep at **, ch 2, dc in next ch-2 space, ch 2, dc in 3rd ch of turning ch, turn.

Row 5: Ch 4 (counts as dc, ch 1), dc in next ch-2 space, ch 2, dc in next ch-2 space, *ch 6, sc in next ch-5 loop, sc in each of next 5 sc, sc in next ch-5 loop, ch 6, dc in next ch-2 space**, (ch 2, dc) in each of next 3 ch-2 spaces; rep from * across, ending last rep at **, ch 2, dc in next ch-2 space of turning ch, ch 1, dc in 3rd ch of turning ch, turn.

Row 6: Ch 5 (counts as dc, ch 2), skip next ch-1 space, dc in next ch-2 space, *ch 6, sc in next ch-6 loop, ch 7, sc in next ch-6 loop, ch 6, dc in next ch-2 space**, (ch 2, dc) in each of next 2 ch-2 spaces; rep from * across, ending last rep at **, ch 2, dc in 3rd ch of turning ch, turn.

Row 7: Ch 4 (counts as dc, ch 1), dc in next ch-2 space, *ch 2, skip next ch-6 loop, (2 tr, ch 1) 6 times in next ch-7 loop, ch 1 more, skip next ch-6 loop, dc in next ch-2 space**, ch 2, dc in next ch-2 loop; rep from * across, ending last rep at **, ch 1, dc in 3rd ch of turning ch, turn.

Row 8: Ch 6 (counts as dc, ch 3), skip next ch-1 space, *2-dc cluster worked across next 2 spaces, (ch 3, starting in same space as last dc made, work 2-dc cluster across next 2 spaces) 5 times, ch 3**, dc in next ch-2 space, ch 3; rep from * across, ending last rep at **, dc in 3rd ch of turning ch. Fasten off.

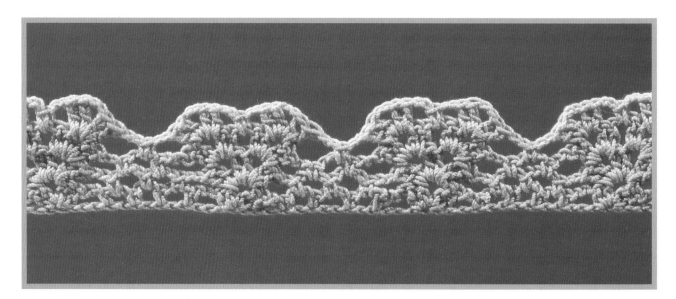

247

Chain multiples of 14 plus 3.

Row 1 (WS): Sc in 4th ch from hook, ch 3, skip next ch, sc in next ch, *ch 2, skip next 3 ch, (2 dc, ch 2, 2 dc) in next ch, ch 2, skip next 3 ch, sc in next ch**, (ch 3, skip next ch, sc in next ch) 3 times; rep from * across, ending last rep at **, ch 3, skip next ch, sc in next ch, ch 1, hdc in last ch, turn.

Row 2: Ch 1, sc in first hdc, ch 3, skip next ch-1 space, sc in next ch-3 loop, *ch 2, skip next ch-2 space, (2 dc, ch 2, 2 dc, ch 2, 2 dc) in next ch-2 space, ch 2, skip next ch-2 space, sc in next ch-3 space**, (ch 3, sc) in each of next 2 ch-3 loops; rep from * across, ending last rep at **, ch 3, sc in 2nd ch of turning ch, turn.

Row 3: Ch 4 (counts as dc, ch 1), sc in next ch-3 loop, *ch 2, skip next ch-2 space, (2 dc, ch 2, 2 dc, ch 1) in each of next 2 ch-2 spaces, ch 1 more, skip next ch-2 space, sc in next ch-3 loop**, ch 3, sc in next ch-3 loop; rep from * across, ending last rep at **, ch 1, dc in last sc, turn.

Row 4: Ch 1, sc in first dc, *ch 2, skip next ch-2 space, (2 dc, ch 2, 2 dc) in next ch-2 space, ch 2, sc in next ch-1 space, ch 2, (2 dc, ch 2, 2 dc) in next ch-2 space, ch 2, skip next ch-2 space, sc in next ch-3 loop; rep from * across, ending with last sc in 3rd ch of turning ch. Fasten off.

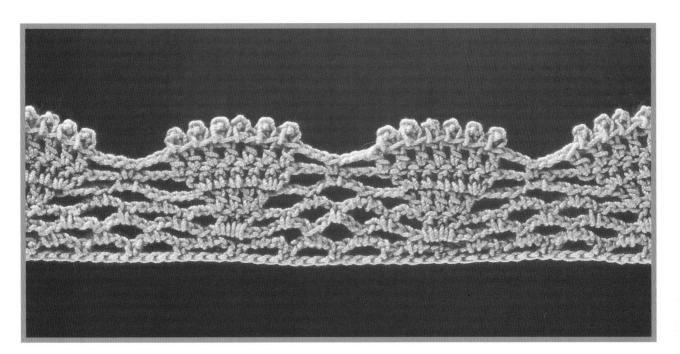

248

Picot: Ch 3, sl st in 3rd ch from hook.

Chain multiples of 16 plus 2.

Row 1 (RS): Sc in 2nd ch from hook, *ch 5, skip next 3 ch, sc in next ch; rep from * across, turn.

Row 2: Ch 5 (counts as dc, ch 2), sc in next ch-5 loop, (ch 5, sc) in each ch-5 loop across to last ch-5 loop, ch 2, dc in last sc, turn.

Row 3: Ch 1, sc in first dc, skip next ch-2 space, *ch 5, sc in next ch-5 loop, ch 3, 3 dc in next ch-5 loop, ch 3, sc in next ch-5 loop, ch 5, sc in next ch-5 loop; rep from * across, ending with last sc in 3rd ch of turning ch, turn.

Row 4: Ch 5 (counts as dc, ch 2), *sc in next ch-5 loop, ch 3, skip next ch-3 loop, 2 dc in next dc, dc in next dc, 2 dc in next dc, ch 3, skip next ch-3 loop, sc in next ch-5 loop**, ch 5; rep from * across, ending last rep at **, ch 2, dc in last sc, turn.

Row 5: Ch 1, sc in first dc, skip next ch-2 space, *ch 3, skip next ch-3 loop, 2 dc in next dc, dc in each of next 3 dc, 2 dc in next dc, ch 3, skip next ch-3 loop, sc in next ch-5 loop; rep from * across, ending with last sc in 3rd ch of turning ch, turn.

Row 6: Ch 1, sc in first sc, *ch 3, skip next ch-3 loop, (dc, picot) in each of next 6 dc, dc in next dc, ch 3, skip next ch-3 loop, sc in next sc; rep from ** across. Fasten off.

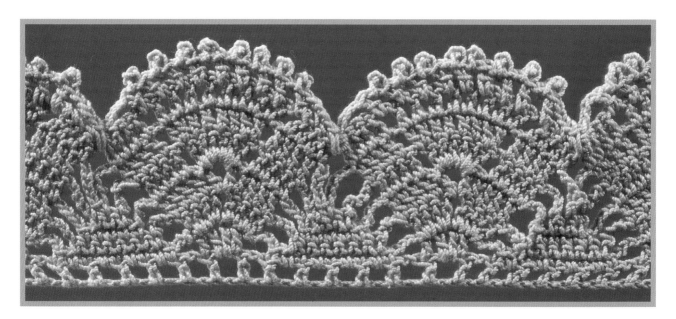

249

Picot: Ch 3, sl st in 3rd ch from hook.

Dc-trtr Cluster: Yo, insert hook in next dc, yo, draw yarn through st, yo, draw yarn through 2 loops on hook, skip next ch-5 loop, yo (4 times), insert hook in last sc, yo, draw yarn through st, (yo, draw yarn through 2 loops on hook) 4 times, yo, draw yarn through 3 loops on hook.

Chain multiples of 14 plus 4.

Row 1 (WS): Dc in 6th ch from hook, *ch 1, skip next ch, dc in next ch; rep from * across, turn.

Row 2: Ch 1, sc in first dc, (sc in next ch-1 space, sc in next dc) twice, *ch 4, skip next ch-1 space, dc in next dc, 2 dc in next ch-1 space, dc in next dc, ch 4, skip next ch-1 space, sc in next dc**, (sc in next ch-1 space, sc in next dc) 4 times; rep from * across, ending last rep at **, sc in next ch-1 space, sc in next dc, sc in ch-1 space of turning ch, sc in 4th ch of turning ch, turn.

Row 3: Ch 1, sc in each of first 4 sc, *ch 4, skip next ch-4 loop, 2 dc in each of next 2 dc, ch 1, 2 dc in each of next 2 dc, ch 4, skip next sc**, sc in each of next 7 sc; rep from * across, ending last rep at **, sc in each of last 4 sc, turn.

Row 4: Ch 1, sc in each of first 3 sc, *ch 4, skip next ch-4 loop, dc in each of next 4 dc, ch 1, (dc, ch 3, dc) in next ch-1 space, ch 1, dc in each of next 4 dc, ch 4, skip next sc**, sc in each of next 5 sc; rep from * across, ending last rep at **, sc in each of last 3 sc, turn.

Row 5: Ch 1, sc in each of first 2 sc, *ch 5, skip next ch-4 loop, dc in each of next 4 dc, ch 1, skip next ch-1 space, dc in next dc, 4 dc in next ch-3 loop, dc in next dc, ch 1, skip next ch-1 space, dc in each of next 4 dc, ch 5, skip next sc**, sc in each of next 3 sc; rep from * across, ending last rep at **, sc in each of last 2 sc, turn.

Row 6: Ch 1, sc in first sc, *ch 5, skip next ch-5 loop, dc in each of next 4 dc, ch 2, skip next ch-1 space, 2 dc in next dc, dc in each of next 4 dc, 2 dc in next dc, ch 2, skip next ch-1 space, dc in each of next 4 dc, ch 5, skip next sc, sc in next sc; rep from * across, turn.

Row 7: Ch 6 (counts as trtr), skip next ch-5 loop, *dc in each of next 4 dc, ch 2, skip next ch-2 space, dc in next dc, (ch 1, dc) in each of next 7 dc, ch 2, skip next ch-2 space, dc in each of next 3 dc**, 2-dc cluster worked across next 2 dc, skipping 2 ch-5 loops in the middle; rep from * across, ending last rep at **, work dc-trtr cluster across next dc and last sc, skipping ch-5 loop in the middle, turn.

Row 8: Ch 1, sc in first cluster, *ch 4, (dc, ch 1, picot) in each of next 8 spaces, dc in next ch-2 space, ch 4, skip next 3 dc, sc in next cluster; rep from * across, ending with last sc in 6th ch of turning ch. Fasten off.

.14.
Lace Patterns

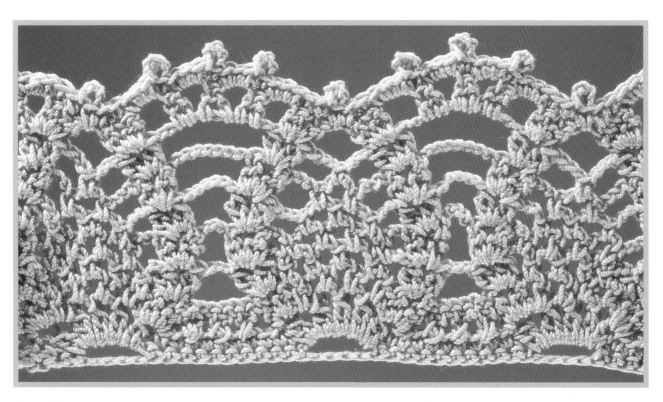

250

Picot: Ch 4, sl st in 4th ch from hook.

Puff st: (Yo, insert hook in next st, yo, draw yarn through st, yo, draw yarn through 2 loops on hook) twice in same st, yo, draw yarn through 3 loops on hook.

Chain multiples of 15 plus 2.

Row 1 (WS): Sc in 2nd ch from hook, sc in each of next 5 ch, *ch 5, skip next 4 ch, sc in each of next 11 ch; rep from * across, ending with sc in each of last 6 ch, turn.

Row 2: Ch 1, sc in each of first 5 sc, *(puff st, ch 3) 4 times in next ch-4 loop, puff st in same ch-4 loop, skip next sc, sc in each of next 9 sc; rep from * across, ending with sc in each of last 5 sc, turn.

Row 3: Ch 3 (counts as dc), skip first 3 sc, dc in next dc, working over last dc made, dc in last skipped ch, *skip next sc, (puff st, ch 1, puff st) bet last skipped sc and next puff st, ch 3, (sc, ch 3) in each of next 4 ch-3 loops, skip next puff st, (puff st, ch 1, puff st) bet last skipped puff st and next sc, skip next 2 sc**, (skip next sc, dc in next sc, working over last dc, dc in last skipped sc) 3 times; rep from * across, ending last rep at **, skip next sc, dc in next sc, working over last dc, dc in last skipped sc, dc in last sc, turn.

Row 4: Ch 3 (counts as dc), skip first 4 sts, *(puff st, ch 1, puff st) in next ch-1 space, ch 3, (sc, ch 3) in each of next 5 ch-3 loops, (puff st, ch 1, puff st) in next ch-1 space**, ch 2, skip next 8 sts; rep from * across, ending last rep at **, skip next 3 sts, dc in 3rd ch of turning ch, turn.

Row 5: Ch 4 (counts as tr), skip first 2 sts, *(puff st, ch 1, puff st) in next ch-1 space, ch 3, skip next ch-3 loop, (sc, ch 3) in each of next 4 ch-3 loops, skip next ch-3 loop, (puff st, ch 1, puff st) in next ch-1 space**, ch 4, skip next ch-2 space; rep from * across, ending last rep at **, tr in 3rd ch of turning ch, turn.

Row 6: Ch 4 (counts as dc, ch 1), skip first 2 sts, *(puff st, ch 1, puff st) in next ch-1 space, ch 3, skip next ch-3 loop, (sc, ch 3) in each of next 3 ch-3 loops, skip next ch-3 loop, (puff st, ch 1, puff st) in next ch-1 space**, ch 6, skip next ch-4 loop; rep from * across, ending last rep at **, ch 1, dc in 4th ch of turning ch, turn.

Row 7: Ch 7 (counts as tr, ch 3), skip next ch-1 space, *(puff st, ch 1, puff st) in next ch-1 space, ch 3, skip next ch-3 loop, (sc, ch 3) in each of next 2 ch-3 loops, skip next ch-3 loop, (puff st, ch 1, puff st) in next ch-1 space**, ch 8, skip next ch-6 loop; rep from * across, ending last rep at **, ch 3, tr in 3rd ch of turning ch, turn.

Row 8: Ch 8 (counts as dc, ch 5), skip next ch-3 loop, *(puff st, ch 1, puff st) in next ch-1 space, ch 3, skip next ch-3 loop, sc in next ch-3 loop, ch 3, skip next ch-3 loop, (puff st, ch 1, puff st) in next ch-1 space**, ch 10, skip next ch-8 loop; rep from * across, ending last rep at **, ch 5, dc in 4th ch of turning ch, turn.

Row 9: Ch 3 (counts as dc), skip next ch, dc in next ch, ch 3, work 2-dc cluster, working first half-closed dc in last ch holding last dc made, skip next 2 ch, work next half-closed dc in next ch, complete cluster, ch 3, *(puff st, ch 1, puff st) in next ch-1 space, skip next 2 ch-3 loops, (puff st, ch 1, puff st) in next ch-1 space, ch 3, work 2-dc cluster, working first half-closed dc in next ch, skip next 2 ch, work next half-closed dc in next ch, complete cluster, ch 3**, (work 2-dc cluster, working first half-closed dc in last ch holding last dc made, skip next 2 ch, work next half-closed dc in next ch, complete cluster, ch 3) twice; rep from * across, ending last rep at **, work 2-dc cluster, working first half-closed dc in last ch holding last dc made, skip next ch, work next half-closed dc in 3rd ch of turning ch, complete cluster, turn.

Row 10: Ch 1, sc in first cluster, (picot, 4 sc in next ch-3 loop) twice, *sc in next puff st, sc in next ch-1 space, picot, sc in next ch-1 space, sc in next puff st**, (4 sc, picot) in each of next 3 ch-3 loops, 4 sc in next ch-3 loop; rep from * across, ending last rep at **, (4 sc, picot) in each of next 2 ch-3 loops, sc in 3rd ch of turning ch. Fasten off.

251

Chain multiples of 8 plus 5.

Row 1 (WS): Sc in 7th ch from hook, *ch 5, skip next 3 ch, sc in next ch; rep from * across to within last 2 ch, ch 2, skip next ch, dc in last ch, turn.

Row 2: Ch 1, sc in first dc, (ch 5, sc) in each ch-5 loop across, ending with last sc in 4th ch of turning ch, turn.

Row 3: Ch 6 (counts as tr, ch 2), sc in next ch-5 loop, (ch 5, sc) in each ch-5 loop across to last ch-5 loop, ch 2, tr in last sc, turn.

Row 4: Ch 1, sc in first tr, (ch 11, sc) twice in next ch-2 space, *ch 2, (sc, ch 3, sc) in next ch-5 loop, ch 2**, (sc, ch 11) 4 times in next ch-5 loop, sc in same ch-5 loop; rep from * across, ending last rep at **, (sc, ch 11) twice in ch-2 space of turning, sc in 4th ch of turning ch, turn.

Row 5: Ch 7 (counts as trtr, ch 1), sc in next ch-11 loop, ch 3, sc in next ch-11 loop, *(sc, ch 3) in each of next 3 ch-11 loops, sc in next ch-11 loop; rep from * across to within last 2 loops, sc in next ch-11 loop, ch 3, sc in next ch-11 loop, ch 1, trtr in last sc, turn.

Row 6: Ch 1, sc in first trtr, (ch 3, sc) in each ch-3 loop across, ending with last sc in 6th ch of turning ch, turn.

Row 7: Ch 1, *4 sc in next ch-3 loop, (sc, hdc, 5 dc, hdc, sc) in next ch-3 loop, 4 sc in next ch-3 loop; rep from * across. Fasten off.

Bottom Edging: With RS facing, working across opposite side of foundation ch, join yarn in first ch, ch 1, 3 sc in first space, (3 sc, ch 3, 3 sc) in each ch-3 loop across, 3 sc in last ch-1 space. Fasten off.

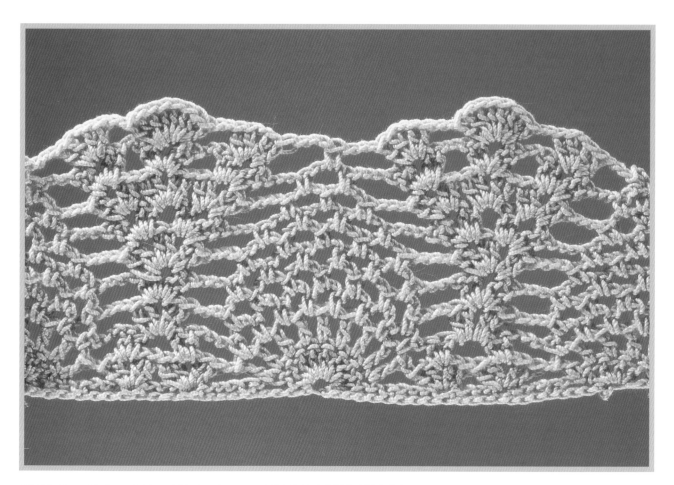

252

Chain multiples of 23 plus 4.

Row 1 (WS): 4 dc in 4th ch from hook, *ch 1, skip next 4 ch, sc in next ch, ch 3, skip next 3 ch, sc in next ch, ch 4, skip next 4 ch, sc in next ch, ch 3, skip next 3 ch, sc in next ch, ch 1, skip next 4 ch**, 9 dc in next ch; rep from * across, ending last rep at **, 5 dc in last ch, turn.

Row 2: Ch 4 (counts as dc, ch 1), skip first dc, (dc, ch 1) in each of next 4 dc, *skip next ch-1 space, (skip next ch-3 loop, [2 dc, ch 1, 2 dc] in next sc) twice, ch 1, skip

next 2 spaces**, (dc, ch 1) in each of next 9 dc; rep from * across, ending last rep at **, (dc, ch 1) in each of next 4 dc, dc in 3rd ch of turning ch, turn.

Row 3: Ch 4 (counts as dc, ch 1), (sc, ch 3) in each of next 4 ch-1 spaces, *skip next ch-1 space, 2 dc in next ch-1 space, ch 1, 2 dc in next ch-1 space, ch 3, skip next ch-1 space**, (sc, ch 3) in each of next 8 ch-1 spaces; rep from * across, ending last rep at **, (sc, ch 3) in each of next 3 ch-1 spaces, sc in next ch-1 space, ch 1, dc in last sc, turn.

Row 4: Ch 1, sc in first dc, ch 3, (sc, ch 3) in each of next 3 ch-3 loops, *skip next ch-3 loop, (2 dc, ch 1, 2 dc) in next ch-1 space, ch 3, skip next ch-3 loop**, (sc, ch 3) in each of next 7 ch-3 loops; rep from * across, ending last rep at **, (sc, ch 3) in each of next 3 ch-3 loops, sc in 3rd ch of turning ch, turn.

Row 5: Ch 4 (counts as dc, ch 1), (sc, ch 3) in each of next 3 ch-3 loops, *skip next ch-3 loop, (2 dc, ch 1, 2 dc) in next ch-1 space, ch 3, skip next ch-3 loop**, (sc, ch 3) in each of next 6 ch-3 loops; rep from * across, ending last rep at **, (sc, ch 3) in each of next 2 ch-3 loops, sc in next ch-3 loop, ch 1, dc in last sc, turn.

Row 6: Ch 1, sc in first dc, ch 3, (sc, ch 3) in each of next 2 ch-3 loops, *skip next ch-3 loop, (2 dc, ch 1, 2 dc, ch 1, 2 dc) in next ch-1 space, ch 3, skip next ch-3 loop**, (sc, ch 3) in each of next 5 ch-3 loops; rep from * across, ending last rep at **, (sc, ch 3) in each of next 2 ch-3 loops, sc in 3rd ch of turning ch, turn.

Row 7: Ch 4 (counts as dc, ch 1), (sc, ch 3) in each of next 2 ch-3 loops, *skip next ch-3 loop, (2 dc, ch 1, 2 dc) in next ch-1 space, ch 1, (2 dc, ch 1, 2 dc) in next ch-1 space, ch 3, skip next ch-3 loop**, (sc, ch 3) in each of next 4 ch-3 loops; rep from * across, ending last rep at **, sc in next ch-3 loop, ch 3, sc in next ch-3 loop, ch 1, dc in last sc, turn.

Row 8: Ch 1, sc in first dc, ch 3, sc in next ch-3 loop, *ch 3, skip next ch-3 loop, (2 dc, ch 1, 2 dc) in each of next 3 ch-1 spaces, ch 3, skip next ch-3 loop**, (sc, ch 3) in each of next 3 ch-3 loops; rep from * across, ending last rep at **, sc in next ch-3 loop, ch 3, sc in 3rd ch of turning ch, turn.

Row 9: Ch 4 (counts as dc, ch 1), sc in next ch-3 loop, *ch 3, skip next ch-3 loop, (2 dc, ch 1, 2 dc, ch 2) in each of next 2 ch-1 spaces, (2 dc, ch 1, 2 dc) in next ch-1 space, ch 3, skip next ch-3 loop**, (sc, ch 3) in each of next 2 ch-3 loops; rep from * across, ending last rep at **, sc in next ch-3 loop, ch 1, dc in last sc, turn.

Row 10: Ch 1, sc in first dc, *ch 3, skip next ch-3 loop, (2 dc, ch 1, 2 dc) in next ch-1 space, ch 2, skip next ch-2 space, 9 dc in next ch-1 space, ch 2, (2 dc, ch 1, 2 dc) in next ch-1 space, ch 3, skip next ch-3 loop, sc in next ch-3 loop; rep from * across, ending with last sc in 3rd ch of turning ch, turn. Fasten off.

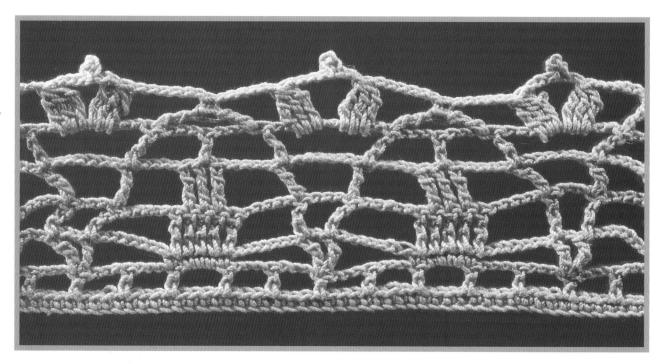

253

Picot: Ch 3, sl st in 3rd ch from hook.

Puff st: (Yo [twice], insert hook in next st, yo, draw yarn through st, [yo, draw yarn through 2 loops on hook] twice) 3 times in same st, yo, draw yarn through 4 loops on hook.

Chain multiples of 20 plus 2.

Row 1 (RS): Sc in 2nd ch from hook, sc in each ch across, turn.

Row 2: Ch 4 (counts as dc, ch 1), skip first 2 sc, dc in next sc, *ch 3, skip next 3 sc, dc in next sc; rep from * across to within last 2 sc, ch 1, skip next sc, dc in last sc, turn.

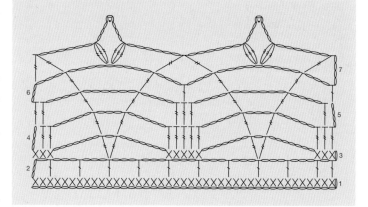

Row 3: Ch 1, sc in first dc, sc in next ch-1 space, sc in next dc, *ch 7, skip next 2 ch-3 loops, (tr, ch 1, tr) in next dc, ch 7, skip next 2 ch-3 loops, sc in next dc**, 3 sc in next ch-3 loop, sc in next dc; rep from * across, ending last rep at **, sc in next ch-1 space of turning ch, sc in 3rd ch of turning ch, turn.

Row 4: Ch 4 (counts as tr), skip first sc, tr in each of next 2 sc, *ch 5, skip next ch-7 loop, tr in next tr, ch 3, skip next ch-1 space, tr in next tr, ch 5, skip next ch-7 loop**, tr in each of next 5 sc; rep from * across, ending last rep at **, tr in each of last 3 sc, turn.

Row 5: Ch 4 (counts as tr), skip first tr, tr in next tr, *ch 4, skip next ch-5 loop, tr in next tr, ch 6, skip next ch-3 loop, tr in next tr, ch 4, skip next tr**, tr in each of next 3 tr; rep from * across, ending last rep at **, tr in next tr, tr in 4th ch of turning ch, turn.

Row 6: Ch 6 (counts as dc, ch 3), *skip next ch-4 loop, tr in next tr, ch 9, skip next ch-6 loop, tr in next tr, ch 3, skip next tr**, tr in next tr, ch 3, skip next ch-4 loop; rep from ** across, ending last rep at **, dc in 4th ch of turning ch, turn.

Row 7: Ch 4 (counts as tr), skip next ch-3 loop, tr in next tr, *ch 6, skip next 4 ch, (puff st, ch 3, picot, ch 3, puff st) in next ch, ch 6, skip next 4 ch**, work 2-tr cluster across next 2 tr, skipping 2 ch-3 loops bet; rep from * across, ending last rep at **, work 2-tr cluster, working first half-closed tr in next tr, skip next 3 ch, work next half-closed tr in 3rd ch of turning ch, complete cluster. Fasten off.

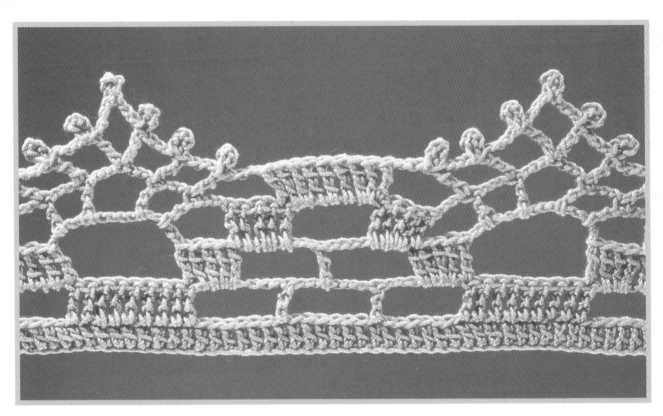

254

Picot: Ch 4, sl st in 4th ch from hook.

Chain multiples of 29 plus 4.

Row 1 (RS): Dc in 4th ch from hook, dc in each ch across, turn.

Row 2: Ch 7 (counts as tr, ch 3), skip first 4 dc, tr in next dc, ch 7, *skip next 6 dc, tr in each of next 9 dc**, (ch 7, skip next 6 dc, tr in next dc) twice, ch 7; rep from * across, ending last rep at **, ch 7, skip next 6 dc, tr in next dc, ch 3, skip next 3 dc, tr in 3rd ch of turning ch, turn.

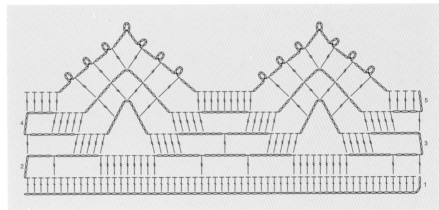

Row 3: Ch 11 (counts as tr, ch 7), skip next ch-3 loop, *4 tr in next ch-7 loop, tr in next tr, ch 15, skip next 7 tr, tr in next tr, 4 tr in next ch-7 loop, ch 7**, tr in next ch-7 loop, ch 7; rep from * across, ending last rep at **, tr in 4th ch of turning ch, turn.

Row 4: Ch 7 (counts as tr, ch 3), *4 tr in next ch-7 loop, tr in next tr, ch 3, skip next 3 ch, tr in next ch, ch 3, skip next 3 ch, (tr, ch 7, tr) in next ch, ch 3, skip next 3 ch, tr in next ch, ch 3, skip next 4 tr, tr in next tr, 4 tr in next ch-7 loop**, ch 7; rep from * across, ending last rep at **, ch 3, tr in 4th ch of turning ch, turn.

Row 5: Ch 4 (counts as tr), 3 tr in next ch-3 loop, *tr in next tr, ch 3, skip next ch-3 loop, (tr, picot, ch 3) in each of next 2 tr, (tr, picot, ch 3, picot, ch 3, tr) in center ch of next ch-7 loop, picot, ch 3, (tr, picot, ch 3) in each of next 2 tr, skip next 4 tr, tr in next tr**, 7 tr in next ch-7 loop; rep from * across, ending last rep at **, 3 tr in ch-3 loop of turning ch, tr in 4th ch of turning ch. Fasten off.

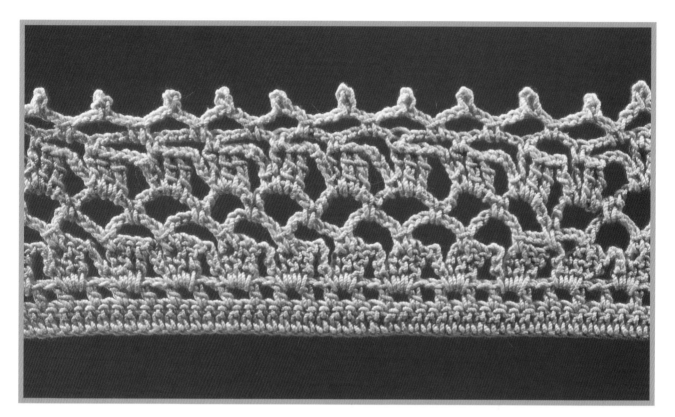

255

Picot: Ch 3, sl st in 3rd ch from hook.

Chain multiples of 4 plus 3.

Row 1 (WS): Dc in 4th ch from hook, dc in each ch across, turn.

Row 2: Ch 4 (counts as dc, ch 1), skip first 2 dc, *dc in next dc, ch 1, skip next dc; rep from * across to turning ch, dc in 3rd ch of turning ch, turn.

Row 3: Ch 1, *(sc, ch 4, 2 tr) in next ch-1 space, ch 5, skip next ch-1 space; rep from * across, sc in 3rd ch of turning ch, turn.

Row 4: Ch 12 (counts as dtr, ch 7), skip next ch-5 loop, sc in next ch-4 loop, *ch 7, skip next ch-5 loop, sc in next ch-4 loop; rep from * across, turn.

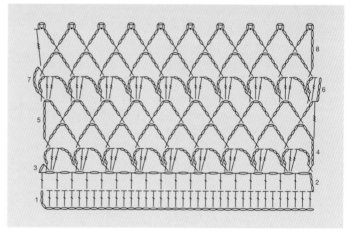

Row 5: Ch 9 (counts as dtr, ch 4), sc in next ch-7 loop, (ch 7, sc) in each ch-7 loop across to last ch-7 loop of turning ch, ch 3, dtr in 5th ch of turning ch, turn.

Row 6: Ch 4 (counts as tr), (tr, ch 4, sc, ch 5) in each loop across, turn.

Row 7: Sc in next ch-4 loop, *ch 7, skip next ch-5 loop, sc in next ch-4 loop; rep from * across, turn.

Row 8: Ch 5 (counts as dtr), picot, ch 3, sc in next ch-5 loop, (ch 3, picot, ch 3, sc) in each ch-5 loop across to last ch-5 loop, ch 3, picot, dtr in last sc. Fasten off.

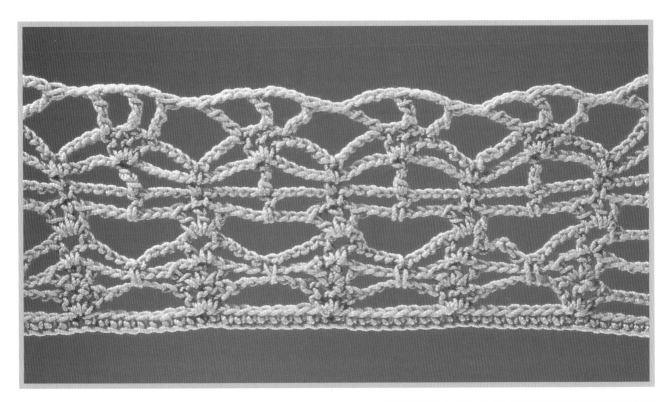

256

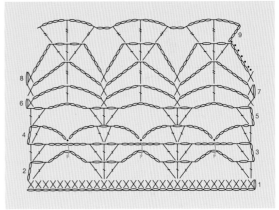

Chain multiples of 10 plus 2.

Row 1 (RS): Sc in 2nd ch from hook, sc in each ch across, turn.

Row 2: Ch 4 (counts as dc, ch 1), dc in first sc, *ch 7, skip next 9 sc**, (dc, ch 1, dc, ch 1, dc) in next sc; rep from * across, ending last rep at **, (dc, ch 1, dc) in last sc, turn.

Row 3: Ch 4 (counts as dc, ch 1), dc in first dc, *ch 6, skip next ch-7 loop, skip next ch-1 space**, (dc, ch 1, dc, ch 1, dc) in next dc; rep from * across, ending last rep at **, (dc, ch 1, dc) in 3rd ch of turning ch, turn.

Row 4: Ch 4 (counts as dc, ch 1), dc in first dc, *ch 5, sl st over next 2 loops, ch 5, skip next ch-1 space, (dc, ch 1 dc) in next dc; rep from * across, ending with last (dc, ch 1, dc) in 3rd ch of turning ch, turn.

Row 5: Ch 4 (counts as dc, ch 1), dc in first dc, *ch 7, skip next 2 ch-5 loops**, (dc, ch 1, dc, ch 1, dc) in next ch-1 space; rep from * across, ending last rep at **, (dc, ch 1, dc) in 3rd ch of turning ch, turn.

Row 6: Ch 1, sc in first dc, *ch 5, skip next ch-1 space, dc in next ch-7 loop, ch 5, skip next ch-1 space, sc in next dc; rep from ** across, ending with last sc in 3rd ch of turning ch, turn.

Row 7: Ch 1, sc in first sc, *ch 6, skip next ch-5 loop, tr in next dc, ch 6, skip next ch-5 loop, sc in next sc; rep from * across, turn.

Row 8: Ch 1, sc in first sc, *ch 5, skip next ch-6 loop, (dc, ch 1, dc, ch 1, dc) in next tr, ch 5, skip next ch-6 loop, sc in next sc; rep from * across, turn.

Row 9: Sl st to first dc, ch 8 (counts as tr, ch 4), skip next ch-1 space, *tr in next dc, ch 4, skip next ch-1 space, tr in next dc**, ch 2, skip next 2 ch-5 loops, tr in next dc, skip next ch-1 space; rep from * across, ending last rep at **. Fasten off.

257

Chain multiples of 7 plus 4.

Row 1 (RS): Tr in 5th ch from hook, tr in each ch across, turn.

Row 2: Ch 9 (counts as dc, ch 6), skip first 7 tr, *tr in next tr, ch 6, skip next 6 tr; rep from * across to turning ch, tr in 4th ch of turning ch, turn.

Row 3: Ch 4 (counts as tr), (4 tr, ch 2, 4 tr) in each ch-7 loop across, turn.

Row 4: Ch 6 (counts as dc, ch 3), *(dc, ch 15) 3 times in next ch-2 space, dc in same ch-2 space, ch 3, skip next 4 tr**, dc bet last skipped and next tr, ch 3; rep from * across, ending last rep at **, dc in 4th ch of turning ch, turn.

Row 5: Ch 11, skip next ch-3 loop, *3 dc in next ch-15 loop, (3 tr, ch 2, 3 tr) in next ch-15 loop, 3 dc in next ch-15 loop**, skip next 2 ch-3 loops; rep from * across, ending last rep at **, turn.

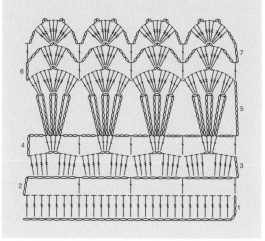

Row 6: Ch 6 (counts as dc, ch 3), *(3 tr, ch 2, 3 tr) in next ch-2 space, ch 3, skip next 5 sts, dc bet last skipped and next dc**, ch 3; rep from * across, ending last rep at ** with last dc in 11th ch of turning ch, turn.

Row 7: Ch 6 (counts as dc, ch 3), skip next ch-3 loop, *(3 tr, ch 2, 3 tr, ch 2, 3 tr) in next ch-2 space, ch 3, skip next ch-3 loop**, dc in next dc, ch 3, skip next ch-3 loop; rep from * across, ending last rep at **, dc in 3rd ch of turning ch. Fasten off.

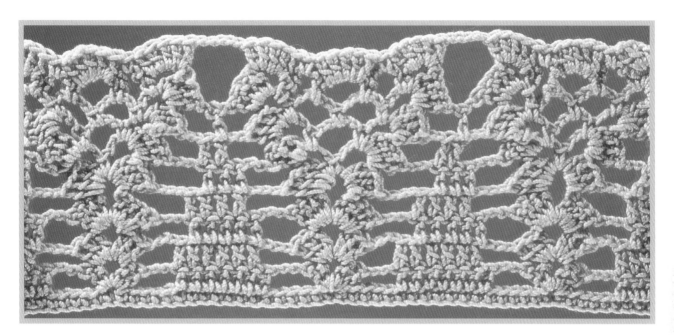

258

Chain multiples of 18 plus 2.

Row 1 (RS): Sc in 2nd ch from hook, sc in each ch across, turn.

Row 2: Ch 3 (counts as dc), skip first sc, dc in each of next 3 sc, *ch 3, skip next 5 sc, (2 dc, ch 2, 2 dc) in next sc, ch 3, skip next 5 sc**, dc in each of next 7 sc; rep from * across, ending last rep at **, dc in each of last 4 sc, turn.

Row 3: Ch 3 (counts as dc), skip first dc, dc in each of next 3 dc, *ch 3, skip next ch-3 loop, (3 dc, ch 3, 3 dc) in next ch-2 space, ch 3, skip next ch-3 loop, skip next dc**, dc in each of next 6 dc; rep from * across, ending last rep at **, dc in each of next 2 dc, dc in 3rd ch of turning ch, turn.

Row 4: Ch 3 (counts as dc), skip first dc, dc in each of next 2 dc, *ch 3, skip next ch-3 loop, (4 dc, ch 5, 4 dc) in next ch-3 loop, ch 3, skip next ch-3 loop, skip next dc**, dc in each of next 5 dc; rep from * across, ending last rep at **, dc in each of next 2 dc, dc in 3rd ch of turning ch, turn.

Row 5: Ch 3 (counts as dc), skip first dc, dc in each of next 2 dc, *ch 3, skip next ch-3 loop, (4 dc, ch 5, sc, ch 5, 4 dc) in next ch-5 loop, ch 3, skip next ch-3 loop, skip next dc**, dc in each of next 4 dc; rep from * across, ending last rep at **, dc in next dc, dc in 3rd ch of turning ch, turn.

Row 6: Ch 3 (counts as dc), skip first dc, dc in next dc, *ch 3, skip next ch-3 loop, (4 dc, ch 5, sc) in next ch-5 loop, ch 5, (sc, ch 5, 4 dc) in next ch-5 loop, ch 3, skip next ch-3 loop, skip next dc**, dc in each of next 3 dc; rep from * across, ending last rep at **, dc in next dc, dc in 3rd ch of turning ch, turn.

Row 7: Ch 3 (counts as dc), skip first dc, dc in next dc, *ch 2, skip next ch-3 loop, (4 dc, ch 5, sc) in next ch-5 loop, ch 5, sc in next ch-5 loop, ch 5, (sc, ch 5, 4 dc) in next ch-5 loop, ch 2, skip next ch-3 loop, skip next dc**, dc in each of next 2 dc; rep from * across, ending last rep at **, dc in 3rd ch of turning ch, turn.

Row 8: Ch 4 (counts as dc, ch 1), skip next ch-2 space, (4 dc, ch 5, sc) in next ch-5 loop, (ch 5, sc) in each of next 2 ch-5 loops, ch 5, (sc, ch 5, 4 dc) in next ch-5 loop, ch 1, skip next ch-2 space, skip next dc, dc in next dc; rep from * across, ending with last dc in 3rd ch of turning ch, turn.

Row 9: Ch 5 (counts as tr, ch 1), skip next ch-1 space, (5 dc in next ch-5 loop, sc in next ch-5 loop) twice, 5 dc in next ch-5 loop**, ch 5, skip next 2 ch-1 spaces; rep from * across, ending last rep at **, ch 1, tr in 3rd ch of turning ch. Fasten off.

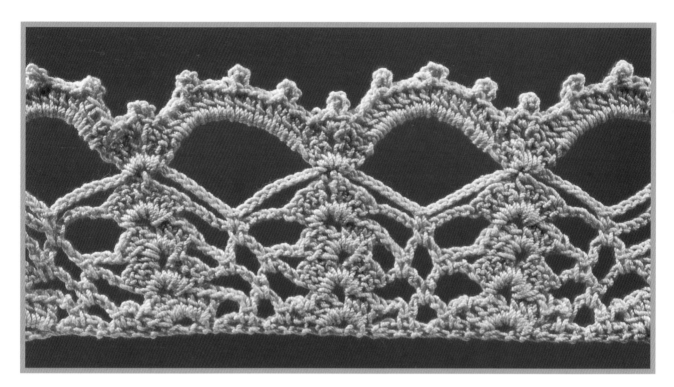

259

Picot: Ch 4, sl st in 4th ch from hook.

No foundation ch needed.

Row 1 (WS): *Ch 4, tr in 4th ch from hook; rep from * a multiple of 3 times for desired length, turn.

Row 2: Ch 3 (counts as dc), working across ch side of Row 1, (4 dc, ch 3, 4 dc) in next ch-3 loop, *ch 3, sc in next ch-3 loop, ch 5, sc in next ch-3 loop, ch 3, (4 dc, ch 3, 4 dc) in next ch-3 loop; rep from * across to last ch-3 loop, dc in next ch, turn.

Row 3: Ch 3 (counts as dc), (4 dc, ch 3, 4 dc) in next ch-3 loop, *ch 5, skip next ch-3 loop, sc in next ch-5 loop, ch 5, skip next ch-3 loop, (4 dc, ch 3, 4 dc) in next ch-3 loop; rep from * across to last ch-3 loop, skip next 4 dc, dc in 3rd ch of turning ch, turn.

Row 4: Ch 3 (counts as dc), (4 dc, ch 3, 4 dc) in next ch-3 loop, *ch 3, sc in next ch-5 loop, ch 5, sc in next ch-5 loop, ch 3, (4 dc, ch 3, 4 dc) in next ch-3 loop; rep from * across to last ch-3 loop, dc in 3rd ch of turning ch, turn.

Row 5: Rep Row 3.

Row 6: Ch 1, sc in first dc, *ch 4, sc in next ch-3 loop, *ch 9, skip next ch-5 loop, sc in next sc, ch 9, skip next ch-5 loop, sc in next ch-3 loop; rep from * across to last ch-3 loop, ch 4, sc in 3rd ch of turning ch, turn.

Row 7: Ch 3 (counts as dc), skip next ch-4 loop, (4 dc, ch 3, 4 dc) in next sc, *ch 12, skip next 2 ch-9 loops, (4 dc, ch 3, 4 dc) in next sc; rep from * across to within last ch-4 loop, skip next ch-4 loop, dc in last sc, turn.

Row 8: Ch 4 (counts as hdc, ch 2), (sc, picot, sc) in next ch-3 loop, *(4 dc, picot) 3 times in next ch-12 loop, 4 dc in same ch-12 loop, (sc, picot, sc) in next ch-3 loop; rep from * across to last ch-3 loop, ch 2, skip next 4 dc, hdc in 3rd ch of turning ch. Fasten off.

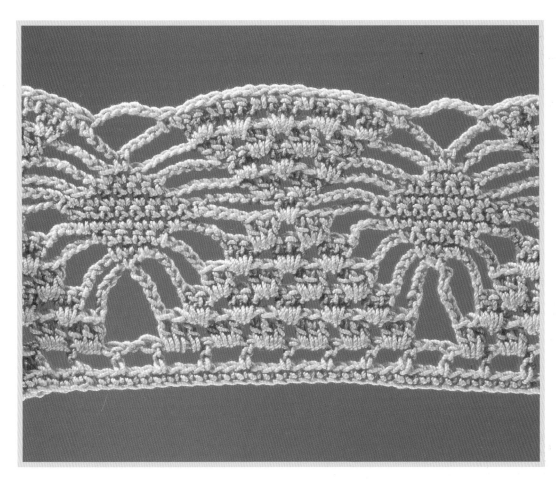

260

Chain multiples of 21 plus 2.

Row 1 (RS): Sc in 2nd ch from hook, sc in each ch across, turn.

Row 2: Ch 5 (counts as dc, ch 2), skip first 3 sc, dc in next sc, *ch 2, skip next 2 sc, dc in next sc; rep from * across, turn.

Row 3: Ch 3 (counts as dc), 3 dc in each of next 3 ch-2 spaces, *ch 13, skip next ch-2 space**, 3 dc in each of next 6 ch-2 spaces; rep from * across, ending last rep at **, 3 dc in each of next 3 ch-2 spaces, dc in 3rd ch of turning ch, turn.

Row 4: Ch 3 (counts as dc), dc in first dc, (skip next 3 dc, 3 dc bet last skipped and next dc) twice, *ch 6, sc in next ch-13 loop, ch 6**, (skip next 3 dc, 3 dc bet last skipped and next dc) 5 times; rep from * across, ending last rep at **, (skip next 3 dc, 3 dc bet last skipped and next dc) twice, skip next 3 dc, dc in 3rd ch of turning ch, turn.

Row 5: Ch 3 (counts as dc), skip first 2 dc, (3 dc bet last skipped and next dc, skip next 3 dc) twice, *ch 6, sc in next ch-6 loop, sc in next sc, sc in next ch-6 loop, ch 6**, (skip next 3 dc, 3 dc bet last skipped and next dc) 4 times; rep from *

across, ending last rep at **, (skip next 3 dc, 3 dc bet last skipped and next dc) twice, skip next dc, dc in 3rd ch of turning ch, turn.

Row 6: Ch 3 (counts as dc), dc in first dc, skip next 3 dc, 3 dc bet last skipped and next dc, *ch 6, sc in next ch-6 loop, sc in each of next 3 sc, sc in next ch-6 loop, ch 6**, (skip next 3 dc, 3 dc bet last skipped and next dc) 3 times; rep from * across, ending last rep at **, skip next 3 dc, 3 dc bet last skipped and next dc, skip next 3 dc, dc in 3rd ch of turning ch, turn.

Row 7: Ch 3 (counts as dc), skip first 2 dc, 3 dc bet last skipped and next dc, *ch 6, sc in next ch-6 loop, sc in each of next 5 sc, sc in next ch-6 loop, ch 6**, (skip next 3 dc, 3 dc bet last skipped and next dc) twice; rep from * across, ending last rep at **, skip next 3 dc, 3 dc bet last skipped and next dc, skip next dc, dc in 3rd ch of turning ch, turn.

Row 8: Ch 3 (counts as dc), dc in first dc, *ch 6, sc in next ch-6 loop, sc in each of next 7 sc, sc in next ch-6 loop, ch 6**, skip next 3 dc, 3 dc bet last skipped and next dc; rep from * across, ending last rep at **, skip next 3 dc, 2 dc in 3rd ch of turning ch, turn.

Row 9: Ch 3, skip first dc, 3 dc in next dc, *ch 6, skip next sc, sc in each of next 7 sc, ch 6, skip next ch-6 loop, 3 dc in next dc**, skip next dc; rep from * across, ending last rep at **, dc in 3rd ch of turning ch, turn.

Row 10: Ch 3 (counts as dc), dc in first dc, *skip next 2 dc, 3 dc in next dc, ch 6, skip next sc, sc in each of next 5 sc, ch 6, skip next ch-6 loop, 3 dc in next dc**, skip next 3 dc, 3 dc bet last skipped and next dc; rep from * across, ending last rep at **, skip next 2 dc, dc in 3rd ch of turning ch, turn.

Row 11: Ch 3, skip first 2 dc, 3 dc bet last skipped and next dc, skip next 2 dc, *3 dc in next dc, ch 6, skip next sc, sc in each of next 3 sc, ch 6, skip next ch-6 loop, 3 dc in next dc, skip next 2 dc, 3 dc bet last skipped and next dc**, skip next 3 dc, 3 dc bet last skipped and next dc, skip next 2 dc; rep from * across, ending last rep at **, skip next dc, dc in 3rd ch of turning ch, turn.

Row 12: Ch 3 (counts as dc), dc in first dc, skip next 3 dc, 3 dc bet last skipped and next dc, *skip next 2 dc, 3 dc in next dc, ch 6, skip next sc, sc in next sc, ch 6, skip next ch-6 loop, 3 dc in next dc, skip next 2 dc, 3 dc bet last skipped and next dc**, (skip next 3 dc, 3 dc bet last skipped and next dc) twice; rep from * across, ending last rep at **, skip next 3 dc, dc in 3rd ch of turning ch, turn.

Row 13: Ch 1, sc in first dc, ch 2, skip next dc, sc bet last skipped and next dc, ch 4, skip next 3 dc, sc bet last skipped and next dc, *ch 4, skip next 2 dc, sc in next dc, ch 7, skip next 2 ch-6 loops, sc in next dc, ch 4, skip next 2 dc, sc bet last skipped and next dc**, (ch 4, skip next 3 dc, sc bet last skipped and next dc) 3 times; rep from * across, ending last rep at **, ch 4, skip next 3 dc, sc bet last skipped and next dc, ch 2, skip next dc, sc in 3rd ch of turning ch. Fasten off.

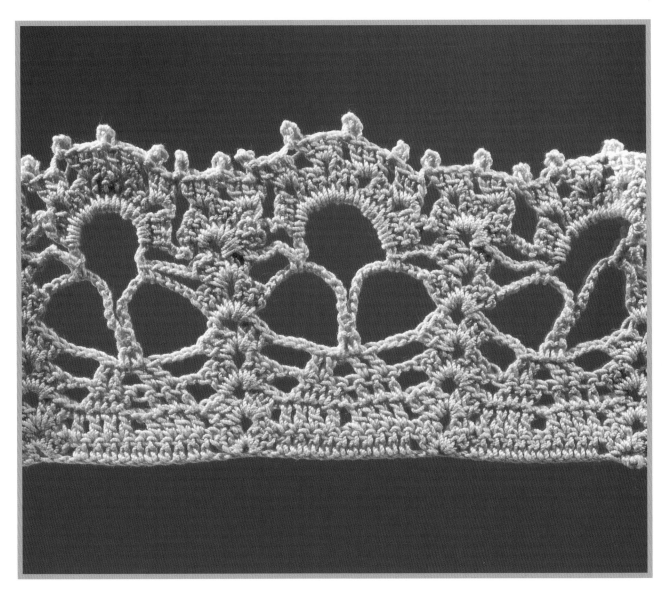

261

Picot: Ch 4, sl st in 4th ch from hook.

Chain multiples of 15 plus 9.

Row 1 (WS): (3 dc, ch 3, 3 dc) in 6th ch from hook, *skip next 2 ch, dc in each of next 10 ch, skip next 2 ch, (3 dc, ch 3, 3 dc) in next ch; rep from * across to within last 3 ch, skip next 2 ch, dc in last ch, turn.

Row 2: Ch 3 (counts as dc), (3 dc, ch 3, 3 dc) in next ch-3 loop, *skip next 3 dc, dc in each of next 4 dc, ch 1, skip next 2 dc, dc in each of next 4 dc, (3 dc, ch 3, 3 dc) in next ch-3 loop; rep from * across to last ch-3 loop, skip next 3 dc, dc in 5th ch of turning ch, turn.

Row 3: Ch 3 (counts as dc), (3 dc, ch 3, 3 dc) in

next ch-3 loop, *ch 2, skip next 4 dc, dc in each of next 3 dc, skip next ch-1 space, dc in each of next 3 dc, ch 2, (3 dc, ch 3, 3 dc) in next ch-3 loop; rep from * across to last ch-3 loop, skip next 3 dc, dc in 3rd ch of turning ch, turn.

Row 4: Ch 3 (counts as dc), (3 dc, ch 3, 3 dc) in next ch-3 loop, *ch 3, skip next ch-2 space, dc in each of next 2 dc, skip next 2 dc, dc in each of next 2 dc, ch 3, skip next ch-2 space, (3 dc, ch 3, 3 dc) in next ch-3 loop; rep from * across to last ch-3 loop, skip next 3 dc, dc in 3rd ch of turning ch, turn.

Row 5: Ch 3 (counts as dc), (3 dc, ch 3, 3 dc) in next ch-3 loop, *ch 12, skip next ch-3 loop, skip next dc, 2-dc cluster worked across next 2 dc, ch 12, skip next ch-3 loop, (3 dc, ch 3, 3 dc) in next ch-3 loop; rep from * across to last ch-3 loop, skip next 3 dc, dc in 3rd ch of turning ch, turn.

Row 6: Ch 3 (counts as dc), (3 dc, ch 3, 3 dc) in next ch-3 loop, *ch 5, sc in next ch-12 loop, ch 13, sc in next ch-12 loop, ch 5, (3 dc, ch 3, 3 dc) in next ch-3 loop; rep from * across to last ch-3 loop, skip next 3 dc, dc in 3rd ch of turning ch, turn.

Row 7: Ch 3 (counts as dc), (3 dc, ch 3, 3 dc, ch 3, 3 dc) in next ch-3 loop, *ch 5, (3 dc, ch 3) 5 times in next ch-13 loop, ch 2 more, skip next ch-5 loop, (3 dc, ch 3, 3 dc, ch 3, 3 dc) in next ch-3 loop; rep from * across to last ch-3 loop, skip next 3 dc, dc in 3rd ch of turning ch, turn.

Row 8: Ch 3 (counts as dc), *(3 dc, picot) in each of next 2 ch-3 loops, skip next ch-5 loop, (3 dc, picot) in each of next 4 ch-3 loops, skip next ch-5 loop; rep from * across to within last 2 ch-3 loop, 3 dc in next ch-3 loop, picot, 3 dc in next ch-3 loop, skip next 3 dc, dc in 3rd ch of turning ch. Fasten off.

.15.
Bobbles

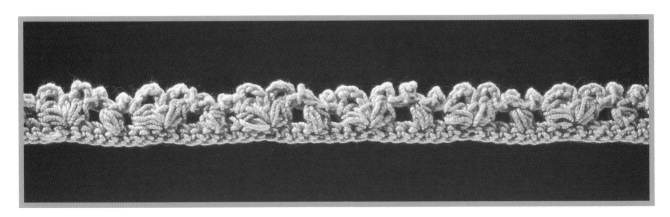

262

Picot: Ch 3, sl st in 3rd ch from hook.

Bobble: (Yo, insert hook in next st, yo, draw yarn through st and up to level of work) 3 times in same st, yo, draw yarn through 7 loops on hook.

Chain multiples of 8 plus 2.

Row 1 (WS): Sc in 2nd ch from hook, sc in each ch across, turn.

Row 2: Ch 5, bobble in first sc, *picot, skip next 3 sc, bobble in next sc, picot, skip next 3 sc**, (bobble, ch 5, sl st, ch 5, bobble) in next sc; rep from * across, ending last rep at **, (bobble, ch 5, sl st) in last sc. Fasten off.

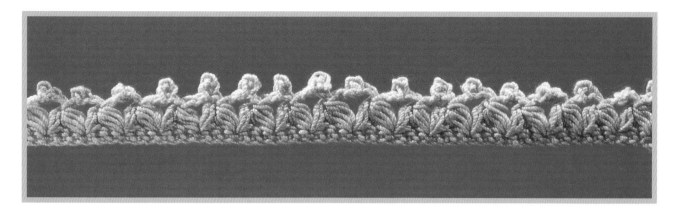

263

Picot: Ch 3, sl st in 3rd ch from hook.

Bobble: (Yo, insert hook in next st, yo, draw yarn through st and up to level of work) 3 times in same sc, skip next 2 sc, (yo, insert hook in next st, yo, draw yarn through st and up to level of work) 3 times in next sc, yo, draw yarn through 13 loops on hook.

Chain multiples of 3 plus 2.

Row 1 (WS): Sc in 2nd ch from hook, sc in each ch across, turn.

Row 2: Ch 4 (counts as dc, ch 1), starting in first sc, work bobble across next 4 sc, *ch 2, picot, ch 1, starting in same sc holding last bobble, work bobble across next 4 sc; rep from * across to last sc, ch 1, dc in last sc holding last bobble. Fasten off.

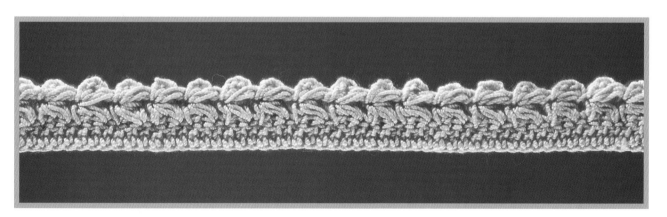

264

Bobble: (Yo, insert hook in 4th ch from hook, yo, draw up a loop to level of work) twice, (yo, insert hook in next dc, yo, draw up a loop to level of work) twice, skip next dc, (yo, insert hook in next dc, yo, draw up a loop to level of work) twice, yo, draw yarn through 13 loops on hook.

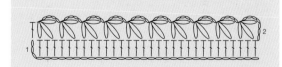

Chain multiples of 3.

Row 1 (WS): Dc in 4th ch from hook, dc in each ch across, turn.

Row 2: Ch 7 (counts as dc, ch 4), bobble worked across (4th ch from hook, first dc, skip next dc, and next dc), *ch 4, bobble; rep from * across to turning ch, dc in 3rd ch of turning ch. Fasten off.

265

Bobble: (Yo, insert hook in next st, yo, draw yarn through st and up to level of work) twice in same st, yo, draw yarn through 5 loops on hook.

Chain multiples of 8.

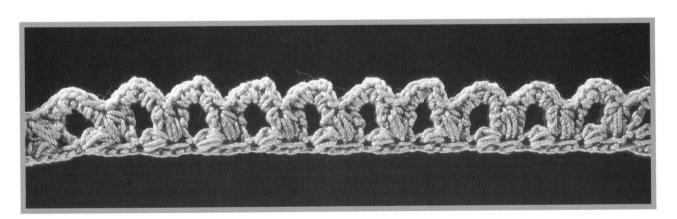

Row 1 (RS): Sc in 12th ch from hook, *ch 4, skip next 3 ch, tr in next ch**, ch 4, skip next 3 ch, sc in next ch; rep from * across, ending last rep at **, turn.

Row 2: Ch 1, sc in first tr, *ch 3, skip next ch-4 loop, bobble in next sc, ch 3, skip next ch-4 loop, sc in next tr; rep from * across, ending with last sc in 7th ch of turning ch, turn.

Row 3: Ch 1, sc in first sc, *ch 3, sc in next ch-3 loop, ch 6, sc in next ch-3 loop, ch 3, sc in next sc; rep from * across. Fasten off.

266

Bobble: (Yo, insert hook in next st, yo, draw yarn through st and up to level of work) 3 times in same st, yo, draw yarn through 7 loops on hook.

Chain multiples of 5 plus 2.

Row 1 (WS): Sc in 2nd ch from hook, *ch 9, bobble in side of last sc made, skip next 4 ch, sc in next ch; rep from * across, turn.

Row 2: Ch 4 (counts as dc), *(2 sc, ch 3, 2 sc) in next ch-9 loop**, bobble in next sc; rep from * across, ending last rep at **, dc in last sc. Fasten off.

267

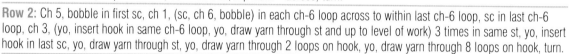

Bobble: *(Yo, insert hook in next st, yo, draw yarn through st and up to level of work) 3 times in same st, yo, draw yarn through 7 loops on hook.*

Chain multiples of 4 plus 2.

Row 1 (RS): Sc in 2nd ch from hook, *ch 6, bobble in side of last sc made, skip next 3 ch, sc in next ch; rep from * across, turn.

Row 2: Ch 5, bobble in first sc, ch 1, (sc, ch 6, bobble) in each ch-6 loop across to within last ch-6 loop, sc in last ch-6 loop, ch 3, (yo, insert hook in same ch-6 loop, yo, draw yarn through st and up to level of work) 3 times in same st, yo, insert hook in last sc, yo, draw yarn through st, yo, draw yarn through 2 loops on hook, yo, draw yarn through 8 loops on hook, turn.

Row 3: Ch 1, sc in first st, ch 6, bobble in next ch-3 loop, (sc, ch 6, bobble) in each ch-6 loop across to last ch-6 loop, sc in 4th ch of turning ch. Fasten off.

268

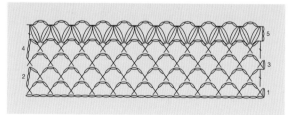

3-looped Bobble: *(Yo, insert hook in next st, yo, draw yarn through st and up to level of work) 3 times in same sc, yo, draw yarn through 7 loops on hook.*

6-looped Bobble: *(Yo, insert hook in next st, yo, draw yarn through st and up to level of work) 3 times in same sc, skip next ch-3 loop, (yo, insert hook in next st, yo, draw yarn through st and up to level of work) 3 times in next sc, yo, draw yarn through 13 loops on hook.*

Chain multiples of 3 plus 2.

Row 1 (RS): Sc in 2nd ch from hook, *ch 3, skip next 2 ch, sc in next ch; rep from * across, turn.

Row 2: Ch 4 (counts as dc, ch 1), sc in next ch-3 loop, (ch 3, sc) in each ch-3 loop across to last ch-3 loop, ch 1, dc in last sc, turn.

Row 3: Ch 1, sc in first dc, (ch 3, sc) in each ch-3 loop across, ending with last sc in 3rd ch of turning ch, turn.

Row 4: Rep Row 2.

Row 5: Ch 3 (counts as dc), skip next ch-1 space, 3-looped bobble in next sc, ch 3, *starting in last sc holding last bobble, work 6-looped bobble across next 2 sc, ch 3; rep from * across to last sc, (yo, insert hook in same sc holding last bobble, yo, draw yarn through st and up to level of work) 3 times in same sc, yo, insert hook in 3rd ch of turning ch, yo, draw yarn through st, yo, draw yarn through 2 loops on hook, yo, draw yarn through 8 loops on hook. Fasten off.

269

Bobble: (Yo, insert hook in next st, yo, draw yarn through st and up to level of work) 3 times in same st, yo, draw yarn through 7 loops on hook.

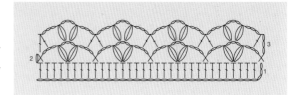

Chain multiples of 8 plus 3.

Row 1 (RS): Dc in 4th ch from hook, dc in each ch across, turn.

Row 2: Ch 1, sc in first dc, *ch 3, skip next 3 dc, (bobble, ch 3, bobble) in next dc, ch 3, skip next 3 dc, sc in next dc; rep from * across, ending with last sc in 3rd ch of turning ch, turn.

Row 3: Ch 3 (counts as dc), dc in next ch-3 loop, *ch 3, (bobble, ch 3, bobble) in next ch-3 loop, ch 3**, 2-dc cluster worked across next 2 ch-3 loops; rep from * across, ending last rep at **, 2-dc cluster worked across last ch-3 loop and last sc. Fasten off.

270

Picot: Ch 4, sl st in 4th ch from hook.

Bobble: (Yo, insert hook in next st, yo, draw yarn through st and up to level of work) 3 times in same st, yo, draw yarn through 7 loops on hook.

Chain multiples of 8 plus 3.

Row 1 (WS): Dc in 4th ch from hook, dc in each ch across, turn.

Row 2: Ch 1, sc in first dc, *ch 1, skip next 3 dc, (bobble, ch 2, bobble, ch 1, picot, ch 1, picot, ch 1, sl st in base of first picot, bobble, ch 2, bobble) in next dc, ch 1, skip next 3 dc, sc in next dc; rep from * across, ending with last sc in 3rd ch of turning ch. Fasten off.

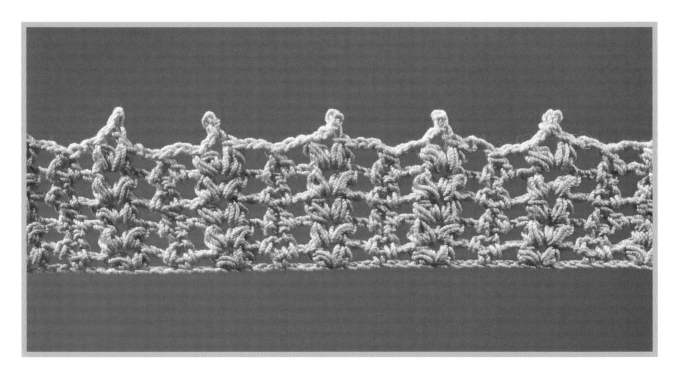

271

Bobble: (Yo, insert hook in next st, yo, draw yarn through st and up to level of work) 3 times in same st, yo, draw yarn through 7 loops on hook.

Picot: Ch 4, sl st in 4th ch from hook.

Chain multiples of 10 plus 2.

Row 1 (RS): Sc in 2nd ch from hook, *ch 2, skip next 4 ch, (bobble, ch 3, bobble) in next ch, ch 3, skip next 4 ch, sc in next ch; rep from * across, turn.

Row 2: Ch 3 (counts as dc), dc in next ch-3 loop, *ch 2, (bobble, ch 3, bobble) in next ch-3 loop, ch 3**, 2-dc cluster worked across next 2 spaces; rep from * across, ending last rep at **, 2-dc cluster, working first half-closed dc in next ch-2 space, work 2nd half-closed dc in last sc, turn.

Rows 3-4: Rep Row 2.

Row 5: Ch 3 (counts as dc), dc in next ch-3 loop, *ch 2, (bobble, ch 1, picot, ch 1, bobble) in next ch-3 loop, ch 3**, 2-dc cluster worked across next 2 spaces; rep from * across, ending last rep at **, 2-dc cluster, working first half-closed dc in next ch-2 space, work 2nd half-closed dc in last sc. Fasten off.

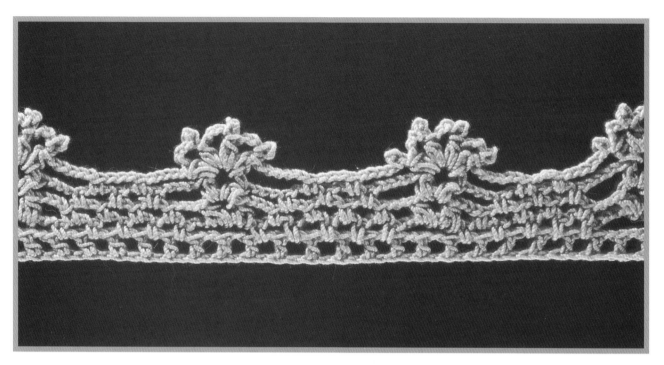

272

Picot: Ch 3, sl st in 3rd ch from hook.

Bobble: (Yo, insert hook in next st, yo, draw yarn through st and up to level of work) twice in same st, yo, draw yarn through 5 loops on hook.

Chain multiples of 14 plus 3.

Row 1 (RS): Dc in 4th ch from hook, *ch 1, skip next ch, dc in next ch; rep from * across to within last ch, dc in last ch, turn.

Row 2: Ch 1, sc in first dc, (ch 3, sc) in each of next 2 ch-1 spaces, *ch 7, skip next 2 ch-1 spaces, sc in next ch-1 space**, (ch 3, sc) in each of next 4 ch-1 spaces; rep from * across, ending last rep at **, ch 3, sc in next ch-1 space, ch 3, skip next dc, sc in 3rd ch of turning ch, turn.

Row 3: Ch 4 (counts as dc, ch 1), sc in next ch-3 loop, ch 3, sc in next ch-3 loop, *ch 3, (bobble, ch 3, bobble) in next ch-7 loop, ch 3, sc in next ch-3 loop**, (ch 3, sc) in each of next 3 ch-3 loops; rep from * across, ending last rep at **, ch 3, sc in next ch-3 loop, ch 1, dc in last sc, turn.

Row 4: Ch 1, sc in first dc, ch 3, skip next ch-1 space, sc in next ch-3 loop, *ch 4, skip next ch-3 loop, (bobble, ch 4, bobble) in next ch-3 loop, ch 4, skip next ch-3 loop, sc in next ch-3 loop**, (ch 3, sc) in each of next 2 ch-3 loops; rep from * across, ending last rep at **, ch 3, sc in 3rd ch of turning ch, turn.

Row 5: Ch 4 (counts as dc, ch 1), sc in next ch-3 loop, *ch 5, (bobble, picot, ch 3) 4 times in next ch-4 loop, ch 2 more, skip next ch-4 loop, sc in next ch-3 loop**, ch 3, sc in next ch-3 loop; rep from * across, ending last rep at **, ch 1, dc in last sc. Fasten off.

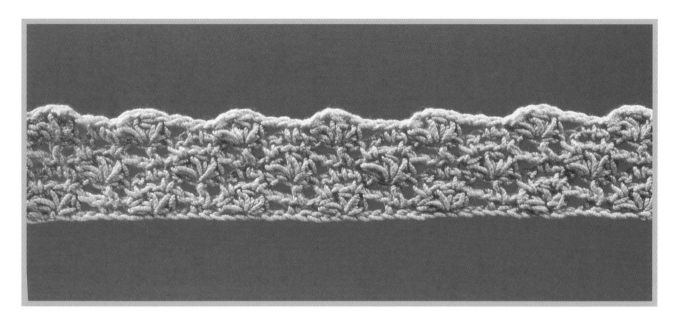

273

Bobble: (Yo, insert hook in next st, yo, draw yarn through st and up to level of work) twice in same st, yo, draw yarn through 5 loops on hook.

Chain multiples of 8 plus 2.

Row 1 (RS): Sc in 2nd ch from hook, *ch 1, skip next 3 ch, (bobble, ch 1, bobble, ch 1, bobble) in next ch, ch 1, skip next 3 ch, sc in next ch; rep from * across, turn.

Row 2: Ch 4 (counts as dc, ch 1), skip next ch-1 space, *sc in next ch-1 space, ch 3, sc in next ch-1 space, ch 1, skip next ch-1 space, dc in next sc**, ch 1; rep from * across, ending last rep at **, turn.

Row 3: Ch 3 (counts as dc), yo, draw up a loop to level of work, yo, draw through 3 loops on hook, ch 1, bobble in first dc, ch 1, skip next ch-1 space, sc in next ch-3 loop, *ch 1, skip next ch-1 space, (bobble, ch 1, bobble, ch 1, bobble) in next dc, ch 1, skip next ch-1 space, sc in next ch-3 loop; rep from * across to last ch-3 loop, ch 1, (bobble, ch 1, bobble) in 3rd ch of turning ch, turn.

Row 4: Ch 3 (counts as hdc, ch 1), *sc in next ch-1 space, ch 1, skip next ch-1 space, dc in next sc, ch 1, skip next ch-1 space, sc in next ch-1 space**, ch 3; rep from * across, ending last rep at **, ch 1, hdc in 3rd ch of turning ch, turn.

Row 5: Ch 1, sc in first hdc, skip next ch-1 space, *ch 1, skip next ch-1 space, (bobble, ch 1, bobble, ch 1, bobble) in next dc, ch 1, skip next ch-1 space, sc in next ch-3 loop; rep from * across, ending with last sc in 2nd ch of turning ch. Fasten off.

274

Bobble: *(Yo, insert hook in next st, yo, draw yarn through st and up to level of work) 3 times in same st, yo, draw yarn through 7 loops on hook.*

Chain multiples of 8 plus 2.

Row 1 (RS): Sc in 2nd ch from hook, *skip next 3 ch, (bobble, ch 3, bobble, ch 3, bobble) in next ch, skip next 3 ch, sc in next ch; rep from * across, turn.

Row 2: Ch 3 (counts as dc), dc in first sc, *ch 2, skip next ch-3 loop, sc in next bobble, ch 2, skip next bobble**, 3 dc in next sc; rep from * across, ending last rep at **, 2 dc in last sc, turn.

Row 3: Ch 3 (counts as dc), (dc, ch 3, bobble) in first dc, *skip next ch-2 space, sc in next sc, skip next dc**, (bobble, ch 3, bobble, ch 3, bobble) in next dc; rep from * across, ending last rep at **, bobble in 3rd ch of turning ch, ch 3, (yo, insert hook in top of turning ch, yo, draw yarn through st and up to level of work) twice in same st, yo, draw yarn through 5 loops on hook. Fasten off.

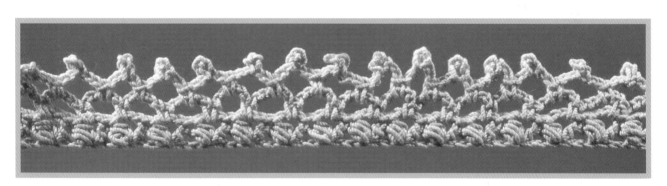

275

Bobble: *(Yo, insert hook in next st, yo, draw yarn through st and up to level of work) 3 times in same st, yo, draw yarn through 7 loops on hook.*

Picot: *Ch 3, sl st in 3rd ch from hook.*

Chain multiples of 3 plus 1.

Row 1 (RS): Dc in 7th ch from hook, ch 2, working over last dc made, skip 2 ch to the right, bobble in next ch to the right, *skip next 2 ch, dc in next ch, ch 2, working over last dc made, skip 2 ch to the right, bobble in next ch to the right already holding a dc; rep from * across to within last ch, dc in last ch, turn.

Row 2: Ch 5 (counts as dc, ch 2), sc in next ch-2 space, (ch 5, sc) in each ch-2 space across to last ch-2 space, ch 2, dc in 3rd ch of turning ch, turn.

Row 3: Ch 1, sc in first dc, *(ch 2, picot, ch 2, sc) in each ch-5 loop across, ending with last sc in 3rd ch of turning ch. Fasten off.

276

Bobble: *(Yo, insert hook in next st, yo, draw yarn through st and up to level of work) 3 times in same st, yo, draw yarn through 7 loops on hook.*

Picot: *Ch 3, sl st in 3rd ch from hook.*

Chain multiples of 6 plus 2.

Row 1 (RS): Sc in 2nd ch from hook, sc in next ch, *ch 6, sc in 2nd ch from hook, hdc in next ch, dc in each of next 3 ch, skip next 3 ch, sc in each of next 3 ch; rep from * across, ending with sc in each of last 2 ch, turn.

Row 2: Ch 7 (counts as dtr, ch 2), skip first sc, *skip next 6 sts, sc in ch-1 space at top of triangle, ch 2, skip next sc, dtr in next sc**, ch 2; rep from * across, ending last rep at **, turn.

Row 3: Ch 3 (counts as dc), picot, (dc, ch 3, bobble) in first dtr, skip next ch-2 space, sc in next sc, skip next ch-2 space, *(bobble, ch 3, bobble, picot, ch 3, bobble) in next dtr, skip next ch-2 space, sc in next sc, skip next ch-2 space; rep from * across to last sc, bobble in 5th ch of turning ch, ch 3, (yo, insert hook in top of turning ch, yo, draw yarn through st and up to level of work) twice in same st, yo, draw yarn through 5 loops on hook, picot. Fasten off.

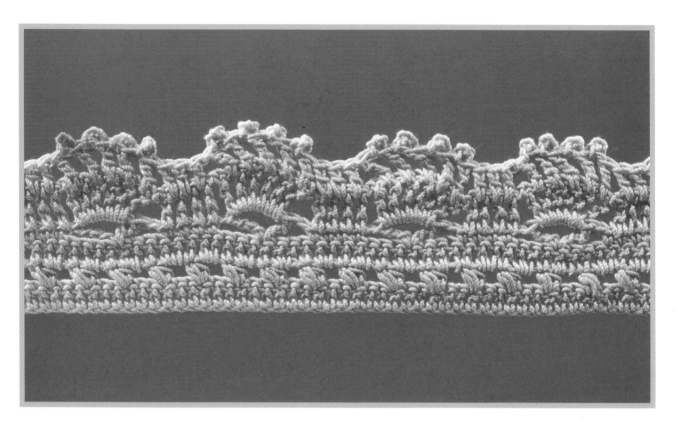

277

Bobble: *(Yo, insert hook in next st, yo, draw yarn through st and up to level of work) 3 times in same st, yo, draw yarn through 7 loops on hook.*

Picot: *Ch 3, sl st in 3rd ch from hook.*

Chain multiples of 33 plus 2.

Row 1 (WS): Dc in 4th ch from hook, dc in each ch across, turn.

Row 2: Ch 4 (counts as dc, ch 1), skip first 2 dc, *bobble in next dc, ch 2, skip next 2 dc; rep from * across to turning ch, bobble in 3rd ch of turning ch, turn.

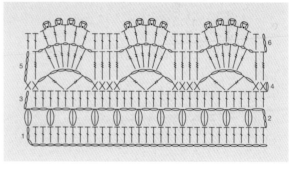

Row 3: Ch 3 (counts as dc), *2 dc in next ch-2 space, dc in next bobble; rep from * across to turning ch, dc in ch-1 space of turning ch, dc in 3rd ch of turning ch, turn.

Row 4: Ch 1, sc in each of first 2 dc, *ch 1, skip next 3 dc, (tr, ch 4, tr) in next dc, ch 1, skip next 3 dc**, sc in each of next 4 dc; rep from * across, ending last rep at **, sc in next dc, sc in 3rd ch of turning ch, turn.

Row 5: Ch 5 (counts as dtr), skip first sc, dtr in next sc, *ch 1, (tr, ch 1) 6 times in next ch-4 loop, skip next ch-1 space**, dtr in each of next 4 sc; rep from * across, ending last rep at **, dtr in each of last 2 sc, turn.

Row 6: Ch 3 (counts as dc), skip first dtr, dc in next dtr, *skip next ch-1 space, (tr, picot) in each of next 4 ch-1 spaces, tr in next ch-1 space, skip next ch-1 space**, dc in each of next 4 dtr; rep from * across, ending last rep at **, dc in next dtr, dc in 3rd ch of turning ch. Fasten off.

.16.
Popcorn Stitches

278

Popcorn (pop): 4 dc in next st, drop loop from hook, insert hook from front to back in first dc of group, pull dropped loop through st.

Chain multiples of 6.

Row 1 (RS): Sc in 9th ch from hook, *ch 3, skip next 2 ch, pop in next ch, ch 3, skip next 2 ch, sc in next ch; rep from * across to within last 3 ch, ch 3, skip next 2 ch, dc in last ch, turn.

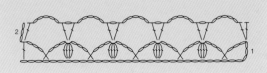

Row 2: Ch 3 (counts as dc), dc in first dc, *ch 5, skip next 2 ch-3 loops**, (dc, ch 1, dc) in next pop; rep from * across, ending last rep at **, 2 dc in 5th ch of turning ch. Fasten off.

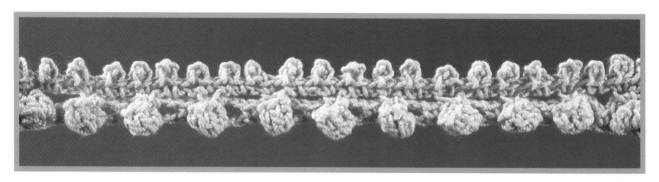

279

Popcorn (pop): 5 dc in next st, drop loop from hook, insert hook from front to back in first dc of group, pull dropped loop through st.

Picot: Ch 3, sl st in 3rd ch from hook.

Chain multiples of 4 plus 2.

Row 1 (RS): Sc in 2nd ch from hook, *ch 3, skip next ch, pop in next ch, ch 3, skip next ch, sc in next ch; rep from * across, turn.

Row 2: Ch 5 (counts as dc, ch 2), skip next ch-3 loop, sc in next pop, *ch 3, skip next 2 ch-3 loops, sc in next pop; rep from * across to last pop, ch 2, dc in last sc, turn.

Row 3: Ch 1, sc in first dc, skip next ch-2 space, *ch 1, picot, sc in next sc, ch 1, picot, sc in next ch-3 loop; rep from * across, ending with last sc in 3rd ch of turning ch. Fasten off.

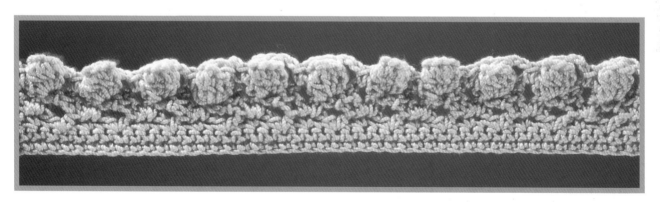

280

Popcorn (pop): 5 dc in next st, drop loop from hook, insert hook from front to back in first dc of group, pull dropped loop through st.

Chain multiples of 4 plus 2.

Row 1 (RS): Sc in 2nd ch from hook, sc in each ch across, turn.

Row 2: Ch 1, sc in each sc across, turn.

Row 3: Ch 1, sc in first sc, *skip next sc, (dc, ch 3, dc) in next sc, skip next sc, sc in next sc; rep from * across, turn.

Row 4: Ch 5 (counts as tr, ch 1), dc in first sc, *sc in next ch-3 loop**, (dc, ch 3, dc) in next sc; rep from * across, ending last rep at **, (dc, ch 1, tr) in last sc, turn.

Row 5: Ch 1, sc in first tr, *ch 3, skip next dc, pop in next sc, ch 3, sc in next ch-3 loop; rep from * across, ending with last sc in 4th ch of turning ch. Fasten off.

281

Popcorn (pop): 5 dc in next st, drop loop from hook, insert hook from front to back in first dc of group, pull dropped loop through st.

Chain multiples of 14 plus 5.

Row 1 (WS): Dc in 4th ch from hook, dc in next ch, *ch 2, skip next 2 ch, sc in next ch, ch 1, skip next 2 ch, (dc, ch 1, dc, ch 1, dc) in next ch, ch 1, skip next 2 ch, sc in next ch, ch 2, skip next 2 ch, dc in each of next 3 ch; rep from * across, turn.

Row 2: Ch 3 (counts as dc), skip first dc, dc in each of next 2 dc, *skip next ch-2 space, (pop, ch 4) in each of next 3 ch-1 spaces, pop in next ch-1 space, skip next ch-2 space, dc in each of next 3 dc; rep from * across, ending with last dc in 3rd ch of turning ch, turn.

Row 3: Ch 3 (counts as dc), skip first dc, dc in each of next 2 dc, *ch 2, sc in next ch-4 loop, (ch 3, sc) in each of next 2 ch-4 loops, ch 2, skip next pop, dc in each of next 3 dc; rep from * across, ending with last dc in 3rd ch of turning ch. Fasten off.

282

Popcorn (pop): 4 dc in next st, drop loop from hook, insert hook from front to back in first dc of group, pull dropped loop through st.

Chain multiples of 12 plus 2.

Row 1 (RS): (Sc, ch 5, sc) in 2nd ch from hook, *ch 5, skip next 5 ch, pop in next ch, ch 6, skip next 5 ch**, (sc, ch 5, sc, ch 5, sc) in next ch; rep from * across, ending last rep at **, (sc, ch 5, sc) in last ch, turn.

Row 2: Ch 9 (counts as dc, ch 6), *skip next 2 loops, (sc, ch 5, sc, ch 5, sc) in next pop, ch 5, skip next 2 ch-5 loops**, pop in next sc, ch 6; rep from * across, ending last rep at **, dc in last sc, turn.

Row 3: Ch 1, (sc, ch 5, sc) in first dc, *ch 5, skip next 2 ch-5 loops, pop in next sc, ch 6, skip next 2 loops**, (sc, ch 5, sc, ch 5, sc) in next pop; rep from * across, ending last rep at **, (sc, ch 5, sc) in 3rd ch of turning ch. Fasten off.

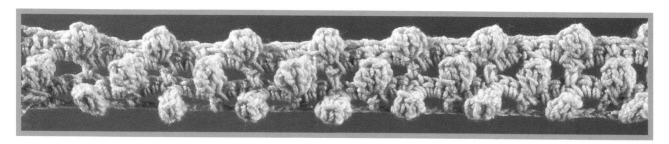

283

Popcorn (pop): 4 dc in next st, drop loop from hook, insert hook from front to back in first dc of group, pull dropped loop through st.

Chain multiples of 6 plus 2.

Row 1 (RS): Sc in 2nd ch from hook, *ch 3, skip next 2 ch, pop in next ch, ch 3, skip next 2 ch, sc in next ch; rep from * across, turn.

Row 2: Ch 1, sc in first sc, 3 sc in each ch-3 loop across, sc in last sc, turn.

Row 3: Ch 3 (counts as dc), dc in first sc, *ch 3, skip next 3 sc, sc bet last skipped and next sc, ch 3, skip next 3 sc, pop bet last skipped and next sc; rep from * across, ending with last pop in last sc, turn.

Row 4: Ch 1, sc in first pop, 3 sc in each ch-3 loop across, sc in 3rd ch of turning ch, turn.

Row 5: Ch 1, sc in first sc, *ch 3, skip next 3 sc, pop bet last skipped and next sc, ch 3, skip next 3 sc, sc bet last skipped and next sc; rep from * across, ending with last sc in last sc. Fasten off.

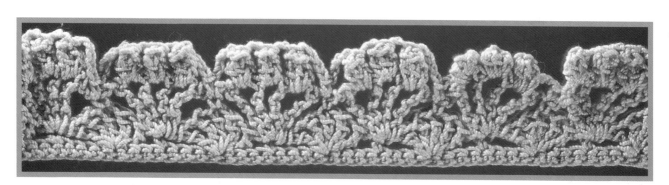

284

Popcorn (pop): 3 dc in next st, drop loop from hook, insert hook from front to back in first dc of group, pull dropped loop through st.

Chain multiples of 8 plus 2.

Row 1 (WS): Sc in 2nd ch from hook, sc in each ch across, turn.

Row 2: Ch 1, sc in first sc, *ch 1, skip next 3 sc, (tr, ch 1) 5 times in next sc, skip next 3 sc, sc in next sc; rep from * across, turn.

Row 3: Ch 8 (counts as dtr, ch 3), dtr in first sc, ch 2, *skip next 3 ch-1 spaces, sc in next tr, ch 2, skip next 3 ch-1 spaces**, (dtr, ch 2) 4 times in next sc; rep from * across, ending last rep at **, (dtr, ch 2, dtr) in last sc, turn.

Row 4: Ch 5 (counts as dc, ch 2), pop in next ch-2 space, *ch 4, skip next ch-2 space, sc in next sc, ch 4, skip next ch-2 space**, (pop, ch 2) in each of next 2 ch-2 spaces, pop in next ch-2 space; rep from * across, ending last rep at **, pop in next ch-3 loop of turning ch, ch 2, dc in 5th ch of turning ch. Fasten off.

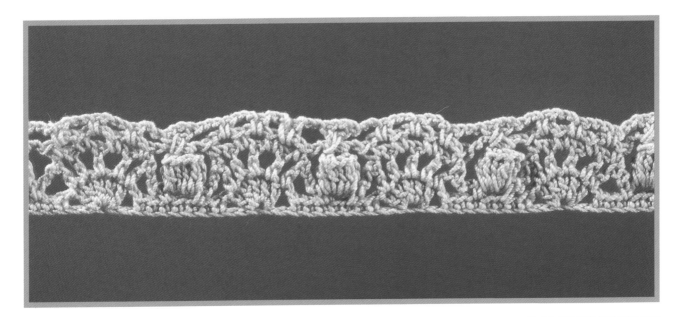

285

Popcorn (pop): 6 dc in next st, drop loop from hook, insert hook from front to back in first dc of group, pull dropped loop through st.

Chain multiples of 12 plus 4.

Row 1 (RS): 2 dc in 4th ch from hook, *skip next 2 ch, sc in each of next 7 ch, skip next 2 ch**, 5 dc in next ch; rep from * across, ending last rep at **, 3 dc in last ch, turn.

Row 2: Ch 5 (counts as dc, ch 2), skip first dc, dc in next dc, ch 2, dc in next dc, *ch 3, skip next 2 sc, sc in next sc, ch 3, skip next sc, sc in next sc, ch 3, skip next 2 sc**, (dc, ch 2) in each of next 4 dc, dc in next dc; rep from * across, ending last rep at **, (dc, ch 2) in each of next 2 dc, dc in 3rd ch of turning ch, turn.

Row 3: Ch 3 (counts as hdc, ch 1), sc in next ch-2 space, ch 3, sc in next ch-2 space, ch 3, *skip next ch-3 loop, pop in next ch-3 loop, ch 3, skip next ch-3 loop**, (sc, ch 3) in each of next 4 ch-2 spaces; rep from * across, ending last rep at **, sc in next ch-2 space, ch 3, sc in next ch-2 space of turning ch, ch 2, hdc in 3rd ch of turning ch, turn.

Row 4: Ch 1, sc in first hdc, ch 3, skip next ch-1 space, sc in next ch-3 loop, ch 3, *skip next ch-3 loop, dc in next ch-3 loop, ch 2, working over last dc made, dc in last skipped ch-3 loop, ch 3**, (sc, ch 3) in each of next 3 ch-3 loops; rep from * across, ending last rep at **, sc in next ch-3 loop, ch 3, sc in 2nd ch of turning ch. Fasten off.

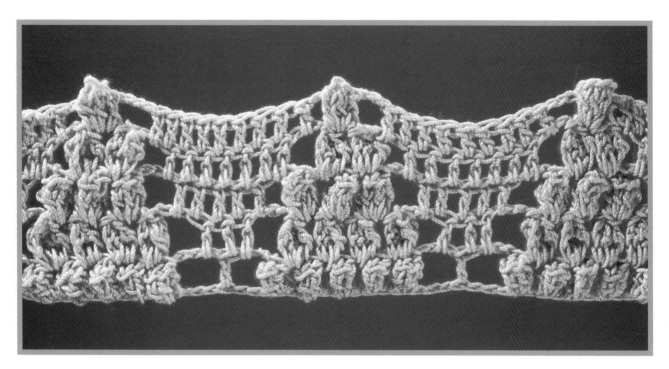

286

Popcorn (pop) (on RS rows): 4 dc in next st, drop loop from hook, insert hook from front to back in first dc of group, pull dropped loop through st.

Popcorn (pop) (on WS rows): 4 dc in next st, drop loop from hook, insert hook from back to front in first dc of group, pull dropped loop through st.

Chain multiples of 16 plus 5.

Row 1 (RS): Dc in 4th ch from hook, *ch 3, skip next 3 ch, (pop, ch 1, skip next ch) 4 times, pop in next ch, ch 3, skip next 3 ch, dc in next ch; rep from * across to within last ch, dc in last ch, turn.

Row 2: Ch 3 (counts as dc), skip first dc, dc in next dc, *dc in next ch-3 loop, ch 3, (pop, ch 1) in each of next 3 ch-1 spaces, pop in next ch-1 space, ch 3, dc in next ch-3 loop, dc in next dc; rep from * across, ending with last dc in 3rd ch of turning ch, turn.

Row 3: Ch 3 (counts as dc), skip first dc, dc in each of next 2 dc, *dc in next ch-3 loop, ch 3, (pop, ch 1) in each of next 2 ch-1 spaces, pop in next ch-1 space, ch 3, dc in next ch-3 loop, dc in each of next 3 dc; rep from * across, ending with last dc in 3rd ch of turning ch, turn.

Row 4: Ch 3 (counts as dc), skip first dc, dc in each of next 3 dc, *dc in next ch-3 loop, ch 3, pop in next ch-1 space, ch 1, pop in next ch-1 space, ch 3, dc in next ch-3 loop**, dc in each of next 5 dc; rep from * across, ending last rep at **, dc in each of next 3 dc, dc in 3rd ch of turning ch, turn.

Row 5: Ch 3 (counts as dc), skip first dc, dc in each of next 4 dc, *dc in next ch-3 loop, ch 3, pop in next ch-1 space, ch 3, dc in next ch-3 loop**, dc in each of next 7 dc; rep from * across, ending last rep at **, dc in each of next 4 dc, dc in 3rd ch of turning ch, turn. Fasten off.

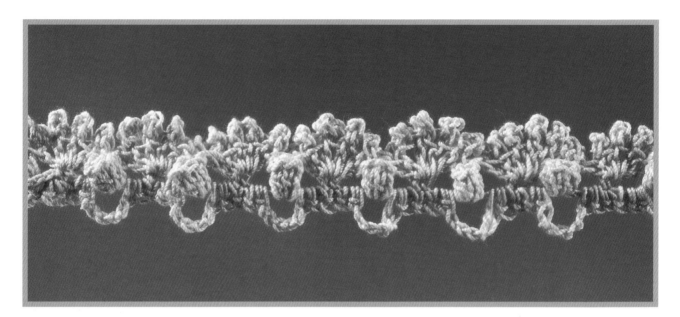

287

Popcorn (pop): *5 dc in next st, drop loop from hook, insert hook from front to back in first dc of group, pull dropped loop through st.*

Picot: *Ch 3, sl st in 3rd ch from hook.*

Chain multiples of 6 plus 2.

Row 1 (RS): Sc in 2nd ch from hook, *ch 3, skip next 2 ch, pop in next ch, ch 3, skip next 2 ch, sc in next ch; rep from * across, turn.

Row 2: Ch 3 (counts as dc), picot, dc in first sc, skip next ch-3 loop, sc in next pop, *skip next ch-3 loop, (dc, picot, dc, picot, dc, picot, dc) in next sc, skip next ch-3 loop, sc in next pop; rep from * across to within last ch-3 loop, skip next ch-3 loop, (dc, picot, dc) in last sc. Fasten off.

Bottom edging: With WS facing, working across opposite side of foundation ch, join yarn in first ch, ch 1, sc in first ch, *2 sc in next ch-2 space, ch 5, 2 sc in next ch-2 space, sc in next ch; rep from * across. Fasten off.

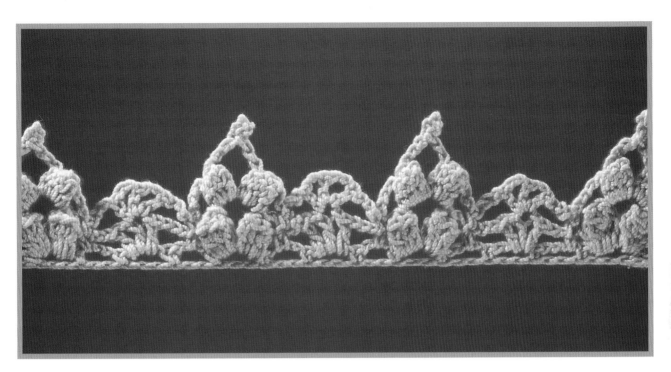

288

Popcorn (pop): 5 dc in next st, drop loop from hook, insert hook from front to back in first dc of group, pull dropped loop through st.

Picot: Ch 4, sl st in 4th ch from hook.

Chain multiples of 12 plus 11.

Row 1 (WS): Sc in 2nd ch from hook, *ch 3, skip next 2 ch, sc in next ch; rep from * across, turn.

Row 2: Ch 1, sc in first sc, 2 sc in next ch-3 loop, *ch 3, (dc, ch 1, dc, ch 1, dc) in next ch-3 loop, ch 3, sc in next ch-3 loop**, ch 2, (pop, ch 5, pop) in next ch-3 loop, ch 2, sc in next ch-3 loop; rep from * across, ending last rep at **, sc in same ch-3 loop, sc in last sc, turn.

Row 3: Ch 1, sc in each of first 3 sc, *ch 3, skip next 2 spaces, (dc, ch 2, dc, ch 2, dc) in next dc, ch 3, skip next 2 spaces, sc in next sc**, ch 3, (pop, ch 3, picot, ch 4, pop) in next ch-5 loop, ch 3, skip next ch-2 space, sc in next sc; rep from * across, ending last rep at **, sc in each of last 2 sc. Fasten off.

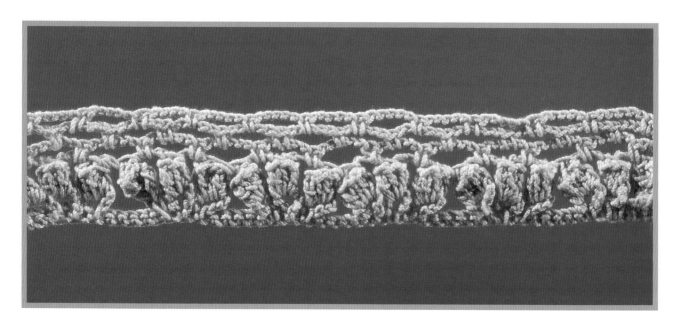

289

Popcorn (pop): 5 dc in next st, drop loop from hook, insert hook from front to back in first dc of group, pull dropped loop through st.

Picot: Ch 7, sl st in 7th ch from hook.

Chain multiples of 8 plus 2.

Row 1 (WS): Sc in 2nd ch from hook, sc in each of next 3 ch, *picot, ch 7, sc in next ch, ch 7**, sc in each of next 7 ch; rep from * across, ending last rep at **, sc in each of last 4 ch, turn.

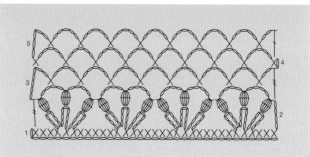

Row 2: Ch 4 (counts as tr), *(pop, ch 4) in each of next 2 ch-7 loop, pop in next picot**, skip next 7 sc; rep from * across, ending last rep at **, skip next 3 sc, tr in last sc, turn.

Row 3: Ch 7 (counts as dtr, ch 2), sc in next ch-4 loop, (ch 5, sc) in each ch-4 loop across to last ch-4 loop, ch 2, skip next pop, dtr in 4th ch of turning ch, turn.

Row 4: Ch 1, sc in first dtr, (ch 5, sc) in each ch-5 loop across, ending with last sc in 5th ch of turning ch, turn.

Row 5: Ch 5 (counts as dc, ch 2), sc in next ch-5 loop, (ch 5, sc) in each ch-5 loop across to last ch-5 loop, ch 2, dc in last sc. Fasten off.

.17.
Puff Stitches

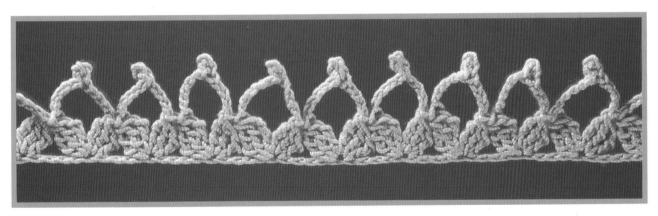

290

Picot: Ch 3, sl st in 3rd ch from hook.

Chain multiples of 5 plus 1.

Row 1 (RS): Work 6-tr cluster, working first 3 half-closed tr in 6th ch from hook, skip next 4 ch, work next 3 half-closed tr in next ch, complete cluster, *ch 5, picot, ch 5, work 6-dc cluster, working first 3 half-closed tr in same ch holding last cluster, skip next 4 ch, work next 3 half-closed tr in next ch, complete cluster; rep from * across to last ch, ch 1, tr in last ch already holding last cluster. Fasten off.

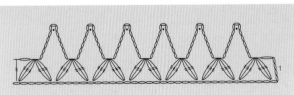

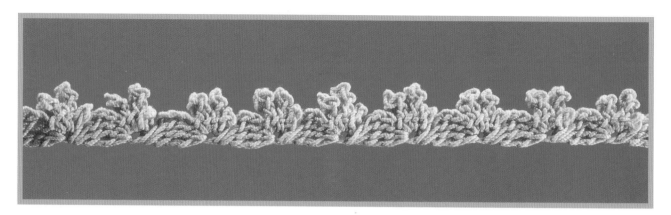

291

Puff st: (Yo [twice], insert hook in next st, yo, draw yarn through st, [yo, draw yarn through 2 loops on hook] twice) 3 times in same st, yo, draw yarn through 4 loops on hook.

Picot: Ch 5, sl st in 5th ch from hook.

No foundation chain needed.

Row 1 (RS): *Work 2 picots, sl st in base of first picot, work 3rd picot, sl st in base of first picot, ch 4, puff st in base of first picot; rep from * for desired length. Fasten off.

292

Puff st: (Yo [twice], insert hook in next st, yo, draw yarn through st, [yo, draw yarn through 2 loops on hook] twice) twice in same st, yo, draw yarn through 3 loops on hook.

No foundation chain needed.

Row 1 (RS): Ch 12, *sl st in 7th ch from hook forming a ring, sc in ring, (ch 4, puff st, ch 4, sc) 5 times in ring**, ch 17; rep from * for desired length, ending last rep at **. Fasten off.

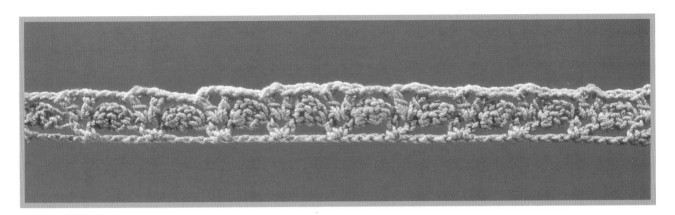

293

Puff st: (Yo, insert hook in next st, yo, draw yarn through st, yo, draw yarn through 2 loops on hook) twice in same st, yo, draw yarn through 3 loops on hook.

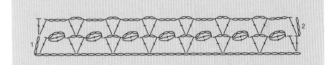

Chain multiples of 5 plus 4.

Row 1 (WS): Dc in 4th ch from hook, *ch 3, puff st in last dc made, skip next 4 ch**, (dc, ch 2, dc) in next ch; rep from * across, ending last rep at **, 2 dc in last ch, turn.

Row 2: Ch 3, (counts as dc), dc in first dc, *ch 3, skip next ch-3 loop**, (dc, ch 2, dc) in next ch-2 space; rep from * across, ending last rep at **, skip next dc, 2 dc in 3rd ch of turning ch. Fasten off.

294

Puff st: (Yo, insert hook in next st, yo, draw yarn through st, yo, draw yarn through 2 loops on hook) twice in same st, yo, draw yarn through 3 loops on hook.

Picot: Ch 7, sl st in 7th ch from hook.

Chain multiples of 18 plus 14.

Row 1 (RS): Sc in 2nd ch from hook, *ch 2, (puff st, ch 5, dc in 5th ch from hook) 3 times in next ch, puff st in same ch, ch 2, skip next 5 ch, sc in next ch**, ch 2, picot, ch 2, skip next 5 ch, sc in next ch; rep from * across, ending last rep at **. Fasten off.

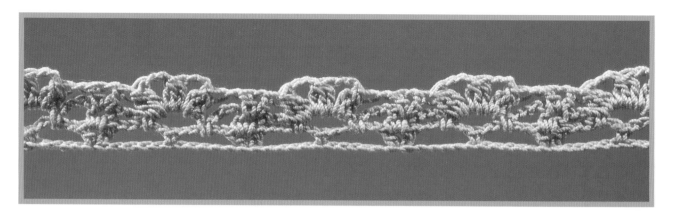

295

Puff st: *(Yo, insert hook in next st, yo, draw yarn through st, yo, draw yarn through 2 loops on hook) 3 times in same st, yo, draw yarn through 4 loops on hook.*

Chain multiples of 12 plus 4.

Row 1 (RS): Dc in 4th ch from hook, *ch 5, skip next 5 ch, sc in next ch, ch 5, skip next 5 ch**, (dc, ch 1, dc) in next ch; rep from * across, ending last rep at **, 2 dc in last ch, turn.

Row 2: Ch 3 (counts as dc), dc in first dc, *ch 3, sc in next ch-5 loop, ch 4, sc in next ch-5 loop, ch 3**, (dc, ch 1, dc) in next ch-1 space; rep from * across, ending last rep at **, skip next dc, 2 dc in 3rd ch of turning ch, turn.

Row 3: Ch 3 (counts as dc), dc in first dc, *skip next ch-3 loop, (puff st, ch 3, puff st, ch 3, puff st) in next ch-4 loop, skip next ch-3 loop**, (dc, ch 1, dc) in next ch-1 space; rep from * across, ending last rep at **, skip next dc, 2 dc in 3rd ch of turning ch. Fasten off.

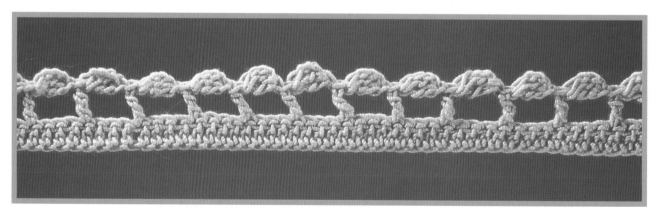

296

Puff st: *(Yo, insert hook in next st, yo, draw yarn through st, yo, draw yarn through 2 loops on hook) twice in same st, yo, draw yarn through 3 loops on hook.*

Chain multiples of 4 plus 3.

Row 1 (WS): Dc in 4th ch from hook, dc in each ch across, turn.

Row 2: Ch 8 (counts as tr, ch 4), puff st in 5th ch from hook, skip first 4 dc, tr in next dc, *ch 4, puff st in last tr made, skip next 3 dc, tr in next dc; rep from * across, ending with last tr in 3rd ch of turning ch. Fasten off.

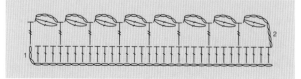

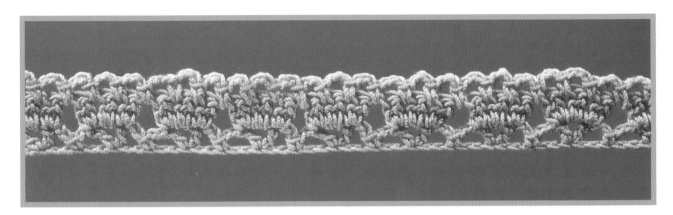

297

Puff st: (Yo, insert hook in next st, yo, draw yarn through st, yo, draw yarn through 2 loops on hook) 3 times in same st, yo, draw yarn through 4 loops on hook.

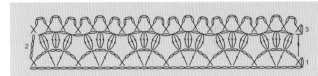

Chain multiples of 6 plus 2.

Row 1 (RS): Sc in 2nd ch from hook, *ch 2, skip next 2 ch, (dc, ch 2, dc) in next ch, ch 2, skip next 2 ch, sc in next ch; rep from * across, turn.

Row 2: Ch 4 (counts as tr), skip next ch-2 space, *puff st in next dc, ch 1, puff st in next ch-2 space, ch 1, puff st in next dc**, ch 1, skip next 2 ch-2 spaces; rep from * across, ending last rep at **, skip next ch-2 space, tr in last sc, turn.

Row 3: Ch 1, sc in first tr, (ch 3, sc) in each ch-1 space across, ending with last sc in 4th ch of turning ch. Fasten off.

298

Puff st: (Yo, insert hook in next st, yo, draw yarn through st, yo, draw yarn through 2 loops on hook) twice in same st, yo, draw yarn through 3 loops on hook.

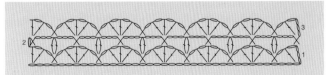

Chain multiples of 6 plus 5.

Row 1 (RS): Dc in 5th ch from hook, *ch 1, skip next 2 ch, sc in next ch, ch 1, skip next 2 ch**, (dc, ch 1, dc, ch 1, dc) in next ch; rep from * across, ending last rep at **, (dc, ch 1, dc) in last ch, turn.

Row 2: Ch 1, sc in first dc, *ch 3, skip next 2 ch-1 spaces, puff st in next sc, ch 3, skip next 2 ch-1 spaces, sc in next dc; rep from * across, ending with last sc in 3rd ch of turning ch, turn.

Row 3: Ch 4 (counts as dc, ch 1), dc in first sc, *ch 1, skip next ch-3 loop, sc in next puff st, ch 1, skip next ch-3 loop**, (dc, ch 1, dc, ch 1, dc) in next sc; rep from * across, ending last rep at **, (dc, ch 1, dc) in last sc. Fasten off.

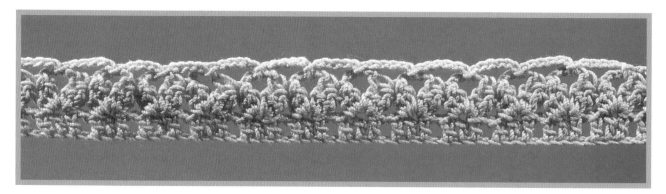

299

Puff st: (Yo, insert hook in next st, yo, draw yarn through st, yo, draw yarn through 2 loops on hook) 3 times in same st, yo, draw yarn through 4 loops on hook.

Chain multiples of 4 plus 3.

Row 1 (RS): Dc in 4th ch from hook, dc in each of next 2 ch, *ch 1, skip next ch, dc in each of next 3 ch; rep from * across to within last ch, dc in last ch, turn.

Row 2: Ch 3 (counts as dc), skip first 2 dc, *(puff st, ch 3, puff st) in next dc**, skip next 3 sts; rep from * across, ending last rep at **, skip next dc, dc in 3rd ch of turning ch, turn.

Row 3: Ch 4, sl st in next ch-3 loop, (ch 5, sl st) in each ch-3 loop across to last ch-3 loop, ch 3, sc in 3rd ch of turning ch. Fasten off.

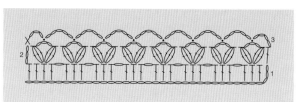

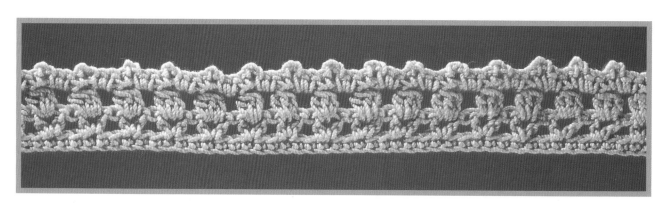

300

Puff st: (Yo, insert hook in next st, yo, draw yarn through st, yo, draw yarn through 2 loops on hook) 3 times in same st, yo, draw yarn through 4 loops on hook.

Chain multiples of 3 plus 1.

Row 1 (RS): Sc in 2nd ch from hook, sc in each ch across, turn.

Row 2: Ch 3 (counts as dc), skip first sc, *(dc, ch 1, dc) in next sc, skip next 2 sc; rep from * across to within last 2 sc, dc in next sc, ch 1, 2-dc cluster worked across last 2 sc, complete cluster, turn.

Row 3: Ch 3 (counts as dc), puff st in next ch-1 space, (ch 2, puff st) in each ch-1 space across to last ch-1 space, skip next dc, dc in 3rd ch of turning ch, turn.

Row 4: Ch 1, sc in first dc, sc in next puff st, *ch 3, 2 sc in next ch-2 space, sc in next puff st; rep from * across to last puff st, ch 3, sc in 3rd ch of turning ch. Fasten off.

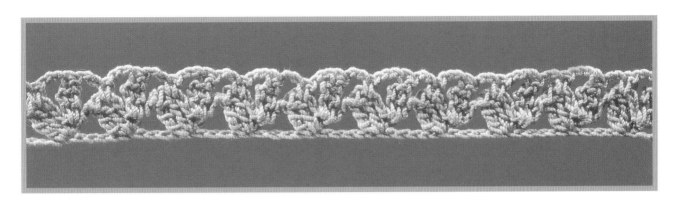

301

Puff st: (Yo [twice], insert hook in next st, yo, draw yarn through st, [yo, draw yarn through 2 loops on hook] twice) twice in same st, yo, draw yarn through 3 loops on hook.

Chain multiples of 5 plus 2.

Row 1 (RS): (Sc, ch 4, puff st) in 2nd ch from hook, *ch 4, skip next 4 ch**, (sc, ch 4, puff st) in next ch; rep from * across, ending last rep at **, sc in last ch, turn.

Row 2: Ch 7 (counts as tr, ch 3), *skip next ch-4 loop, sc in next ch-4 loop, ch 3**, puff st in next sc, ch 3; rep from * across, ending last rep at **, tr in last sc. Fasten off.

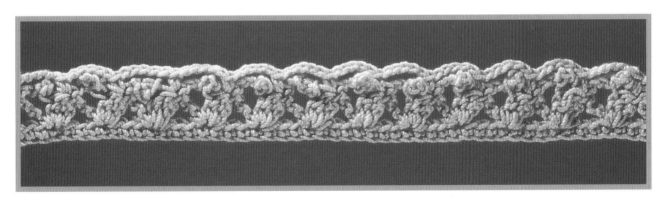

302

Puff st: (Yo, insert hook in next st, yo, draw yarn through st, yo, draw yarn through 2 loops on hook) 3 times in same st, yo, draw yarn through 4 loops on hook.

Picot: Ch 3, sl st in 3rd ch from hook.

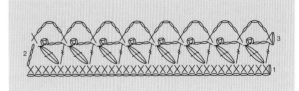

Chain multiples of 4 plus 2.

Row 1 (RS): Sc in 2nd ch from hook, sc in each ch across, turn.

Row 2: Ch 4 (counts as tr), skip first 4 sc, *(puff st, picot, ch 2, tr) in next sc**, skip next 3 sc; rep from * across, ending last rep at **, turn.

Row 3: Ch 1, sc in first tr, (ch 5, sc) in each tr across, ending with last sc in 4th ch of turning ch. Fasten off.

303

Puff st: (Yo, insert hook in next st, yo, draw yarn through st, yo, draw yarn through 2 loops on hook) twice in same st, yo, draw yarn through 3 loops on hook.

Chain multiples of 4 plus 2.

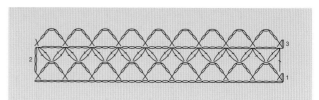

Row 1 (RS): Sc in 2nd ch from hook, *ch 5, skip next 3 ch, sc in next ch; rep from * across, turn.

Row 2: Ch 3 (counts as dc), puff st in next ch-5 loop, *ch 3, work 4-dc cluster, working first 2 half-closed dc in same ch-5 loop as last 2 dc, work next 2 half-closed dc in next ch-5 loop, complete cluster; rep from * across to last ch-5 loop, ch3 work 3-dc cluster, working first 2 half-closed dc in last ch-5 loop holding last 2 dc, work next half-closed dc in last sc, complete cluster, turn.

Row 3: Ch 1, sc in first cluster, (ch 5, sc) in each cluster across, ending with last sc in 3rd ch of turning ch. Fasten off.

304

Puff st: (Yo, insert hook in next st, yo, draw yarn through st, yo, draw yarn through 2 loops on hook) 3 times in same st, yo, draw yarn through 4 loops on hook.

Chain multiples of 12 plus 2.

Row 1 (WS): Sc in 2nd ch from hook, sc in each of next 3 ch, *ch 7, skip next 5 ch, sc in each of next 7 ch; rep from * across, ending with sc in each of last 4 ch, turn.

Row 2: Ch 1, sc in first sc, *ch 1, (puff st, ch 2) 4 times in next ch-7 loop, puff st in same ch-7 loop, ch 1, skip next 3 sc, sc in next sc; rep from * across, turn.

Row 3: Ch 1, sc in first sc, skip next ch-1 space, *(ch 3, sc) in each of next 5 spaces, sc in next ch-1 space; rep from * across to within last 5 space, (ch 3, sc) in each of next 4 ch-2 spaces, ch 3, skip next ch-1 space, sc in last sc. Fasten off.

305

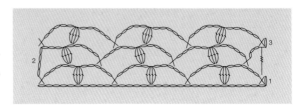

Puff st: (Yo, insert hook in next st, yo, draw yarn through st, yo, draw yarn through 2 loops on hook) 4 times in same st, yo, draw yarn through 5 loops on hook.

Chain multiples of 10 plus 2.

Row 1 (RS): Sc in 2nd ch from hook, *ch 5, skip next 4 ch, puff st in next ch, ch 5, skip next 4 ch, sc in next ch; rep from * across, turn.

Row 2: Ch 7 (counts as tr, ch 3), *puff st in next ch-5 loop, ch 5, sc in next ch-5 loop**, ch 5; rep from * across, ending last rep at **, ch 3, dtr in last sc, turn.

Row 3: Ch 1, sc in first dtr, *ch 5, puff st in next ch-5 loop, ch 5, sc in next ch-5 loop; rep from * across, ending with last sc in 4th ch of turning ch. Fasten off.

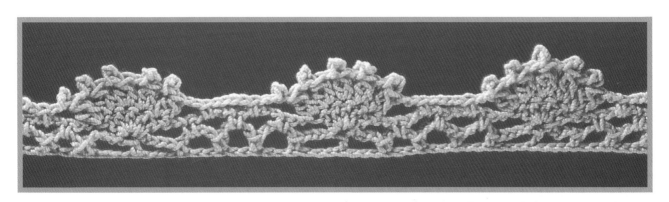

306

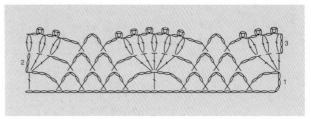

Puff st: (Yo, insert hook in next st, yo, draw yarn through st, yo, draw yarn through 2 loops on hook) twice in same st, yo, draw yarn through 3 loops on hook.

Chain multiples of 17 plus 7.

Row 1 (RS): Sc in 11th ch from hook, *(ch 4, skip next 2 ch, sc in next ch) 3 times, ch 4, skip next 3 ch, dc in next ch, ch 4 **, skip next 3 ch, sc in next ch; rep from * across, ending last rep at ** turn.

Row 2: Ch 3 (counts as dc), 2 dc in first dc, *ch 2, skip next ch-4 loop, sc in next ch-4 loop, (ch 4, sc) in each of next 2 ch-4 loops, ch 2, skip next ch-4 loop**, 5 dc in next dc; rep from * across, ending last rep at **, 3 dc in 6th ch of turning ch, turn.

Row 3: Ch 3 (counts as dc), dc in first dc, (picot, ch 1, puff st) in each of next 2 dc, picot, ch 2, *sc in next ch-4 loop, ch 4, sc in next ch-4 loop, ch 2, skip next ch-2 space**, (puff st, picot, ch 1) in each of next 5 dc, ch 1 more; rep from * across, ending last rep at **, (puff st, picot, ch 1) in each of next 2 dc, puff st in 3rd ch of turning ch. Fasten off.

307

2-Dc Puff st: (Yo, insert hook in next st, yo, draw yarn through st, yo, draw yarn through 2 loops on hook) twice in same st, yo, draw yarn through 3 loops on hook.

3-Dtr Puff st: (Yo [3 times], insert hook in next st, yo, draw yarn through st, [yo, draw yarn through 2 loops on hook] 3 times) 3 times in same st, yo, draw yarn through 4 loops on hook.

Chain multiples of 16 plus 14.

Row 1 (RS): Sc in 2nd ch from hook, sc in each ch across, turn.

Row 2: Ch 1, sc in first sc, *ch 5, skip next 3 sc, sc in next sc; rep from * across, turn.

Row 3: Ch 3, (counts as dc), sc in next ch-5 loop, (ch 5, sc) in each ch-5 loop across to last ch-5 loop, ch 2, dc in last sc; rep from * across, turn.

Row 4: Ch 1, sc in first dc, *(ch 5, sc) in each of next 3 ch-5 loops**, ch 9, dc in 6th ch from hook, ch 3, sc in next ch-5 loop; rep from * across, ending last rep at ** with last sc in 3rd ch of turning ch, turn.

Row 5: Ch 9 (counts as tr, ch 5), *2-dc puff st in each of next 3 ch-5 loops**, ch 1, skip next ch-3 loop, (3-dtr puff st, ch 4) 3 times in next ch-5 loop, 3-dtr puff st in same ch-5 loop, ch 1, skip next ch-3 loop; rep from * across, ending last rep at **, ch 5, tr in last sc. Fasten off.

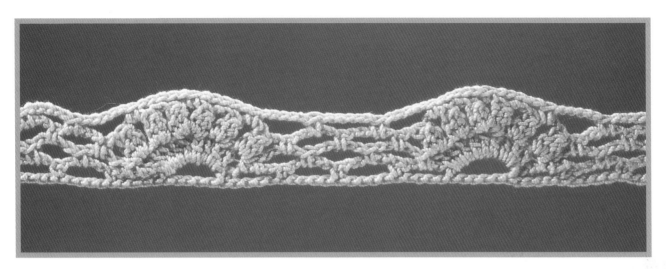

308

Puff st: (Yo, insert hook in next st, yo, draw yarn through st, yo, draw yarn through 2 loops on hook) 3 times in same st, yo, draw yarn through 4 loops on hook.

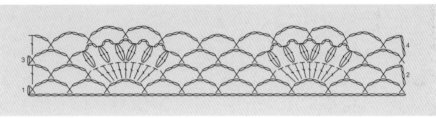

Chain multiples of 25 plus 2.

Row 1 (WS): Sc in 2nd ch from hook, *ch 5, skip next 4 ch, sc in next ch; rep from * across, turn.

Row 2: Ch 5 (counts as dc, ch 2), sc in next ch-5 loop, ch 5, sc in next ch-5 loop, *9 dc in next ch-5 loop, sc in next ch-5 loop**, (ch 5, sc) in each of next 3 ch-5 loops; rep from * across, ending last rep at **, ch 5, sc in next ch-5 loop, ch 2, dc in last sc, turn.

Row 3: Ch 1, sc in first dc, *ch 5, sc in next ch-5 loop, ch 1, (puff st, ch 3, skip next dc) twice, (puff st, ch 3, puff st) in next dc, (ch 3, skip next dc, puff st in next dc) twice, ch 1, sc in next ch-5 loop, ch 5, sc in next ch-5 loop; rep from * across, ending with last sc in 3rd ch of turning ch, turn.

Row 4: Ch 5 (counts as dc, ch 2), *sc in next ch-5 loop, (ch 5, skip next space, sc in next loop) 4 times**, ch 5; rep from * across, ending last rep at **, ch 2, dc in last sc. Fasten off.

309

2-Dc Puff st: (Yo, insert hook in next st, yo, draw yarn through st, yo, draw yarn through 2 loops on hook) twice in same st, yo, draw yarn through 3 loops on hook.

3-Dc Puff st: (Yo, insert hook in next st, yo, draw yarn through st, yo, draw yarn through 2 loops on hook) 3 times in same st, yo, draw yarn through 4 loops on hook.

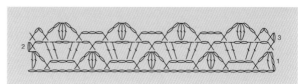

Chain multiples of 8 plus 4.

Row 1 (RS): Dc in 4th ch from hook, *ch 2, skip next ch, sc in next ch, ch 3, skip next 3 ch, sc in next ch, ch 2, skip next ch**, 3-dc puff st in next ch; rep from * across, ending last rep at **, 2-dc puff st in last ch, turn.

Row 2: Ch 1, sc in first puff st, *ch 1, skip next ch-2 space, (2 dc, ch 2, 2 dc) in next ch-3 loop, ch 1, skip next ch-2 space, sc in next puff st; rep from * across, ending with last sc in 3rd ch of turning ch, turn.

Row 3: Ch 1, sc in first sc, ch 2, skip next ch-1 space, *sc in next dc, ch 2, 3-dc puff st in next ch-2 space, ch 2, skip next dc, sc in next dc**, ch 3, skip next 2 ch-1 spaces; rep from * across, ending last rep at **, ch 2, skip next ch-1 space, sc in next sc. Fasten off.

310

Puff st: (Yo, insert hook in next st, yo, draw yarn through st, yo, draw yarn through 2 loops on hook) 3 times in same st, yo, draw yarn through 4 loops on hook.

Chain multiples of 8 plus 5.

Row 1 (RS): (Puff st, ch 1, puff st) in 9th ch from hook, *ch 2, skip next 3 ch, dc in next ch**, ch 2, skip next 3 ch, (puff st, ch 1, puff st) in next ch; rep from * across, ending last rep at **, turn.

Row 2: Ch 5 (counts as dc, ch 2), skip next ch-2 space, *(puff st, ch 1, puff st) in next ch-1 space, ch 2, skip next ch-2 space**, dc in next dc, ch 2, skip next ch-2 space; rep from * across, ending last rep at **, dc in 6th ch of turning ch, turn.

Row 3: Ch 5 (counts as dc, ch 2), skip next ch-2 space, *(puff st, ch 1, puff st) in next ch-1 space, ch 2, skip next ch-2 space**, dc in next dc, ch 2, skip next ch-2 space; rep from * across, ending last rep at **, dc in 3rd ch of turning ch. Fasten off.

311

Puff st: (Yo, insert hook in next st, yo, draw yarn through st, yo, draw yarn through 2 loops on hook) 3 times in same st, yo, draw yarn through 4 loops on hook.

Picot: Ch 3, sl st in 3rd ch from hook.

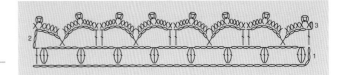

Chain multiples of 10.

Row 1 (RS): Puff st in 4th ch from hook, *ch 5, skip next 4 ch, puff st in next ch; rep from * across to within last ch, dc in last ch, turn.

Row 2: Ch 7 (counts as dc, ch 4), sc in next ch-5 loop, *ch 6, 2 dc in next ch-5 loop, ch 6, sc in next ch-5 loop; rep from * across to last ch-5 loop, ch 4, dc in 3rd ch of turning ch, turn.

Row 3: Ch 1, sc in first dc, picot, 5 sc in next ch-4 loop, *(5 sc, picot, 4 sc) in next ch-6 loop, sc in each of next 2 dc, (4 sc, picot, 5 sc) in next ch-6 loop; rep from * across to turning ch, 5 sc in next ch-4 loop of turning ch, picot, sc in 3rd ch of turning ch. Fasten off.

312

Puff st: (Yo, insert hook in next st, yo, draw yarn through st, yo, draw yarn through 2 loops on hook) twice in same st, yo, draw yarn through 3 loops on hook.

Chain multiples of 3 plus 2.

Row 1 (RS): Sc in 2nd ch from hook, *ch 3, skip next 2 ch, sc in next ch; rep from * across, turn.

Row 2: Ch 4 (counts as dc, ch 1), sc in next ch-3 loop, (ch 4, sc) in each ch-3 loop across to last ch-3 loop, ch 1, dc in last sc, turn.

Row 3: Ch 1, sc in first dc, (ch 5, sc) in each ch-4 loop across, ending with last sc in 3rd ch of turning ch, turn.

Row 4: Ch 5 (counts as tr, ch 1), puff st in next ch-5 loop, (ch 2, puff st) in each ch-5 loop across to last ch-5 loop, ch 1, dc in last sc, turn.

Row 5: Ch 1, sc in first dc, sc in next ch-1 space, (sc, ch 3, sc) in each ch-2 space across to last ch-2 space, sc in next ch-1 space of turning ch, sc in 4th ch of turning ch. Fasten off.

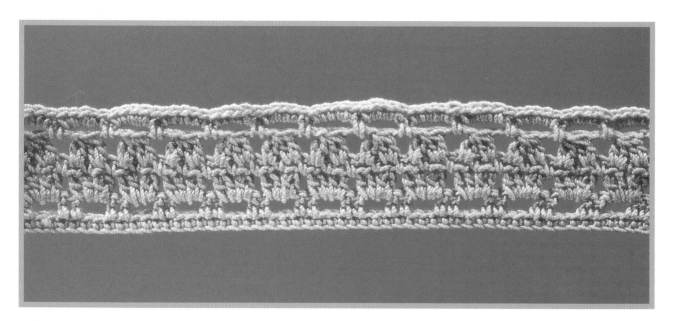

313

Chain multiples of 4 plus 3.

Row 1 (RS): Sc in 2nd ch from hook, sc in each ch across, turn.

Row 2: Ch 3 (counts as dc), skip first sc, dc in next sc, *ch 2, skip next 2 sc, dc in each of next 2 sc; rep from * across, turn.

Row 3: Ch 3 (counts as dc), (2 dc, ch 1, 2 dc) in each ch-2 space across to last ch-2 space, skip next dc, dc in 3rd ch of turning ch, turn.

Row 4: Ch 1, sc in first dc, *ch 1, sc in next ch-1 space, ch 1, skip next 2 dc, sc bet last skipped and next dc; rep from * across, ending with last sc in 3rd ch of turning ch, turn.

Row 5: Ch 4 (counts as dc, ch 1), *work 4-dc cluster, working first 2 half-closed dc in next ch-1 space, work next 2 half-closed dc in next ch-1 space, complete cluster**, ch 3; rep from * across, ending last rep at **, ch 1, dc in last sc, turn.

Row 6: Ch 1, sc in first dc, skip next ch-1 space, (ch 4, sc) in each ch-3 loop across, ending with last sc in 3rd ch of turning ch, turn.

Row 7: Ch 1, 5 sc in each ch-4 loop across. Fasten off.

314

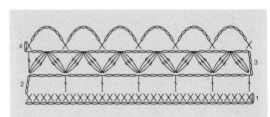

Chain multiples of 5 plus 2.

Row 1 (RS): Sc in 2nd ch from hook, sc in each ch across, turn.

Row 2: Ch 7 (counts as dc, ch 4), skip first 5 sc, dc in next sc, *ch 4, skip next 4 sc, dc in next sc; rep from * across, turn.

Row 3: Ch 6 (counts as tr, ch 2), work 6-tr cluster, working first 3 half-closed tr in first dc, skip next ch-4 loop, work next 3 half-closed tr in next dc, complete cluster, *ch 4, work 6-tr cluster, working first 3 half-closed tr in same dc holding last cluster, skip next ch-4 loop, work next 3 half-closed tr in next dc, complete cluster; rep from * across to turning ch, work 6-tr cluster, working first 3 half-closed tr in same dc holding last cluster, skip next ch-4 loop of turning ch, work next 3 half-closed tr dc in 3rd ch of turning ch, complete cluster, ch 2, tr in 3rd ch of turning ch, turn.

Row 4: Ch 1, sc in first tr, skip next ch-2 space, (ch 7, sc) in each ch-4 loop across, ending with last sc in 4th ch of turning ch. Fasten off.

315

Puff st: (Yo, insert hook in next st, yo, draw yarn through st, yo, draw yarn through 2 loops on hook) 3 times in same st, yo, draw yarn through 4 loops on hook.

Picot: Ch 3, sl st in 3rd ch from hook.

Chain multiples of 5 plus 1.

Row 1 (RS): Sc in 2nd ch from hook, sc in each ch across, turn.

Row 2: Ch 4 (counts as hdc, ch 2), skip first 2 sc, sc in next sc, *ch 5, skip next 4 sc, sc in next sc; rep from * across to within last 2 sc, ch 2, skip next sc, hdc in last sc, turn.

Row 3: Ch 1, sc in first hdc, skip next ch-2 space, *ch 3, puff st in next sc, picot, ch 3, sc in next ch-5 loop; rep from * across, ending with last sc in 2nd ch of turning ch. Fasten off.

316

Puff st: *(Yo, insert hook in next st, yo, draw yarn through st, yo, draw yarn through 2 loops on hook) 3 times in same st, yo, draw yarn through 4 loops on hook.*

Picot: *Ch 3, sl st in 3rd ch from hook.*

Chain multiples of 4 plus 2.

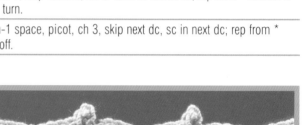

Row 1 (RS): Sc in 2nd ch from hook, sc in each ch across, turn.

Row 2: Ch 3 (counts as dc), skip first sc, dc in next sc, *ch 1, skip next sc, dc in each of next 3 sc; rep from * across to within last 3 sc, ch 1, skip next sc, sc in each of last 2 sc, turn.

Row 3: Ch 1, sc in first dc, *ch 3, picot, puff st in next ch-1 space, picot, ch 3, skip next dc, sc in next dc; rep from * across, ending with last sc in 3rd ch of turning ch. Fasten off.

317

2-Dc Puff st: *(Yo, insert hook in next st, yo, draw yarn through st, yo, draw yarn through 2 loops on hook) twice in same st, yo, draw yarn through 3 loops on hook.*

3-Dc Puff st: *(Yo, insert hook in next st, yo, draw yarn through st, yo, draw yarn through 2 loops on hook) 3 times in same st, yo, draw yarn through 4 loops on hook.*

Picot: *Ch 3, sl st in 3rd ch from hook.*

Chain multiples of 8 plus 2.

Row 1 (RS): Sc in 2nd ch from hook, sc in each ch across, turn.

Row 2: Ch 1, sc in first sc, *ch 4, skip next 3 sc, puff st in next sc, ch 4, skip next 3 sc, sc in next sc; rep from * across, turn.

Row 3: Ch 3 (counts as dc), 2-dc puff st in first sc, *ch 4, skip next ch-4 loop, sc in next puff st, ch 4, skip next ch-4 loop, puff st in next sc; rep from * across, turn.

Row 4: Ch 1, sc in first puff st, *ch 4, skip next ch-4 loop, puff st in next sc, ch 4, skip next ch-4 loop, sc in in next puff st; rep from * across, ending with last sc in 3rd ch of turning ch, turn.

Row 5: Ch 1, sc in first sc, *4 sc in next ch-4 loop, sc in next puff st, picot, 4 sc in next ch-4 loop, sc in next sc; rep from * across. Fasten off.

318

Puff st: (Yo, insert hook in next st, yo, draw yarn through st, yo, draw yarn through 2 loops on hook) twice in same st, yo, draw yarn through 3 loops on hook.

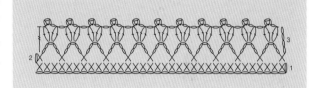

Chain multiples of 3 plus 2.

Row 1 (RS): Sc in 2nd ch from hook, sc in each ch across, turn.

Row 2: Ch 1, sc in first sc, *ch 5, skip next 2 sc, sc in next sc; rep from * across, turn.

Row 3: Ch 4 (counts as tr), (puff st, ch 1, picot, puff st) in next ch-5 loop, *ch 1, (puff st, ch 1, picot, puff st) in next ch-5 loop; rep from * across to last ch-5 loop, tr in last sc. Fasten off.

319

Puff st: (Yo [3 times], insert hook in next st, yo, draw yarn through st, [yo, draw yarn through 2 loops on hook] twice) 3 times in same st, yo, draw yarn through 4 loops on hook.

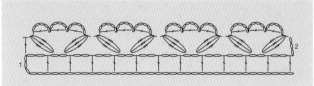

Picot: Ch 4, dc in 4th ch from hook.

Chain multiples of 9 plus 5.

Row 1 (WS): Dc in 8th ch from hook, *ch 2, skip next 2 ch, dc in next ch; rep from * across, turn.

Row 2: Ch 3 (counts as dc), skip next ch-2 space, *(puff st, work 3 picots, puff st) in next ch-2 space**, skip next 2 ch-2 spaces; rep from * across, ending last rep at **, skip next 2 ch of turning ch, dc in 5th ch of turning ch. Fasten off.

320

Puff st: (Yo, insert hook in next st, yo, draw yarn through st, yo, draw yarn through 2 loops on hook) 3 times in same st, yo, draw yarn through 4 loops on hook.

Chain multiples of 10 plus 2.

Row 1 (RS): Sc in 2nd ch from hook, sc in each ch across, turn.

Row 2: Ch 1, sc in first sc, *ch 3, skip next 4 sc, (dc, ch 3, dc, ch 3, dc) in next sc, ch 3, skip next 4 sc, sc in next sc; rep from * across, turn.

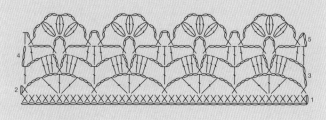

Row 3: Ch 6 (counts as dc, ch 3), *skip next ch-3 loop, 3 dc in next ch-3 loop, ch 3, sc in next dc, ch 3, 3 dc in next ch-3 loop, ch 3, skip next ch-3 loop, dc in next sc**, ch 3; rep from * across, ending last rep at **, turn.

Row 4: Ch 3 (counts as dc), *dc in next ch-3 loop, ch 3, sc in next ch-3 loop, ch 4, sc in next ch-3 loop, ch 3, dc in next ch-3 loop**, dc in next dc; rep from * across, ending last rep at **, dc in 3rd ch of turning ch, turn.

Row 5: Ch 3 (counts as hdc, ch 1), skip first dc, sc in next dc, *ch 3, skip next ch-3 loop, (puff st, ch 3, puff st, ch 3, puff st) in next ch-4 loop, ch 3, skip next ch-3 loop, sc in next dc**, ch 3, skip next dc, sc in next dc; rep from * across, ending last rep at **, ch 1, hdc in 3rd ch of turning ch. Fasten off.

321

Puff st: (Yo [twice], insert hook in next st, yo, draw yarn through st, [yo, draw yarn through 2 loops on hook] twice) 3 times in same st, yo, draw yarn through 4 loops on hook.

Chain multiples of 5 plus 2.

Row 1 (RS): Dc in 4th ch from hook, dc in each ch across, turn.

Row 2: Ch 4 (counts as dc, ch 1), skip first 2 dc, *(dc, ch 3, dc) in next dc**, ch 3, skip next 4 dc; rep from * across, ending last rep at **, ch 1, skip next dc, dc in 3rd ch of turning ch, turn.

Row 3: Ch 7 (counts as dtr, ch 2), skip next ch-1 space, (puff st, ch 5, puff st) in next ch-3 loop**, ch 4, skip next ch-3 loop; rep from * across, ending last rep at **, ch 2, dtr in 3rd ch of turning ch, turn.

Row 4: Ch 1, sc in first dtr, *ch 1, (hdc, dc, tr, dtr, tr, dc, hdc) in next ch-5 loop, ch 1, sc in next ch-4 loop; rep from * across, ending with last sc in 5th ch of turning ch. Fasten off.

322

Puff st: (Yo [3 times], insert hook in next st, yo, draw yarn through st, [yo, draw yarn through 2 loops on hook] 3 times) 3 times in same st, yo, draw yarn through 4 loops on hook.

Picot: Ch 3, sl st in 3rd ch from hook.

Chain multiples of 11 plus 2.

Row 1 (RS): Sc in 2nd ch from hook, sc in each ch across, turn.

Row 2: Ch 1, sc in first sc, *ch 6, picot, ch 6, skip next 10 sc, sc in next sc; rep from * across, turn.

Row 3: Ch 7, skip next ch-6 loop, *(puff st, ch 5, puff st, ch 5, puff st) in next picot**, work 2-dtr cluster over next 2 ch-6 loops; rep from * across, ending last rep at **, ch 7, sl st in last sc. Fasten off.

323

2-Dc Puff st: (Yo, insert hook in next st, yo, draw yarn through st, yo, draw yarn through 2 loops on hook) twice in same st, yo, draw yarn through 3 loops on hook.

3-Tr Puff st: (Yo [twice], insert hook in next st, yo, draw yarn through st, [yo, draw yarn through 2 loops on hook] twice) 3 times in same st, yo, draw yarn through 4 loops on hook.

Picot: Ch 5, sl st in 5th ch from hook.

Chain multiples of 6.

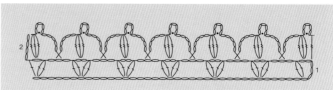

Row 1 (RS): 2-dc puff st in 6th ch from hook, *ch 3, skip next 5 ch**, (2-dc puff st, ch 2, 2-dc puff st) in next ch; rep from * across, ending last rep at **, (2-dc puff st, ch 2, dc) in last ch, turn.

Row 2: Ch 4 (counts as tr), 3-tr puff st in next ch-1 space, picot, *ch 5, sc in next ch-3 loop, ch 5, 3-tr puff st in next ch-2 space, picot; rep from * across to turning ch, tr in 3rd ch of turning ch. Fasten off.

324

Puff st: *(Yo [twice], insert hook in next st, yo, draw yarn through st, [yo, draw yarn through 2 loops on hook] twice) twice in same st, yo, draw yarn through 3 loops on hook.*

Chain multiples of 5 plus 3.

Row 1 (RS): Sc in 2nd ch from hook, sc in each ch across, turn.

Row 2: Ch 7 (counts as dc, ch 4), skip first 3 sc, sc in next sc, *ch 7, skip next 4 sc, sc in next sc; rep from * across to within last 3 sc, ch 4, skip next 2 sc, dc in last sc, turn.

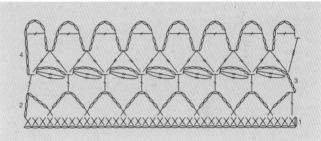

Row 3: Ch 9, puff st in 6th ch from hook, skip next ch-4 loop, *dc in next ch-7 loop, ch 5, puff st in last dc made; rep from * across to last ch-7 loop, dc in 3rd ch of turning ch, turn.

Row 4: Ch 9, dc in 5th ch from hook, ch 2, work 2-tr cluster, working first half-closed tr in first dc, skip next ch-5 loop, work next half-closed tr in next dc, complete cluster, *ch 7, dc in 5th ch from hook, ch 2, work 2-dc cluster, working first half-closed tr in last dc holding last tr made, skip next ch-5 loop, work next half-closed tr in next dc, complete cluster; rep from * across, ending with last half-closed dc in 4th ch of turning ch, ch 7, dc in 5th ch from hook, dtr in 4th ch of turning ch. Fasten off.

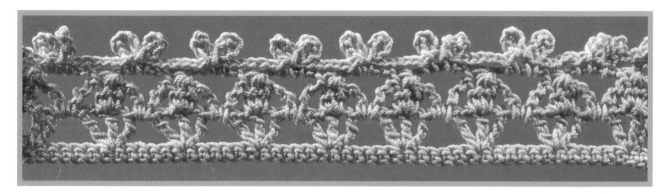

325

Picot: Ch 6, sl st in 6th ch from hook.

Chain multiples of 6 plus 2.

Row 1 (WS): Sc in 2nd ch from hook, sc in each ch across, turn.

Row 2: Ch 4 (counts as tr), skip first 3 sc, *(tr, ch 1, tr, ch, tr) in next sc**, ch 1, skip next 5 sc; rep from * across, ending last rep at **, skip next 2 sc, tr in last sc, turn.

Row 3: Ch 6 (counts as tr, ch 2), *work 5-st cluster, working first half-closed dtr in first tr, skip next ch-1 space, work 3 half-closed dc in next tr, skip next ch-1 space, work next half-closed dtr in next ch-1 space, complete cluster, *ch 5, work 5-st cluster, working first half-closed dtr in last ch-1 space holding last dtr made, skip next ch-1 space, work 3 half-closed dc in next tr, skip next ch-1 space, work next half-closed dtr in next ch-1 space, complete cluster; rep from * across, ending with last half-closed dtr in 4th ch of turning ch, ch 2, tr in 4th ch of turning ch, turn.

Row 4: Ch 1, (sc, picot, sc) in first tr, skip next ch-2 space, *ch 5, (sc, 2 picots, sl st in base of first picot, sc) in next ch-5 loop; rep from * across to last ch-5 loop, ch 5, (sc, picot, sc) in 4th ch of turning ch. Fasten off.

326

Puff st: (Yo [twice], insert hook in next st, yo, draw yarn through st, [yo, draw yarn through 2 loops on hook] twice) 3 times in same st, yo, draw yarn through 4 loops on hook.

Picot: Ch 3, sl st in 3rd ch from hook.

Chain multiples of 8 plus 2.

Row 1 (RS): Sc in 2nd ch from hook, *ch 5, skip next 3 ch, puff st in next ch, ch 5, skip next 3 ch, sc in next ch; rep from * across, turn.

Row 2: Ch 3 (counts as hdc, ch 1), *sc in next ch-5 loop, ch 10, sc in next ch-5 loop**, ch 3; rep from * across, ending last rep at **, hdc in last sc, turn.

Row 3: Ch 1, (5 sc, picot, 3 sc, picot, 3 sc, picot, 5 sc) in next ch-10 loop**, 3 sc in next ch-3 loop; rep from * across, ending last rep at **, sc in 2nd ch of turning ch. Fasten off.

327

Puff st: *(Yo, insert hook in next st, yo, draw yarn through st, yo, draw yarn through 2 loops on hook) 3 times in same st, yo, draw yarn through 4 loops on hook.*

Chain multiples of 9 plus 2.

Row 1 (RS): Sc in 2nd ch from hook, sc in each ch across, turn.

Row 2: Ch 5 (counts as dc, ch 2), skip first 3 sc, dc in next sc, *ch 2, skip next 2 sc, dc in next sc; rep from * across, turn.

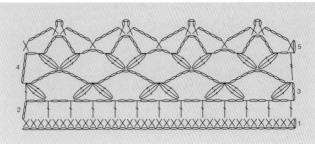

Row 3: Ch 3 (counts as dc), skip next ch-2 space, puff st in next dc, *ch 9, skip next ch-2 space**, work 6-dc cluster, working first 3 half-closed dc in next dc, skip next 2 ch-2 spaces, work next 3 half-closed dc in next dc, complete cluster; rep from * across, ending last rep at **, work 4-dc cluster, working first 3 half-closed dc in next dc, skip next 2 ch of turning ch, work next half-closed dc in 3rd ch of turning ch, complete cluster.

Row 4: Ch 5 (counts as tr, ch 1), *(puff st, ch 7, puff st) in next ch-9 loop**, ch 3; rep from * across, ending last rep at **, ch 1, tr in 3rd ch of turning ch, turn.

Row 5: Ch 1, sc in first tr, *ch 4, (sc, ch 3, sc) in next ch-7 loop, ch 4, sc in next ch-3 loop; rep from * across, ending with last sc in 4th ch of turning ch. Fasten off.

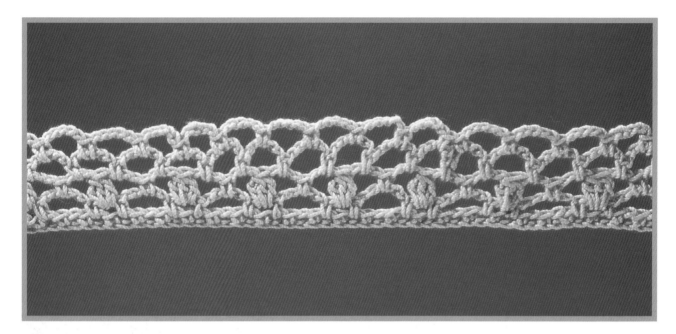

328

2-Dc Puff st: (Yo, insert hook in next st, yo, draw yarn through st, yo, draw yarn through 2 loops on hook) twice in same st, yo, draw yarn through 3 loops on hook.

3-Dc Puff st: (Yo, insert hook in next st, yo, draw yarn through st, yo, draw yarn through 2 loops on hook) 3 times in same st, yo, draw yarn through 4 loops on hook.

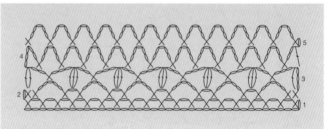

Chain multiples of 6 plus 2.

Row 1 (RS): Sc in 2nd ch from hook, *ch 1, skip next ch, sc in next ch; rep from * across, turn.

Row 2: Ch 1, sc in first sc, sc in next ch-1 space, *ch 5, skip next ch-1 space, sc in next ch-1 space**, ch 1, sc in next ch-1 space; rep from * across, ending last rep at **, sc in last sc, turn.

Row 3: Ch 3 (counts as dc), dc in first sc, *ch 3, sc in next ch-5 loop, ch 2**, 3-dc puff st in next ch-1 space; rep from * across, ending last rep at **, skip next sc, 2-dc puff st in last sc, turn.

Row 4: Ch 5 (counts as dc, ch 2), sc in next ch-2 space, (ch 5, sc) in each space across, ch 2, dc in 3rd ch of turning ch, turn.

Row 5: Ch 1, sc in first dc, (ch 5, sc) in each ch-5 loop across, ending with last sc in 3rd ch of turning ch. Fasten off.

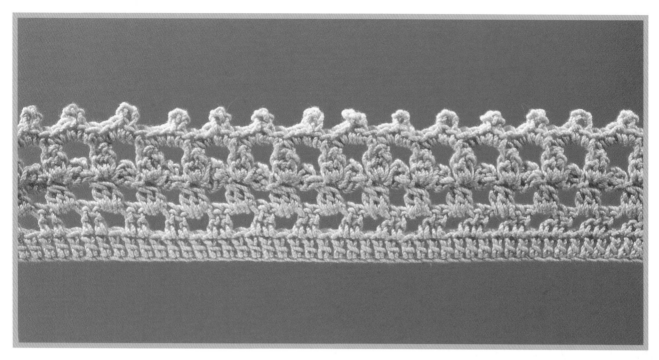

329

2-Dc Puff st: (Yo, insert hook in next st, yo, draw yarn through st, yo, draw yarn through 2 loops on hook) twice in same st, yo, draw yarn through 3 loops on hook.

3-Dc Puff st: (Yo, insert hook in next st, yo, draw yarn through st, yo, draw yarn through 2 loops on hook) 3 times in same st, yo, draw yarn through 4 loops on hook.

Picot: Ch 4, sl st in 4th ch form hook.

Chain multiples of 6 plus 2.

Row 1 (RS): Dc in 4th ch from hook, dc in each ch across, turn.

Row 2: Ch 4 (counts as dc, ch 1), skip first 2 dc, *dc in each of next 2 dc, ch 2, skip next dc**, dc in each of next 2 dc, ch 1, skip next dc; rep from * across, ending last rep at **, dc in 3rd ch of turning ch, turn.

Row 3: Ch 3 (counts as dc), *3-dc puff st in next ch-2 space, ch 3, 2-dc puff st in last puff st made, skip next ch-1 space; rep from * across to turning ch, dc in 3rd ch of turning ch, turn.

Row 4: Ch 6 (counts as dc, ch 3), *skip next ch-3 loop, 3-dc puff st in next puff st**, ch 4; rep from * across, ending last rep at **, dc in 3rd ch of turning ch, turn.

Row 5: Ch 1, sc in first dc, (2 sc, picot, 2 sc) in each ch-4 loop across to turning ch, (2 sc, picot, sc) in ch-3 loop of turning ch, sc in 3rd ch of turning ch. Fasten off.

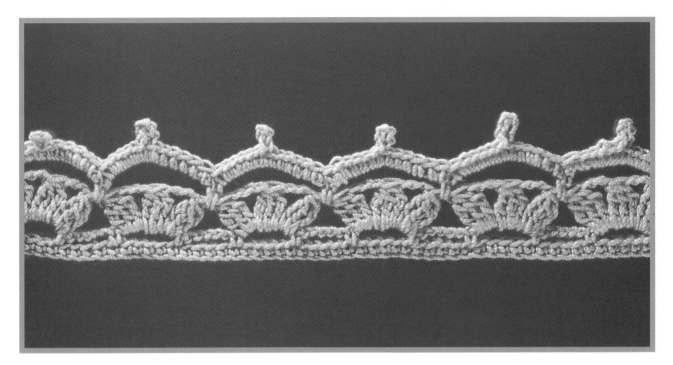

330

Puff st: (Yo twice, insert hook in next st, yo, draw yarn through st, [yo, draw yarn through 2 loops on hook] twice) 3 times in same st, yo, draw yarn through 4 loops on hook.

Picot: Ch 5, sl st in 5th ch from hook.

Chain multiples of 10 plus 1.

Row 1 (RS): Sc in 2nd ch from hook, sc in each ch across, turn.

Row 2: Ch 1, sc in each of first 3 sc, *ch 5, skip next 4 sc, sc in next sc; rep from * across to within last 2 sc, sc in each of last 2 sc, turn.

Row 3: Ch 3 (counts as dc), (puff st, ch 3, puff st, ch 3, puff st) in next ch-5 loop**, skip next ch-5 loop; rep from * across, ending last rep at **, skip next 2 sc, dc in last sc, turn.

Row 4: Ch 1, sc in first dc, *ch 11, skip next 3 puff sts, sc bet last skipped and next puff st; rep from * across, ending with last sc in 3rd ch of turning ch, turn.

Row 5: Ch 1, sc in first sc, (6 sc, picot, 6 sc) in each ch-11 loop across, sc in last sc. Fasten off.

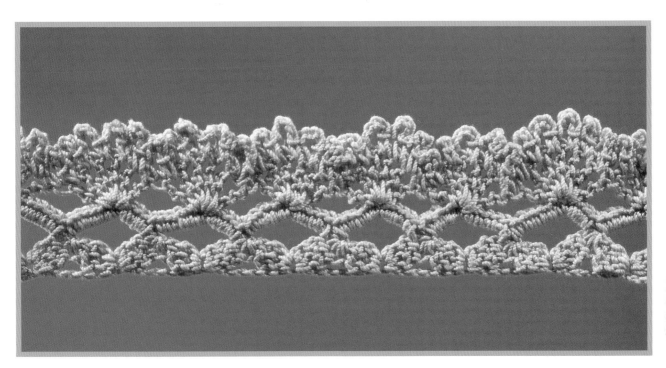

331

Puff st: *(Yo [twice], insert hook in next st, yo, draw yarn through st, [yo, draw yarn through 2 loops on hook] twice) 3 times in same st, yo, draw yarn through 4 loops on hook.*

Chain multiples of 7 plus 4.

Row 1 (WS): Puff st in 7th ch from hook, *ch 7, work 6-dc cluster, working first 3 half-closed dc in same ch as last puff st made, skip next 6 ch, work next 3 half-closed dc in next ch, complete cluster; rep from * across to within last 4 ch, ch 7, puff st in same ch as last cluster made, skip next 3 ch, dc in last ch, turn.

Row 2: Ch 1, sc in first dc, 11 sc in each ch-7 loop across, sc in last sc, turn.

Row 3: Ch 4 (counts as tr), skip first 6 sc, (tr, ch 1) 5 times in next sc, tr in same sc**, skip next 10 sc; rep from * across, ending last rep at **, skip next 5 sc, tr in last sc, turn.

Row 4: Ch 1, sc in first tr, (ch 3, sc) in each ch-1 space across, ending with last sc in 4th ch of turning ch. Fasten off.

332

Puff st: (Yo [twice], insert hook in next st, yo, draw yarn through st, [yo, draw yarn through 2 loops on hook] twice) 3 times in same st, yo, draw yarn through 4 loops on hook.

Picot: Ch 4, sl st in 4th ch from hook.

Chain multiples of 14 plus 8.

Row 1 (WS): Tr in 5th ch from hook, tr in each of next 3 ch, *ch 5, skip next 4 ch, tr in next ch, ch 5, skip next 4 ch, tr in each of next 5 ch; rep from * across, turn.

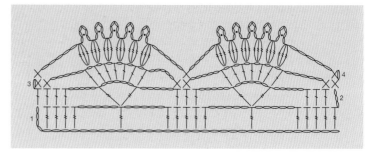

Row 2: Ch 3 (counts as dc), skip first dc, dc in each of next 3 tr, *ch 5, skip next ch-5 loop, (tr, ch 5, tr) in next tr, ch 5, skip next tr, dc in each of next 3 tr; rep from * across to turning ch, dc in 4th ch of turning ch, turn.

Row 3: Ch 1, sc in each of first 2 dc, *ch 5, skip next ch-5 loop, dc in next tr, ch 1, (dc, ch 1) 5 times in next ch-5 loop, dc in next tr, ch 5, skip next ch-5 loop**, sc in each of next 2 dc; rep from * across, ending last rep at **, skip next 2 sc, sc in next dc, sc in 3rd ch of turning ch, turn.

Row 4: Ch 1, sc in first sc, *ch 5, skip next ch-5 loop, (puff st, ch 1, picot, ch 1) in each of next 5 ch-1 spaces, puff st in next ch-1 space, ch 5, skip next ch-5 loop, sc in next sc; rep from * across, ending last rep at **, skip next sc, sc in last sc. Fasten off.

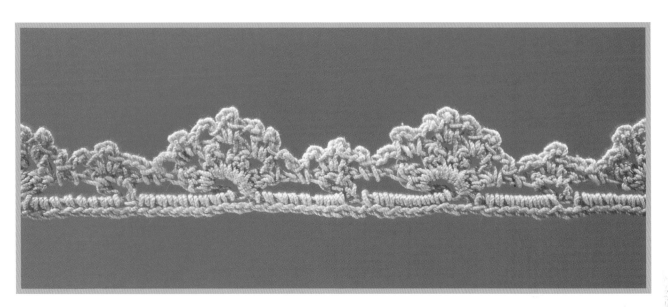

333

Puff st: (Yo, insert hook in next st, yo, draw yarn through st, yo, draw yarn through 2 loops on hook) 3 times in same st, yo, draw yarn through 4 loops on hook.

Picot: Ch 8, sl st in 8th ch from hook.

No foundation ch needed.

Row 1 (RS): Ch 1, picot, *ch 7, picot; rep from * for desired length, working an odd number of picots, ch 1. Fasten off.

Row 2: With WS facing, join yarn in first picot of Row 1, ch 1, (sc, ch 3, sc) in first picot, *ch 3, skip next ch-7 loop, (puff st, ch 3) 4 times in next picot, skip next ch-7 loop, (sc, ch 3, sc) in next picot; rep from * across, turn.

Row 3: Ch 2, (sc, ch 3, sc) in next ch-3 loop, ch 3, sc in next ch-3 loop, *(ch 3, sc, ch 3, sc) in each of next 3 ch-3 loops, ch 3, sc in next ch-3 loop; rep from * across to within last ch-3 loop, ch 3, (sc, ch 3, sc) in last ch-3 loop. Fasten off.

Bottom Edging: With RS facing, working across opposite side of Row 1, join yarn in first ch, ch 1, sc in first ch, *ch 3, skip next sl st at base of picot**, 7 sc in next ch-7 loop; rep from * across, ending last rep at **, sc in last ch. Fasten off.

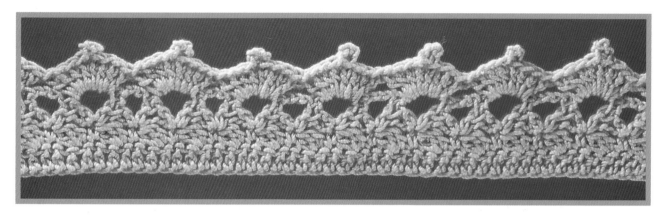

334

Puff st: (Yo, insert hook in next st, yo, draw yarn through st, yo, draw yarn through 2 loops on hook) 3 times in same st, yo, draw yarn through 4 loops on hook.

Chain multiples of 8 plus 3.

Row 1 (WS): Dc in 4th ch from hook, dc in each ch across, turn.

Row 2: Ch 1, sc in first dc, *ch 3, puff st in next dc, skip next 2 dc, sc in next dc; rep from * across, ending with last sc in 3rd ch of turning ch, turn.

Row 3: Ch 4 (counts as dc, ch 1), dc in first sc, *sc in next ch-3 loop**, (dc, ch 3, dc) in next sc; rep from * across, ending last rep at **, (dc, ch 1, dc) in last sc, turn.

Row 4: Ch 1, sc in first dc, skip next ch-1 space, (4 dc, picot, 4 dc) in next ch-3 loop**, skip next ch-3 loop; rep from * across, ending last rep at **, sc in 3rd ch of turning ch. Fasten off.

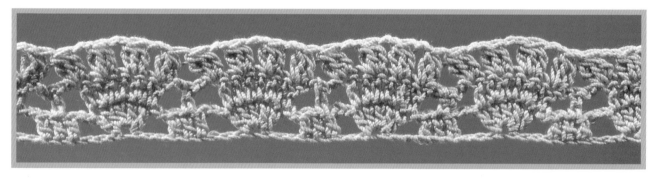

335

Puff st: (Yo, insert hook in next st, yo, draw yarn through st, yo, draw yarn through 2 loops on hook) 3 times in same st, yo, draw yarn through 4 loops on hook.

Chain multiples of 10 plus 3.

Row 1 (RS): Dc in 4th ch from hook, *ch 2, skip next 3 ch, 5 dc in next ch, ch 2, skip next 3 ch, dc in each of next 3 ch; rep from * across, ending with dc in each of last 2 ch, turn.

Row 2: Ch 5 (counts as dc, ch 2), *skip next ch-2 space, (dc in next dc, 2 dc in next dc) twice, dc in next dc, ch 2, skip next dc, dc in next dc; rep from * across, ending with last dc in 3rd ch of turning ch, turn.

Row 3: Ch 3 (counts as dc), skip next ch-2 space, *(puff st in next dc, ch 2, skip next dc) 3 times, puff st in next dc**, skip next 2 ch-2 spaces; rep from * across, ending last rep at **, dc in 3rd ch of turning ch. Fasten off.

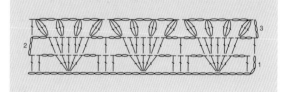

336

Puff st: (Yo, insert hook in next st, yo, draw yarn through st, yo, draw yarn through 2 loops on hook) 3 times in same st, yo, draw yarn through 4 loops on hook.

Chain multiples of 9 plus 3.

Row 1 (RS): 5 dc in 8th ch from hook, *ch 4, skip next 8 ch, 5 dc in next ch; rep from * across to within last 4 ch, ch 1, skip next 3 ch, dc in last ch, turn.

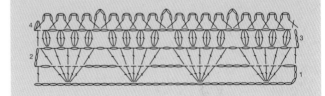

Row 2: Ch 3 (counts as dc), skip next ch-1 space, *(dc, ch 1) in each of next 5 dc, skip next ch-4 loop; rep from * across, omitting last ch-1, dc in 6th ch of turning ch, turn.

Row 3: Ch 3 (counts as dc), *(puff st, ch 1) in each of next 3 ch-1 space, puff st in next ch-1 space**, ch 2; rep from * across, ending last rep at **, dc in 3rd ch of tunring ch, turn.

Row 4: Ch 1, sc in first dc, *(ch 3, sc) in each of next 3 ch-1 spaces, ch 3**, (sc, ch 4, sc) in next ch-2 space; rep from * across, ending last rep at **, sc in 3rd ch of turning ch. Fasten off.

337

Puff st: (Yo, insert hook in next st, yo, draw yarn through st, yo, draw yarn through 2 loops on hook) 3 times in same st, yo, draw yarn through 4 loops on hook.

Picot: Ch 7, sl st in 7th ch from hook.

Chain multiples of 8 plus 1.

Row 1 (RS): Sc in 2nd ch from hook, sc in each ch across, turn.

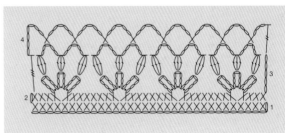

Row 2: Ch 1, sc in each of first 4 sc, *work 3 picots, sc in each of next 8 sc; rep from * across, ending with sc in each of last 4 sc, turn.

Row 3: Ch 5 (counts as dtr), *(puff st, ch 5) in each of next 2 picots, puff st in next picot**, skip next 8 sc; rep from * across, ending last rep at **, skip next 3 sc, dtr in last sc, turn.

Row 4: Ch 7 (counts as tr, ch 3), sc in next ch-5 loop, (ch 5, sc) in each ch-5 loop across to last ch-5 loop, ch 3, tr in 5th ch of turning ch. Fasten off.

338

Puff st: (Yo, insert hook in next st, yo, draw yarn through st, yo, draw yarn through 2 loops on hook) twice in same st, yo, draw yarn through 3 loops on hook.

Chain multiples of 8 plus 3.

Row 1 (RS): Dc in 4th ch from hook, *ch 1, skip next ch, dc in next ch; rep from * across to within last ch, dc in last ch, turn.

Row 2: Ch 5 (counts as dc, ch 2), puff st in first dc, skip next ch-1 space, *dc in next dc, dc in next ch-1 space, dc in next dc, skip next ch-1 space**, (puff st, ch 4, puff st) in next ch-1 space, skip next ch-1 space; rep from * across, ending last rep at **, (puff st, ch 2, dc) in 3rd ch of turning ch, turn.

Row 3: Ch 3 (counts as hdc, ch 1), sc in next ch-2 space, *ch 3, skip next puff st, sc in next dc, ch 3, skip next dc, sc in next dc, ch 3**, (sc, ch 3, sc) in next ch-4 loop; rep from * across, ending last rep at **, sc in ch-2 space of turning ch, ch 1, hdc in 3rd ch of turning ch, turn.

Row 4: Ch 1, sc in first hdc, skip next ch-1 space, *ch 1, skip next ch-3 loop, (puff st, ch 1, puff st, ch 1, puff st) in next ch-3 loop in next ch-3 loop, ch 1, skip next ch-3 loop, sc in next ch-3 loop; rep from * across, ending with last sc in 2nd ch of turning ch, turn.

Row 5: Ch 1, sc in first sc, *ch 3, (sc, ch 3, sc, ch 3) in each of next 2 ch-3 loops, skip next ch-1 space, sc in next sc; rep from * across. Fasten off.

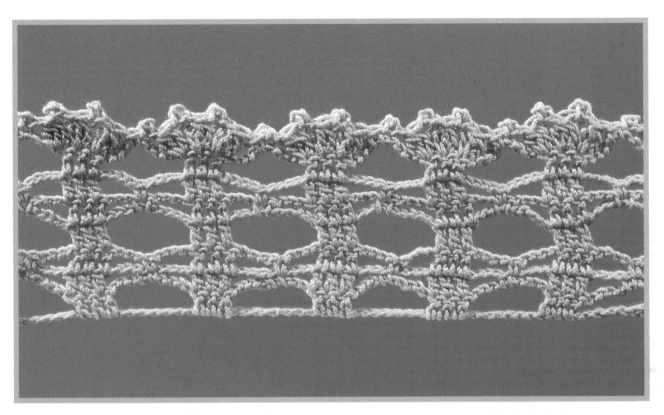

339

Puff st: (Yo, insert hook in next st, yo, draw yarn through st, yo, draw yarn through 2 loops on hook) 3 times in same st, yo, draw yarn through 4 loops on hook.

Picot: Ch 3, sl st in 3rd ch from hook.

Chain multiples of 9 plus 5.

Row 1 (WS): Dc in 4th ch from hook, dc in next ch, *ch 9, skip next 6 ch, dc in each of next 3 ch; rep from * across, turn.

Row 2: Ch 3 (counts as dc), skip first dc, dc in each of next 2 dc, *ch 3, sc in next ch-9 loop, ch 3, dc in each of next 3 dc; rep from * across, ending with last dc in 3rd ch of turning ch, turn.

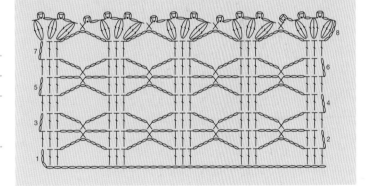

Row 3: Ch 3 (counts as dc), skip first dc, dc in each of next 2 dc, *ch 4, skip next ch-3 loop, sc in next sc, ch 4, skip next ch-3 loop, dc in each of next 3 dc; rep from * across, ending with last dc in 3rd ch of turning ch, turn.

Row 4: Ch 3 (counts as dc), skip first dc, dc in each of next 2 dc, *ch 9, skip next 2 ch-4 loops, dc in each of next 3 dc; rep from * across, ending with last dc in 3rd ch of turning ch, turn

Rows 5-7: Rep Rows 2-4.

Row 8: Ch 4, puff st in first dc, *(ch 1, picot, puff st) in each of next 2 dc, ch 1, picot, sc in next ch-9 loop, puff st in next dc; rep from * across, ch 1, picot, puff st in next dc, ch 1, picot, puff st in 3rd ch of turning ch. Fasten off.

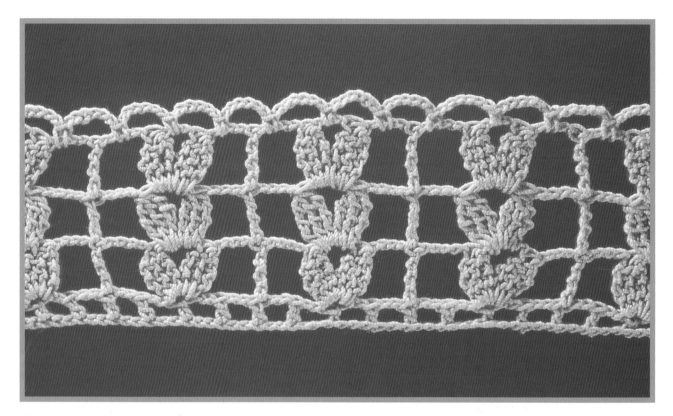

340

Puff st: (Yo [3 times], insert hook in next st, yo, draw yarn through st, [yo, draw yarn through 2 loops on hook] 3 times) 3 times in same st, yo, draw yarn through 4 loops on hook.

Chain multiples of 12 plus 5.

Row 1 (RS): Dc in 8th ch from hook, *ch 2, skip next 2 ch, dc in next ch; rep from * across, turn.

Row 2: Ch 9 (counts as dtr, ch 4), skip next 2 ch-2 spaces, *(puff st, ch 3, puff st) in next dc, ch 4, skip next 2 ch-2 spaces, dtr in next dc; rep from * across, ending with last dtr in 5th ch of turning ch, turn.

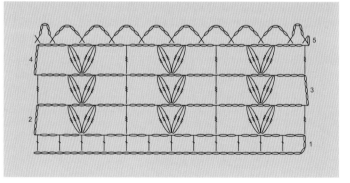

Rows 3-4: Ch 9 (counts as dtr, ch 4), skip next ch-4 loop, (puff st, ch 3, puff st) in next ch-3 loop, ch 4, skip next ch-4 loop, dtr in next dtr; rep from * across ending with last dtr in 5th ch of turning ch, turn.

Row 5: Ch 1, sc in first dtr, (ch 5, sc) in each loop across, to ch-4 loop of turning ch, ch 5, sc in 5th ch of turning ch. Fasten off.

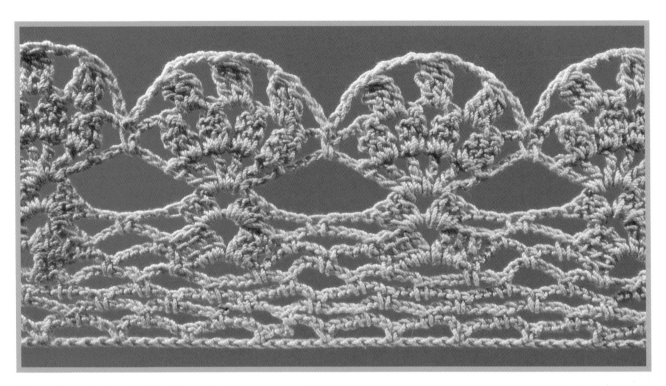

341

Puff st: (Yo [twice], insert hook in next st, yo, draw yarn through st, [yo, draw yarn through 2 loops on hook] twice) 3 times in same st, yo, draw yarn through 4 loops on hook.

Chain multiples of 10 plus 2.

Row 1 (WS): Sc in 2nd ch from hook, *ch 7, skip next 4 ch, sc in next ch; rep from * across, turn.

Row 2: Ch 7 (counts as tr, ch 3), sc in next ch-7 loop, (ch 7, sc) in each ch-7 loop across to last ch-7 loop, ch 3, tr in last sc, turn.

Row 3: Ch 1, sc in first tr, (ch 7, sc) in each ch-7 loop across, ending with last sc in 4th ch of turning ch, turn.

Rows 4-5: Rep Rows 2-3.

Row 6: Ch 7 (counts as tr, ch 3), *sc in next ch-7 loop, (3 tr, ch 3, 3 tr) in next sc, sc in next ch-7 loop**, ch 7; rep from * across, ending last rep at **, ch 3, tr in last sc, turn.

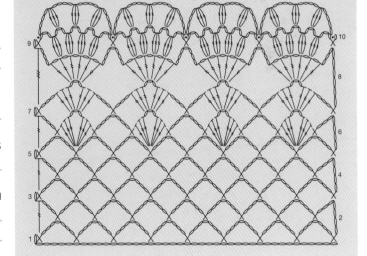

Row 7: Ch 1, sc in first tr, ch 3, skip next ch-3 loop, *(3 tr, ch 3, 3 tr) in next ch-3 loop, ch 3**, sc in next ch-7 loop, ch 3; rep from * across, ending last rep at **, sc in 4th ch of turning ch, turn.

Row 8: Ch 9 (counts as trtr, ch 3), skip next ch-3 loop, *(tr, ch 1) 5 times in next ch-3 loop, tr in same ch-3 loop**, ch 5, skip next 2 ch-3 loops; rep from * across, ending last rep at **, ch 3, skip next ch-3 loop, trtr in last sc, turn.

Row 9: Ch 1, sc in first trtr, *skip next tr, (ch 3, puff st) in each of next 4 tr, ch 3, skip next ch-1 space, sc in next ch-7 loop; rep from * across, ending with last sc in 6th ch of turning ch, turn.

Row 10: Ch 1, sl st in first sc, *ch 4, skip next ch-3 loop, (puff st, ch 4) in each of next 3 ch-3 loops, skip next ch-3 loop, sl st in next sc; rep from * across. Fasten off.

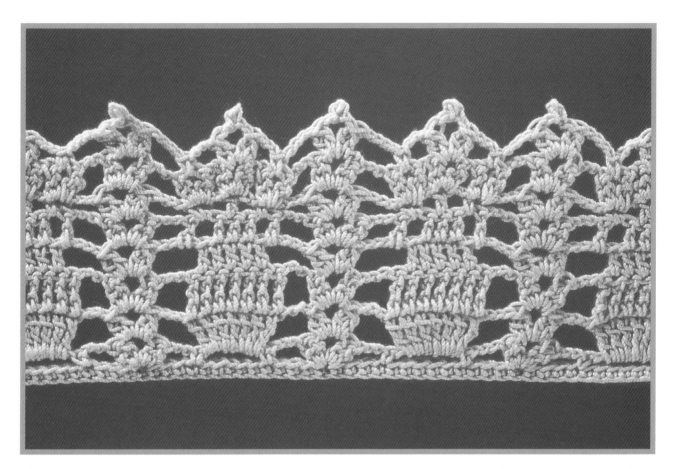

342

Puff st: (Yo, insert hook in next st, yo, draw yarn through st, yo, draw yarn through 2 loops on hook) twice in same st, yo, draw yarn through 3 loops on hook.

Picot: Ch 3, sl st in 3rd ch from hook.

Chain multiples of 14 plus 2.

Row 1 (RS): Sc in 2nd ch from hook, sc in each ch across, turn.

Row 2: Ch 4 (counts as dc, ch 1), puff st in first sc, *ch 3, skip next 3 sc, sc in next sc, ch 5, skip next 5 sc, sc in next sc, ch 3, skip next 3 sc**, (puff st, ch 3, puff st) in next sc; rep from * across, ending last rep at **, (puff st, ch 1, dc) in last sc, turn.

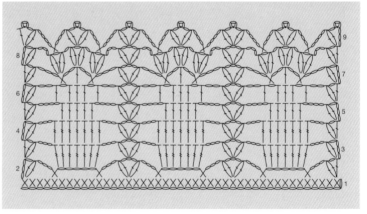

Row 3: Ch 4 (counts as dc, ch 1), puff st in first dc, *ch 3, skip next ch-3 loop, 7 tr in next ch-5 loop, ch 3, skip next ch-3 loop**, (puff st, ch 3, puff st) in next ch-3 loop; rep from * across, ending last rep at **, (puff st, ch 1, dc) in 3rd ch of turning ch, turn.

Row 4: Ch 4 (counts as dc, ch 1), puff st in first dc, *ch 3, skip next ch-3 loop, tr in each of next 7 tr, ch 3, skip next ch-3 loop**, (puff st, ch 3, puff st) in next ch-3 loop; rep from * across, ending last rep at **, (puff st, ch 1, dc) in 3rd ch of turning ch, turn.

Row 5: Ch 4 (counts as dc, ch 1), puff st in first dc, *ch 4, skip next ch-3 loop, skip next tr, dc in each of next 5 tr, ch 4, skip next ch-3 loop**, (puff st, ch 3, puff st) in next ch-3 loop; rep from * across, ending last rep at **, (puff st, ch 1, dc) in 3rd ch of turning ch, turn.

Row 6: Ch 4 (counts as dc, ch 1), puff st in first dc, *ch 2, dc in next ch-4 loop, ch 1, skip next dc, dc in each of next 3 dc, ch 1, dc in next ch-4 loop, ch 2**, (puff st, ch 3, puff st) in next ch-3 loop; rep from * across, ending last rep at **, (puff st, ch 1, dc) in 3rd ch of turning ch, turn.

Row 7: Ch 4 (counts as dc, ch 1), puff st in first dc, *ch 3, skip next ch-2 space, sc in next ch-1 space, ch 2, skip next dc, dc in next dc, ch 2, sc in next ch-1 space, ch 3**, (puff st, ch 3, puff st) in next ch-3 loop; rep from * across, ending last rep at **, (puff st, ch 1, dc) in 3rd ch of turning ch, turn.

Row 8: Ch 4 (counts as dc, ch 1), puff st in first dc, *ch 3, skip next ch-3 loop, (puff st, ch 1, puff st) in next sc, ch 1, skip next ch-2 space, (puff st, ch 1, puff st) in next dc, ch 1, skip next ch-2 space, (puff st, ch 1, puff st) in next sc, ch 3, skip next ch-3 loop**, (puff st, ch 3, puff st) in next ch-3 loop; rep from * across, ending last rep at **, (puff st, ch 1, dc) in 3rd ch of turning ch, turn.

Row 9: Ch 3 (counts as dc), picot, ch 1, puff st in first sc, *ch 4, skip next ch-3 loop, sc in next ch-1 space, ch 3, skip next ch-1 space, (puff st, ch 1, picot, ch 1, puff st) in next ch-1 space, ch 3, skip next ch-1 space, sc in next ch-1 space, ch 4, skip next ch-3 loop**, (puff st, ch 3, puff st) in next ch-3 loop; rep from * across, ending last rep at **, (puff st, ch 1, picot, dc) in 3rd ch of turning ch. Fasten off.

■ Acknowledgments ■

I'd like to thank Charles Nurnberg, president of Sterling Publishing Company in New York, who very kindly remembered me from 20 years ago, when I wrote my first crochet books, and gave me the wonderful opportunity of reprising them with Lark Books and passing on again these timeless techniques and my own love of crochet.

I'd also like to thank the Lark team who helped me through the revision of this book and who brought the entire project together — my editor Susan Kieffer, technical editor Karen Manthey, and art director Shannon Yokeley. I appreciate your dedication and vision.

■ Author Biography ■

Linda Schapper's artistic vision is expressed in a wide range of media, from patchwork quilts and crochet, to painting and liturgical textiles, all of which are characterized by a folk-art style. She has traveled and taught extensively around the world in more than 30 countries, speaks four languages, and has had some 100 exhibits of her patchwork quilts. She has written eight books, four of them on crochet. She now divides her time between painting and writing about her liturgical work.

Crochet Terms and Abbreviations

Abbreviations

alt	alternate	oz	ounce(s)
Alt lp st	alternate loop stitch	prev	previous
approx	approximately	rem	remaining
beg	begin, beginning	rep	repeat
BL	back loop	reverse sc	reverse single crochet
BP	back post	RS	right side
Bbl st	Bobble stitch	rnd(s)	round(s)
ch	chain	sc	single crochet
ch-sp	chain space	sk	skip
cont	continue	sl st	slip stitch
dc	double crochet	sp	space(s)
dec	decrease(s/ing)	st(s)	stitch(es)
dtr	double treble crochet	tch	turning chain
ea	each	tog	together
FL	front loop	tr	treble crochet
FP	front post	Tss	Tunisian simple stitch
hdc	half double crochet	Tsl	Tunisian slip stitch
hk	hook	WS	wrong side
inc	increase(s/ing)	V-st	V-stitch
lp(s)	loop(s)	yo	yarn over
Lp st	loop stitch		

* Repeat directions following * as many times indicated

[] Repeat directions inside brackets as many times as indicated

() Work directions inside parentheses into stitch indicated

U.S. Term	U.K./AUS Term
sl st slip st	**sc** single crochet
sc single crochet	**dc** double crochet
hdc half double crochet	**htr** half treble crochet
dc double crochet	**tr** treble crochet
tr treble crochet	**dtr** double treble crochet
dtr double treble crochet	**trip tr** or **trtr** triple treble crochet
trtr triple treble crochet	**qtr** quadruple treble crochet
rev sc reverse single crochet	**rev dc** reverse double crochet
yo yarn over	**yoh** yarn over hook

■ Index ■